E G L

Research in Human Geography

Introductions and Investigations

Edited by John Eyles

Basil Blackwell

Copyright © Basil Blackwell Ltd., 1988

First published 1988

Basil Blackwell Ltd.
108 Cowley Road, Oxford, OX4 1JF, UK

Basil Blackwell Inc.
432 Park Avenue South, Suite 1503
New York, NY 10016, USA

British Library Cataloguing in Publication Data
    Eyles, John
    Research in human geography: introductions
    and investigations
    1. Human Geography
    I. Title
    304.2
    ISBN 0-631-15009-9

Library of Congress Cataloging-in-Publication Data
Research in human geography : introductions and investigations /
    edited by John Eyles.
        p.   cm.
    Includes index.
    ISBN 0-631-15009-9
    1. Anthropo-geography—Research.   I. Eyles, John.
GF26.R47 1988
307—dc19   87-29390
                                                                CIP

Typeset in 10 on 11.5 pt Plantin
by Photo·graphics, Honiton, Devon
Printed in Great Britain

Contents

Contributors

Keith Beavon, Department of Geography and Environmental Studies, University of Witwatersrand, Johannesburg, South Africa

John Eyles, Department of Geography, McMaster University, Hamilton, Ontario, Canada

Dean Forbes, Department of Human Geography, Research School of Pacific Studies, Australian National University, Canberra, Australia

Barry Garner, Department of Geography, University of New South Wales, Kensington, Australia

John Goddard, Centre for Urban and Regional Development Studies, University of Newcastle-upon-Tyne, Newcastle-upon-Tyne, England

Peter Gould, Department of Geography, Pennsylvania State University, University Park, PA, USA

Ron Johnston, Department of Geography, University of Sheffield, Sheffield, England

David Ley, Department of Geography, University of British Columbia, Vancouver, BC, Canada

Linda McDowell, Faculty of Social Sciences, Open University, Milton Keynes, England

Phil O'Keefe, Department of Town Planning, Newcastle Polytechnic, Newcastle-upon-Tyne, England

Richard Peet, School of Geography, Clark University, Worcester, Mass, USA

Chris Rogerson, Department of Geography and Environmental Studies, University of Witwatersrand, Johannesburg, South Africa

David Smith, Department of Geography and Earth Science, Queen Mary College, London, England

Preface

Editors of all collections of essays have many debts to acknowledge. I must firstly thank all the contributors. They not only agreed to write to a set of guidelines, which may have seemed quite daunting, but they also showed great patience while I performed various editorial tasks. This volume has been rather slow in the making, being conceived in early 1985 and finally sent to the publisher in early 1987. I must thank John Davey and Virginia Murphy at Basil Blackwell for their understanding and patience.

Because the creative period has been somewhat protracted, I, as editor and, during the period, with access to more and more of the essays – the first arriving in October 1985 and that last in December 1986 – have been able to reflect on the purpose of the volume and alter my perspective accordingly. I can briefly share these reflections because, as Peter Gould notes, the first paragraphs readers see are usually written last. And these are no exception. As the papers were delivered, I saw their great variability and individuality which are the hallmarks of the research process. I increasingly recognized that no definitive statement of the research process would emerge. If in my wilder moments I have expected them, I was a fool. I had wanted the individuality – the 'humanity' – of research to shine through, and had got it. And reading and re-reading the essays, I became more conscious of what is and should be considered when beginning or continuing research. So while the papers cannot be definitive in the literal sense of that word, they can and do inform in general terms about motivations and contexts, discovery and routine and problems and linkages. By telling us part of their biographies, the contributors have given us the raw materials to do that. And they give us story-lines, not a story, variability, not uniformity, in approach. I have found it extremely useful in my reading and re-reading of the papers to consider these disagreements, to consider the story-line of person A in the contexts of those of B, C, D and so on. I hope that readers (and perhaps the authors themselves) find this a useful task as well. Such interrogation is another element in learning how research is done: it may enable us to make our human geographies better, and more consciously for ourselves and our audience.

John Eyles
Collingtree

1

Introduction: Geography in the Making

John Eyles

This is not a book about method in that blow-by-blow accounts of how to carry out pieces of research are not provided. It is rather about how human geography is made in the sense of being constructed through individual endeavour. It is an attempt to expose that which is often suppressed not by deliberate connivance but by the ways in which research is usually presented to its audience. In this reporting we are seldom told what were the motivations or problems (excepting technical ones) of carrying out a project. While these motivations and problems (and much else besides) have been explored by other social scientists (e.g. Hammond, 1964; Bell and Newby, 1977; Bell and Encel, 1978; Roberts, 1981; Bell and Roberts, 1984), there has been little such exploration in human geography. The mid-to-late 1980s seems to be an appropriate time to examine the nature of human geographical research, because the problems of starting research, maintaining momentum and completion are now made worse by the various competing 'paradigms' of conceptualization, explanation and validation. It is hoped that this collection will help demonstrate the suitability of different approaches to research problems. Further, along with the other social sciences, human geography has come under increasing scrutiny in various countries because, it would seem, of an apparent lack of policy relevance and of a distinctive image of what it contributes to knowledge. It is not the intention of this volume to attempt to demonstrate the impossible, namely that geography is unique. It is simply to demonstrate its distinctive style and problem focus, a style and focus shared with several (but no one) discipline. And also along with other disciplines, human geography, particularly in Britain, has been criticized for a slow and poor completion rate amongst its graduate students. The critics tend to overlook the individualism of the research enterprise. The student or continuing researcher may be helped to confront this individualism (i.e. the isolation, start, relationship between self and subject, keeping going) by being shown how specific individuals have overcome their 'individual' problems in the context of a specific research task. The intention of the volume is, therefore, to show how the individual contributors tackle or tackled specific problems. The thought processes behind individual pieces of research are sometimes demonstrated, as are the chains of reason, leaps of fancy, uses of contacts and so on. In this way the 'humanity' behind research documents may be in part seen. The essays are then part of the biographies of those that have written them and, in this, help us recognize the connections between the personal and the research process. Yet while personal accounts of geographical research are provided, all the contributors talk of theory and/or policy. They necessarily remain within social science – 'inside the whale' in Bell and Encel's (1978) graphic terms – but it is to be hoped that their accounts, by employing what Mills (1956) called the sociological imagination to locate research in its variety of contexts, help break down the emasculating separations concerning theory, method, observation and the personal.

It must be said that some of the inspiration for deciding to put such a collection together comes from such employment in social research in general. There seemed to be particular parallels between what Bell and Newby (1977) identified as the methodological pluralism of sociology and what is presently occurring, at both a theoretical and a methodological level, in human geography. The theoretical extravaganza, documented elsewhere (see Eyles, 1986), has brought the growing realization that disciplinary development must be based on empirical investigation of concrete reality – the examination of the operations and effects of social, economic and political processes in and on specific localities, for example. This realization has been admirably described and put into practice in the fields of industrial geography (see Massey, 1984) and of health care analysis (see Cornwell, 1984). But such practice does rely on a methodological pluralism in which the strengths and limitations of different methods are recognized. In this way it may be possible to avoid what Bell and Newby (1977), following Bernstein (1974), regard as possible consequences of such pluralism:

In a subject where theories and methods are weak, intellectual shifts are likely to arise out of the conflicts between *approaches* rather than conflicts between explanations, for by definition, most explanations will be weak and often non-comparative, because they are approach-specific. The weakness of the explanation is likely to be attributable to the approach, which is analysed in terms of its ideological stance. Once the ideological stance is exposed, then all the work may be written off. Every new approach becomes a social movement or sect which immediately defines the nature of the subject by redefining what is to be admitted and what is beyond the pale, so that with every new approach the subject starts almost from scratch (Bernstein, 1974, p. 154).

The theoretical debate of the past 10–15 years suggested this almost constant renewal of human geographical endeavour. But recognition of methodological pluralism (and its constraints) is leading to greater empirical endeavour and debates on the kinds of knowledge different methods produce. Eyles and Smith (1988) have put together a collection of the variety of qualitative and interpretative methods in geography, and studies in industrial geography have also directly examined the broad issues of 'the meaning of "a case-study"; the validity of components of change analysis; the kind of data sources required (and considered valid) by different approaches; the questioning whether interviews should be informally structured and interactive or structured and replicable; and so forth' (Massey and Meegan, 1985a, p. 12). Important in setting these questions is the distinction made by Harré (1979) and used by Sayer (1984) between intensive and extensive research, the two approaches asking different sorts of questions, using different techniques and method and defining their objects and boundaries differently (see table 1.1 and Sayer and Morgan, 1985).

In concluding their collection, Massey and Meegan (1985b, p. 170) suggest that the most difficult research question of all is what exactly is the research question you are trying to answer and elaborate thus:

What kind of an explanation are you looking for? – where do you expect it to be located? – how is it structured? – are you looking for patterns or processes? – what does that mean for your research design? – are the categories and concepts you are looking for consistent with these aims? – in what way do you want your data to be comprehensive – in coverage of areas or industries? – in the detail of investigation of individual corporations perhaps? – in the range of actors you investigate? – if you see the necessity for different levels of analysis, what exactly do you want from each level? – how are the levels to be linked? – and (to avoid the age-old problem of feeling one ought to be studying the cosmos) how is each to be delimited? – if there are different actors involved in the issues you are studying how are you to structure the interaction between them? – how do you propose to analyse any conflicts of interest or information which may exist between them? – how and in what way do you want your conclusions to be generalizable?

While such comments help guide the research process, and suggest that different methods need to be considered, a further distinction must be made; one which points up the importance of the approach adopted in this book. It is that made by Gouldner (1967) between method and methodolatry (see also Bell and Newby, 1977). Gouldner (1967, p. 338) argues, with comments that could be directed explicitly to particular forms of statistical geography, that method 'sacrifices the venturesome but chancy insight for the security of controllable routine, the penetrating novelty for the shallow familiarity, the broader for the narrow circumstances'. Gouldner is not suggesting that we abandon method, but that we avoid becoming methodolatorous or compulsively preoccupied with a method of knowing, which is exalted without serious consideration of how successful it is in producing knowledge. This consideration involves

Table 1.1 Intensive and extensive research: a summary

	Intensive	Extensive
Research question	How does a process work in a particular case or small number of cases? What *produces* a certain change? What did the agents actually do?	What are the regularities, common patterns, distinguishing features of a population? How widely are certain characteristics or processes distributed or represented?
Relations	Substantial relations of connection.	Formal relations of similarity.
Type of groups studied	Causal groups.	Taxonomic groups.
Type of product produced	Causal explanation of the production of certain objects or events, though not necessarily a representative one.	Descriptive 'representative' generalizations, lacking in explanatory penetration.
Typical methods	Study of individual agents in their causal contexts, interactive interviews, ethnography. Qualitative analysis.	Large-scale survey of population or representative sample, formal questionnaires, standardized interviews. Statistical analysis.
Are the results generalizable?	Actual concrete patterns and contingent relations are unlikely to be 'representative', 'average' or generalizable. *Necessary* relations discovered will exist wherever their relata are present, e.g. causal powers of objects are generalizable to other contexts as they are necessary features of these objects.	Although representative of a whole population, they are unlikely to be generalizable to other populations at different times and places. Problem of ecological fallacy in making inferences about individuals.
Disadvantages	Problem of representativeness.	Lack of explanatory power. Ecological fallacy in making inferences about individuals.

Source: Sayer and Morgan 1985, p. 151. Reproduced with kind permission of the author.

the examination of the routines and contexts within which research takes place. These contexts are institutional (see, for example, Bell's (1984) discussion of the significance of the British social research council), disciplinary (in that its shifting boundaries and frontiers – not always in the same place – can influence research endeavour), societal (see, for example, Horowitz's (1967) account of the role of liberal US in preventing research on social upheaval in Latin America from occurring) and personal (which Clarke (1975) outlines perceptively and which forms one of the bases of methodological texts in the social sciences, e.g. Burgess, 1984). Part of the personal context is an awareness of the significance of what Gouldner (1967) calls 'intuitive insight with enriching novelty'. And to show how geography is made, those insights must be shared. At the risk of self-indulgence 'confession is good for ideas' (Watkins, quoted in Bell and Newby, 1977, p. 13).

Some contributors have found the concentration on confession and the personal easier than others. The guidelines for contributors asked them to consider covering, among other things, the following points: how the researcher became interested in the problem and how the specific topic arose; whether the focus of interest was broad or narrow; how the research was initially tackled; did the approach adopted square with intentions and expectations; were specific methods/methodologies/philosophies adopted and with what impact; was the research independent or sponsored or contract, and with what implications for the nature of the research; what happened as the research progressed – did ideas, emphases, methods change; how were 'data' sought, obtained and confronted; were the 'data' published statistics, individuals in a survey, decision-makers or key personnel, or a combination; were there conscious stages in the research, were these adhered to and what happened at them; were 'gaps' discovered in the 'data' or in ideas and what was done; how was analysis carried out; were the findings easily explained, and how; how was the research concluded; did it lead on to any further projects? Throughout, the feelings of the researcher should be assessed. Was there fear (of statistics, or interviewing for example), mundaneness and boredom (in, say, data collection or specific stages of research process), excitement and elation (at the findings or completion), commitment, revelation, satisfaction?

I concluded that such a listing would perhaps put off any intended contributor, although in the end of the 11 people asked to write, only one failed to deliver. I am saddened that there is no contribution on local government-oriented research (although John Goddard's account covers this topic in part) and no historical geographical one (although some of its particular concerns are addressed by Chris Rogerson and Keith Beavon). I was in fact keen to show the variety of contexts in which research in human geography is carried out, e.g. research with or for organizations and with or for private business; research carried out overseas (in non-English-speaking societies); historical research; contemporary statistically based research; social geographical research using formal social surveys and qualitative techniques; and contemplative/ critical (i.e. theory-laden) research. I asked people known personally to me, and recognize that this choice constrains the story of how human geography is made, although we must recognize practical considerations such as book length and so on.

The opening essay by Peter Gould (chapter 2) begins by freeing the research process of much of its cant in an exposure of the rituals and forms that much research appears to take but seldom can. So it is usually impossible to know what we are going to find out, let alone how we are going to achieve that, before we start our research programme. He highlights curiosity, discovery and calling to geography (see also Gould, 1985; Buttimer, 1983) as dimensions of the research task. He then goes on to relate 'the story of mental maps' through residential preferences to patterns of geographical information with their emerging problems and linkages. Throughout, he illustrates the significance of a quantitative approach to particular geographical research problems. The quantitative approach and solution to problems are also found in chapter 3 by Barry Garner who, in his work for the private sector – the coalmining industry of New South Wales, Australia – had to forecast the likely indirect employment and housing effects of a new mine in an environmental impact statement. He shows the different pressures on, and requirements of, the researcher working in private industry as opposed to doing conventional university-based research. Research involves time and financial costs, and there is a vested interest in the success of the proposed venture (and perhaps, therefore, in certain kinds of results). But Garner points not only to these difficulties but also to the importance of the cross-fertilization of ideas for scientific understanding and advancement, and to the way a research programme builds up over time.

This last feature is also illustrated in chapter 4, by John Goddard, who shows how his interest in industrial and office location developed from his Ph.D. to his directorship of the Centre for Urban and Regional Development Studies. His research on contact patterns among groups of offices broadened to consider the significance of communication systems and new technology in regional development, particularly with respect to the Northern Region of England. Goddard's contribution also shows the importance of contacts to enable research to progress in particular directions and of team research, often of a multi-disciplinary kind. Like Garner's essay, a major feature of Goddard's is policy-oriented research, but mainly for public bodies. He also demonstrates the convincing cases that have to be made to these bodies – local, national, statutory and European – so that sponsorship can be obtained. Different forms of sponsorship and research orientation are found in chapter 5. While Goddard's orientation is to react swiftly to the requirements of policy-makers so that problems may be ameliorated and the workings of an industrial society better understood, that of Phil O'Keefe and Dick Peet is derived from radical geography. The nature of this principally marxist orientation is now well known through the pages of *Antipode*, in Peet (1977), and in summary form from Gregory (1986). Methodologically, marxists have used a great range of methods, 'many of them reflecting an unremitting positivism' and using 'official statistics with an abandon matched only by orthodox positivism' (Bell and Newby, 1977, p. 27). But O'Keefe and Peet are at pains to demonstrate in a case study (world view – including research – as practice) the need to reconstruct energy accounting. The locale of their work, the Southern Africa Frontline States, points to the importance of political context not just in affecting the nature of the research process but in deciding where research is to be carried out. Their work indicates that 'the radical tradition yields different research methodologies and brings different policy and planning conclusions than conventional social science'.

The sixth chapter, by Chris Rogerson and Keith Beavon, is also based on research in Southern Africa but this time in the Republic itself. Because of how their research has changed, they explicitly point to the events and contexts in which their work was and is now located. They demonstrate that the conventional approaches in Anglo-American human geography – the academic context – acted as a straitjacket. The impacts of black struggle and political change on their work are described. Black South Africa was largely unknown: its subsequent exploration being shaped by work on the informal sector in South-east Asia and elsewhere and indigenous studies of the history of 'common people' in the Republic. Rogerson and Beavon chart their tentative and careful steps to explore the contemporary informal sector and their use of archival material to rediscover the past. The informal sector is also the topic of research for Dean Forbes in the seventh chapter. He describes the academic antecedents that aroused his interest and curiosity in this sector, the reasons behind the choice of Indonesia and Ujung Pandang for the research and many of the practical problems of field investigations, e.g. learning a foreign language and different customs, the problems of heat and climate, the political limitations that can be placed on researchers and the changes likely to be brought about in the researcher's own character by his/her time in the field. Forbes also discusses the methodological issues that faced him, i.e. the relative merits (including 'ease' of carrying out a procedure) of surveys, life histories and informal and depth interviewing. The last-named strategy was the approach mainly used by David Ley who, in the eighth chapter, outlines some of the moral and ethical issues arising from participant observation. Ley points to the importance of a reciprocal relationship between the researcher and the community that he/she is investigating, and of the significance of the formative tasks of making contact and settling in (and how he accomplished these). He also places his work, albeit as he admits with hindsight, in its conceptual context, the 'interpretive traditions'. His reflections on his own work in 'Monroe', Philadelphia, and on the work of others, lead him to conclude that 'thick description' (Geertz, 1973) or interpretation should create new knowledge and make the unquestioned questionable not just to researchers but to the community at large.

The next two essays certainly try to make the unquestioned questionable for researchers at least by exposing to their (and our) critical gaze the nature of particular research orientations. Why then does, or should, the research process take a particular form? In the ninth chapter, David Smith explores the academic framework and personal context that led to the development and elaboration of the welfare approach. He points to the importance of people and places in its development and to the series of studies (again the cumulative nature of research) that resulted in its elaboration. Smith suggests that certain pressures – his desire to write and love of writing, publishing commitments – also shape research and with more time (and therefore reading and thinking) the welfare approach may have been somewhat differently made. And he demonstrates that the institutional context – the university and its funding – may not only constrain the nature of research but also stop it altogether, not by censorship but by ensuring through its demands 'the demise of the creative spirit'.

In the tenth chapter, Linda McDowell argues the case for a particular research orientation, feminism. While the problems of gender-blindness are discussed by O'Keefe and Peet, and by Rogerson and Beavon (see also Bowlby *et al.*, 1986), this collection has a similar male bias to that of Bell and Newby (1977), a bias not unnoticed by the editors of a later collection (Bell and Roberts, 1984). McDowell herself addresses the issue of bias, locating feminist research in broader social movements and changes. She highlights the problems of research on women and their activities, and of choosing a topic, commenting that the key task is to deepen 'knowledge of the *variety* of women's experience'. Before looking at how feminist research can enhance theoretical developments, McDowell examines the problems of doing research, exploring the attempts to develop feminist method. However, the aim is not to create a 'supermethodology', but to work together for change by challenging the construction and validity of knowledge. In other words, what is made by the research process must be itself fully interrogated.

In the final essay, Ron Johnston examines the different ways in which knowledge is made, i.e. the philosophical bases that order and promote different varieties of science. But his main aim is to explore how research is disseminated through geographical writing. He readily admits that much of his discussion refers to publishing in the geographical literature which enables us to pose the question that if the findings of research are not published, is geography truly made? The answer must surely be that research that remains as an unpublished Ph.D. or known only to a few peers is only partly made. Important as such research is for self-development and awareness, scientific practice demands that we share our work with our community of scholars, and perhaps the community at large. Johnston points to the values that scientists use to evaluate contributions to the advancement of knowledge, how particular versions of science shape this advancement (including the norm of research process and dissemination in human geography) and the role of 'gatekeepers' in affecting what is produced and published. With these gatekeepers we have in a way come full circle because Ron Johnston's 'journal editor' has a similar power to Peter Gould's 'research committee' in influencing the making and re-making of human geography.

In conclusion, I would like to ask myself a question. Did the contributors succeed in carrying out the tasks I set them in the guidelines for the volume? Collectively, I think that they did. Further, I do not consider it realistic to expect all to inform in similar fashion on every respect. Patently, some of the aspects are irrelevant to some of the approaches described. But in providing personal accounts of research or case studies from an avowedly distinctive perspective, they try to tell us how they practised (and continue to practise) research. They, therefore, enable a greater understanding of epistēmē as well as technē (Gouldner, 1967). The practice and reporting of human geographical research have provided a grounding in technē, the lessons of experience, of clever skills refined through diligent practice, while that in epistēmē, awareness of the known, of the knower and of the knowing, is only now emerging through theoretical debate and methodological pluralism. It may be that the development of epistēmē will finally depend upon the analytical dissection of the known, knower and knowing, although the implications in this context – research on research – seem rather introspective (but see Baldamus, 1972). And while self-portraiture may be regarded as an indulgence, the pursuit of epistēmē and analytic dissection is enhanced by exposing the research process to the critical gaze so we may all understand it better and interrogate our own ways of making geography.

References

Baldamus, W. (1972) The role of discoveries in social science. In T. Shanin (ed.), *The Rules of the Game*. Tavistock, London.
Bell, C. (1984) The SSRC: restructured and defended. In Bell and Roberts (1984), 14–31.

Bell, C. and Encel, S. (eds) (1978) *Inside the Whale: ten personal accounts of social research*. Allen & Unwin, Sydney.

Bell, C. and Newby, H. (eds) (1977) *Doing Sociological Research*. Allen & Unwin, London.

Bell, C. and Roberts, H. (eds) (1984) *Social Researching: politics, problems, practice*. Routledge & Kegan Paul, London.

Bernstein, B. (1974) Sociology and the sociology of education. In J. Rex (ed.), *Approaches to Sociology*. Routledge & Kegan Paul, London.

Bowlby, S. R., Foord, J. and McDowell, L. (1986) The place of gender in locality studies. *Area*, 18, 327–31.

Burgess, R. G. (1984) *In the Field*. Allen & Unwin, London.

Buttimer, A. (ed.) (1983) *The Practice of Geography*. Longman, London.

Clarke, M. (1975) Survival in the field: implications of personal experience in field work. *Theory and Society*, 2, 95–123.

Cornwell, J. (1984) *Hard-earned Lives*. Tavistock, London.

Eyles, J. (1986) Britain. In J. Eyles (ed.), *Social Geography in International Perspective*. Croom Helm, London.

Eyles, J. and Smith, D. M. (eds) (1988) *Qualitative Methods in Human Geography*. Polity Press, Cambridge.

Geertz, C. (1973) *The Interpretation of Cultures*. Harper, New York.

Gould, P. (1985) *The Geographer at Work*. Routledge & Kegan Paul, London.

Gouldner, A. W. (1967) *Enter Plato*. Routledge & Kegan Paul, London.

Gregory, D. (1986) Marxist geography. In R. J. Johnston (ed.), *The Dictionary of Human Geography*. Blackwell, Oxford.

Hammond, P. (1964) *Sociologists at Work*. Basic Books, New York.

Harré, R. (1979) *Social Being*. Blackwell, Oxford.

Horowitz, I. (1967) *The Rise and Fall of Project Camelot*. MIT Press, Cambridge, Mass.

Massey, D. (1984) *Spatial Divisions of Labour*. Macmillan, London.

Massey, D. and Meegan, R. (1985a) Introduction: the debate. In D. Massey and R. Meegan (eds), *Politics and Method*. Methuen, London.

Massey, D. and Meegan, R. (1985b) Postscript: doing research. In D. Massey and R. Meegan (eds), *Politics and Method*. Methuen, London.

Mills, C. W. (1956) *The Sociological Imagination*. Oxford University Press, New York.

Peet, R. (ed.) (1977) *Radical Geography*. Maaroufa Press, Chicago.

Roberts, H. (ed.) (1981) *Doing Feminist Research*. Routledge & Kegan Paul, London.

Sayer, A. (1984) *Method in Social Science*. Hutchinson, London.

Sayer, A. and Morgan, K. (1985) A modern industry in a declining region: links between method, theory and policy. In D. Massey and R. Meegan (eds), *Politics and Method*. Methuen, London.

2

Expose Yourself to Geographic Research

Peter Gould

'Is the scientific paper a fraud?' (Title of a paper by Peter Medawar in *The Listener*)

[Answer: You better believe it!]

By Way of a Somewhat Lengthy Preamble

If you take a course on Research Methods, it is unlikely that you will be told that introductory paragraphs of papers, or first chapters of books and theses, are often written last. As we shall see, you will normally be obliged to set out the entire form and structure of what you want to say long before you know what it is that you are going to say. That this ritualistic requirement is all back-to-front and topsy-turvy is . . . well, precisely the point of this essay. And in writing this essay I have been forced to come back to the beginning just as I was ending it. This is because the Truth, whether derived from experience, thoughtful reflection, or research (often in various combinations), sometimes makes its own demands upon us. John Eyles, the editor of this volume, asked me to set out how I *actually* went about a piece of research, what were the ideas, what were the real difficulties, what were the joys and sorrows of a concrete piece of geographic inquiry. But as I was setting down some of the things that happen during a research project, I started to think. This, of course, is often fatal. In thinking about research, what I came to see was the enormous amount of pretentious ritual that students are made to wallow through before they can undertake imaginative inquiry about something they find intriguing. So to be Truthful, I really felt I had to undertake a sort of intellectual slash-and-burn operation, and make a clearing in which people might start to think afresh about inquiry – *all* inquiry, including the geographic.

The Joys and Sorrows of a Geographer

I am going to assume that you have been 'called to geography', although I will be the first to admit that this expression has a rather funny ring to it these days. The idea of being *called* to a particular way of looking at the world may be appropriate for people in some form of religious or artistic life, but it seems a bit excessive for others. Most of us can accept that poets are called, at least the really good ones who disclose and sing with words; and so are the artists who paint, sculpt, etch, and draw simply because they must. Dancers, too, those who are driven by a disciplining, rhythmic demon inside of them; and composers and musicians, the ones who seem to have no choice but to set down what they hear, to bring forth for others what has been granted to them. Religious and artistic ways of life have a certain feeling about them that makes the notion of a 'calling' appropriate. But can it really be applied to geographers?

Of course it can, although only you can tell whether you feel that sense of calling, that compulsive drive that tells you that you do not want to do anything else. Only you know whether you will become a professional geographer, despite the obstacles in your path. Which means you have already seen a clear distinction between commendable amateur enthusiasm and truly professional dedication, and have decided that you will be responsible for pointing your own life in the direction of the latter. After all, life is not a rehearsal – one performance only.

Your decision to follow this particular calling gives you great freedom. It also, quite paradoxically, imposes some considerable constraints. The freedom is given to you because the geographic way of looking places few bounds upon the actual subject-matter you may inquire about. There are few things of interest at the human scale that cannot be illuminated by thinking about them as a geographer. However, that same decision also places some constraints upon you. The first is sheer, professional responsibility. The very eclecticism of geographic inquiry, and the feeling that many different things are connected together, can easily lead to superficiality. Geography, as a way of looking at the world, touches upon many other, much more limited and specialized, ways of considering people and things. Along the geographic way you are going to meet many others with a particular passion for inquiry in much more limited domains. If you choose to look at these things from your own geographic perspective, you owe it to yourself, and to the way of looking to which you have been called, to gain a reasonable grasp of what is already known in these more limited areas.

Unfortunately, by taking on the responsibility to inform your own inquiries with the more specialized knowledge of others, you immediately expose yourself to another danger. That same specialized knowledge you acquire from others can also constrain your own inquiries from a geographic perspective, and severely limit your thinking by channelling it down a certain way of already established procedures that address already established questions. So at this point things look pretty bleak; you may feel that there is no way you can win, that you are damned if you do, and damned if you do not. If you do *not* expose yourself to more specialized and established ways of thinking and inquiring, you may miss something important, and so be labelled superficial; but if you *do* thoroughly investigate these more specialized ways of inquiry, then your thinking may be so conditioned that you end up as a psychologist, hydrologist, or even an economist. At this point, genuine and open *geographic* inquiry becomes practically impossible, because your thinking now has become trapped in those particular paradigmic ways of accepted procedures that metamorphose genuine inquiry into the rituals and forms of professionally accepted research. These rituals and forms have the capacity to shape severely the questions, procedures, methods and presentations, and we should take a moment to look at them more carefully.

Rituals and Forms

It must be difficult being a student today. There seems to be so little freedom to go your own way, to choose your own questions, and to make your own mistakes. It always seems that there is a right way of doing things, an approved-by-your-adviser-or-tutor-or-committee way of doing things. Follow *their* way and all will be well, but stray from the path of righteousness, and you will be crunched. Of course, this do-as-I-say way is fine for the person who likes being told what to do. In fact, if you do it well, you can even plot all the way to a PhD. Unfortunately, it is a way almost guaranteed to frustrate the really imaginative and curious person, and nowhere is conformity more apparent than in the outlining and writing of research proposals, whether for an undergraduate paper or thesis, or for a postdoctoral research programme funded by a national agency.

The problem is that no-one is allowed to say openly and honestly 'Well, what I really want to do is poke around in this area and see what I can find.' Before you can do what you want to do, you will have to posture, pose and distort as you formalize and disguise your geographic curiosity in the great ritual of the Research Proposal. This document may have little to do with what you really want to accomplish, or the way you will actually go about it when your adviser or committee have been lulled into thinking that it is all right to unleash you. Perhaps the great Research Proposal is really designed to protect the adviser, committee, or the 'dispenser of funds'. The 'system' holds them responsible for judging whether you can be unleashed or not, and the best way for them to cover themselves is to make you tell them what you think you are going to do, how you are going to do it, and what you are going to find . . . *before* you have done it. Yes, I know, it all seems a bit backwards, but I am trying to be honest about what actually takes place. You will be told that all this is designed to help and protect you, but as you struggle to squeeze your enthusiastic curiosity into thoroughly irksome ritualistic forms, the feeling will grow upon you that this cannot possibly be right. And you will certainly be partly correct. What you are going through is a *rite de passage* to ensure that you conform to the accepted (ahem!) *paradigm*. Invariably, this paradigm is the one into which your adviser was inculcated when he or she was a graduate student. This is why most academic research is so sluggish and slow to change. The priests of one generation train the acolytes of the next.

What are the pieces of such a proposal? First of all, you will have to outline it, and the more formally you do it the better. A detailed hierarchical structure, with all the Roman numerals and subsections of subsections, will do much to convince Them that you are on the right track. Of course, you will have to fill in all those hierarchical subsections with things that you invent out of thin air, for the simple reason that you have not done the research yet. How can you possibly know whether you will find X when you have not looked, or that method Y will work when you have not tried it? If it all seems senseless and back-to-front, just remember, there are people in the academic world who spend their lives doing this. They outline, collect bibliographic references, and do literature searches, because they are much more intrigued with the forms of the ritual dances than actual inquiry. All too often, those who do little research themselves are the ones who teach others how to do it.

Now quite obviously the time to outline and structure your thinking and findings is *after* you have done the research, when you really have something to say, and so have the responsibility to say it clearly, fluently and well to your reader. But I doubt that anyone will tell you this. It would undermine one of the great rituals of the day, a ritual that can only make you feel fraudulent, uncomfortable, and perhaps humiliated. I use the last word advisedly. When I first started to teach, one of the 'Great Figures' of the day said, with characteristically unquestioned authority, that 'the purpose of writing research proposals, and holding doctoral examinations, is to give the student a good dose of humility'. I cannot think of a more inappropriate or humanly disgusting attitude for a teacher to have, and I despised the man from that day on.

Secondly, you may be forced to pose hypotheses, no matter how banal these seem, although what you *really* want to do is observe carefully, closely, openly, and with as little prejudice as you can muster, and then describe, with insight, skill, and thoughtful imagination, the topic you have chosen. In the process, you hope that along the way all sorts of interesting things turn up that you could not possibly have anticipated. But such a natural hope and expectation that things might come to light that were not seen before is something that the 'formalists' do not talk about. Hypotheses it must be, even if these have to be winkled out on the end of a blunt paradigmic pin.

One problem with such hypothetical mouthings is that they tend to be dissimulating. After all, what on earth is the use of posing a hypothesis if you are pretty sure it is going to fail? If you think it is going to fail, why pose it in the first place? Still, you can always get around this by posing the alternative hypothesis as your original hypothesis, and with this intellectual pirouette demonstrate your positive approach to scientific research. Unfortunately, there is another problem: once you set the hypothesis down in the accepted form, you find yourself trapped into having to test the wretched thing in some way that is equally acceptable. This, almost invariably, means Statistical Methodology these days. This is because we increasingly confuse this highly constrained and limited way of marshalling certain types of evidence with *the* Scientific Method. This confusion, and how it came to be, is a deep and important topic for the intellectual historian of the 20th century, but we cannot pursue it any further here. Still, it is worth pointing out that science made splendid progress for 300 years before the statisticians came along, and that most of the really great names in the history of science never posed a statistically testable hypothesis in their lives. Of course, they certainly had hunches, and they pursued these with great skill, imagination, and diligence; but few of them ever set down a formal hypothesis, and then went on to test it at the five per cent level of significance. Most really good scientists have the intellectual self-confidence to put this limited domain of methodology firmly in its place, and only bring it out when it is needed. Only people who are intellectually insecure hang on to the coat tails of the statistician in order to make their often banal questions and findings acceptable to Them. I have the uncomfortable feeling that the more statistical tests of significance are reported, the more banal, plodding and pedestrian the research is likely to be. What is continually ignored by those who cling to the forms and rituals is that most *eureka* experiences come from *descriptions* of the physical, biological and human worlds that allow us to see something we did not see before – like $e = mc^2$, models of DNA molecules, huge water ripples in Washington scablands, gaps in chemical tables, jumping genes, and subducting plates. The *eureka* experience does not have to be exactly Archimedean in its explosive power – there is no need to expose yourself to that extent –

but it should mean that something not seen before emerges into the open clearing of our thinking. Something *dawns* on us, we say 'Oh, I *see!*', and I think it is worth pausing for a moment and thinking about the phrases we use when something like this happens.

Notice how we constantly use images of light whenever we try to express our own sense of coming-to-understand-something. We direct our thinking, which means we direct ourselves, like an illuminating beam to light up something that was there all along, only *we did not see it before*. In every science, and in all successful research, there are moments of sudden seeing when something that was concealed from us becomes unconcealed. Which is exactly why *aletheia* for the Greeks was the word for truth, the *a* negating the *Lethe*, the dark underworld of concealment, to make truth un-concealment.

Statistical Significance and Meaning

Now contrary to what you may be thinking at this point, this is not a tirade against statistical methods and statisticians. Sometimes these ways of marshalling evidence are perfectly appropriate, and may be the only feasible possibility of bringing evidence to bear on a particular question. But this *possibility* should not force all research into it. We have to be very careful to distinguish between what is simply significant in a statistical sense, and what is meaningful. Often, in a statistical approach, something, sometime, somewhere will seem worth reporting as 'significant', simply because 'significance' is tautologically defined within the totally closed system of statistical thinking. Something is significant because the N (sample size) and the p (probability level) say it is so. And N and p say it is so because that is what has been defined as significant. The trouble is that *significant* does not mean *meaningful*, and 'meaningful' means capable of being given persuasive interpretation – at least for the historically contingent moment.

What do we *really* do when we undertake a piece of research? First, there is no point in undertaking research at all unless the topic, the general area of inquiry, fascinates you. To do research simply because some requirement for an academic degree says you must is one of the most anti-intellectual and soul-destroying things I can think of. Secondly, interesting research, the sort that discloses unexpected things and perspectives, is nearly always a difficult-to-talk-about and strange mixture of successes and failures, hopes and disappointments, times when you wish a day had a hundred hours, and other times when you groan because you know it does. In any research, there are times when you have to grit your teeth to get through some miserable task at hand (gathering, coding, plotting, drawing, programming, computing, etc.).

But perhaps the best way to demonstrate this is to tell you the story of one piece of research. Not because it was particularly meritorious (no DNAs or $e = mc^2$s), but simply because it was my own and I know it best.

The Story of Mental Maps

It really started one afternoon in 1966, fiddling around on a blackboard, and thinking in what I can only call a 'gravity model mood'. Like many geographers I nearly always have to draw pictures when I think, or before I can convince myself that I really understand something. I was wondering how so many forms of human interaction were predicted quite well by very simple gravity model ideas. In those days (long before Alan Wilson was to derive the entropy maximizing version), these were straightforward Newtonian, $I = P_1 . P_2/D$ analogies, used to describe journey-to-work, shopping, and air traffic movements. These were rooted in the 19th-century tradition of Reilly's migration studies and Comte's social physics.

The early 1960s were the days when geographers were starting to drive the questions back to the human beings who were actually doing the deciding about locating, moving, growing, making, investing, buying, and so on, and notions like decision-making, optimization, normative models, information, satisficing behaviour, and things like that were in the air (Billinge, Gregory and Martin, 1984). It was out of this intellectual flux that something called Behavioral Geography was to emerge, and in this embryonic context it seemed quite reasonable to ask individuals where they might like to live if they had an absolutely free choice. To what extent were broad patterns of movement simply a result of many people doing what they wanted to do? Could you get them to rank places in order of preference? Could you actually *measure* people's preferences? And what would you do with the responses if you got them?

The last question was interesting to someone who was intrigued with methodology for its own sake, although you never actually dared to admit this. Remember, you started in the great Research Proposal tradition, posed a problem in a pretentious series of null hypotheses, and only then decided 'what was the most suitable methodology' – a phrase intoned in a solemn voice of quite impeccable transcendental seriousness that nearly always means the established way of doing things is driving you rapidly towards thoughtless hypocrisy. In fact, it often worked the other way around: you came across a then-new and intriguing method, cast around for a problem (usually with a body of readily-available numerical data that would let you use it), and then proceeded to work things through, hoping that something interesting and interpretable would emerge at the other end. Not surprisingly, it often did, and some of the most imaginative and illuminating research of those days came from precisely this much scorned and disparaged 'methodology first' way of going about things. Actually, if you are really prepared to think about it, rather than simply pouring scorn on it, it is really not so surprising that some 'illumination' of a problem should appear. When we look at something in a different *way*, from a different perspective, we often see things that we did not see before. And the reason I italicized *way* in that last sentence is precisely because methodology means a way (*hodos*) towards knowledge (*logos*). If you explore a new *way*, if you take a different path, it seems quite likely that you will see something from a different angle. And if a definition of scientific research does not encompass seeing things differently along new ways, then I submit that there is no hope for any of us. It means that today's Establishment, bred in the graduate schools of the late 1960s and early 1970s, have got such a grip on our thinking that we can no longer call it our own.

Now these were factor analytic days, when the world was a great data cube of things, places, and times (Berry, 1968), and depending upon how you sliced the cube, you could run the gamut from O to T modes (Cattell, 1966). So people and their preferences for places immediately suggested an m-places versus n-people data matrix, and although places were unique (and, therefore, according to the Traditional Authorities, were not capable of being studied *scientifically*), and although everyone knew that people were also unique (and, therefore, according to the TAs, not capable of being studied *scientifically*), it was rather fun thinking about what it might *mean* if you factor analysed such a places v people matrix.[1] At least it seemed worth a try, and since I already had a PhD, and did not have to write Research Proposals, but could just say to myself 'I wonder what would happen if . . . ' I went ahead and did what I wondered. At least a PhD is good for something.

So I asked students in a beginning class to put themselves in a mood of totally free, money-doesn't-matter choice, and then to rank order their preferences for the states of the USA. I then factor analysed the preference matrix, doing all sorts of totally forbidden and undefined mathematical operations, computed the scores for the states, and plotted them on a map (Abler, Adams and Gould, 1972). It was that map of the 'preference surface' that was the interesting thing to drop out of the other end. I then got kind colleagues at Minnesota and Berkeley to do similar 'where-would-you-like-to-live' surveys, and at that point some really very interesting and unexpected things started to appear. Although taken from groups of young adults thousands of miles apart, the mental maps from Pennsylvania, Minnesota and California were almost identical except for a dome of residential desirability right around the local area. A little later, I found the same thing in Britain, thanks to Rod White (Gould and White, 1968, 1986), who did most of the dirty work, and Peter Haggett, who arranged for the school teachers attending the Madingley Lectures at Cambridge to take part. In Nigeria, Dan Ola (Gould and Ola, 1970), found the same sort of thing, and also uncovered the possibility that young people were learning about places in rather regular and predictable ways.

As a result of this rather haphazard poking around, factor analysing, and 'wondering if . . . ', I reached the point where I wanted to undertake a full-fledged study, a study that would allow me to ask all sorts of questions whose answers could not even be contemplated without lots of data. For this I needed a reasonably small country, with a good schooling system, and a tradition of geographers being involved in practical and useful research. To cut a very long story short, I found such a country in Sweden, together with a group of geographers at Lund who could open some very necessary doors to get people high in the educational system to grant me permission to approach principals and teachers for their help. But for this I needed money, and so I found myself back in the grip of the great Research Proposal. Although it was eventually dressed up in the necessarily pretentious phrases, implying that if the research were not conducted the intellectual life of all humankind would be greatly impoverished, what it really said between the lines was 'I want to go to Sweden, gather very large quantities of data relating to people's preferences and geographic information, and then see what I can find.' But, of course, I could not just say that honestly and openly. One reviewer objected to the proposal with the question 'But where is the *model?*' meaning, in essence, where were the equations that should have been hypothesized before any research had been done to explain why Person X at Place Y liked Place Z – at least to a certain degree of probability. As usual, all these equations had to be written down beforehand, and it did not matter particularly whether they made any sense ultimately or not. The important thing was that you had something in the accepted *form* that could be tested with equally accepted statistical procedures. No one really gave a damn whether you accepted or rejected your essentially meaningless null hypotheses and intellectual pirouettes at the end of the research. Form was everything, and trying to uncover the Truth was not only a poor and distant second, but was considered by the *cognoscenti* to be really quite distressingly naïve as well. After all, *everyone* knew that Truth was either relative, or really did not exist anyway. The important thing was to put forward a model, and then accept or reject it at the five per cent level. Fortunately, there were enough reviewers who thought that trying to find out something new was still acceptable science, so eventually some money came through.

The Expected and the Unexpected[2]

What came out of this research, research based on about 11,000 returns of residential preferences and geographic information from Swedes living in 58 of the 70 regions, ranging from seven-and-a-half-year-olds to adults? First of all, things that were expected, expected in the sense that what was found confirmed some of the things that we already suspected from the USA, UK, and Nigeria. It was clear that most people, by the time they became adults, had developed a preference surface that displayed marked similarities to those generated by people at other locations (68). These collective images of people's likes and dislikes for places had so many things in common that it seemed legitimate to construct a 'National Perception Surface' (70). Then a particular regional surface, generated by people from a particular location, could be composed of this shared, national view convoluted with a 'Local Dome of Desirability'.

But it was here that the North of Sweden started to be troublesome by refusing to fit. The 'awkward' viewpoints from the Northerners also raised the question of the strength of the preference 'signal', and this seemed to be measured nicely, but quite fortuitously, by something that was at the heart of the principal component methodology (45). Very strong agreement about residential desirability meant a large eigenvalue (λ_1) associated with the first component, and a correspondingly much smaller one (λ_2) measuring the second. So if the ratio were large, it meant a very strong preference signal, while a small ratio implied that there were at least two major viewpoints that were construed as quite independent of each other. I expected that as people went from childhood to adulthood, the rather fuzzy, and not very well informed, preferences of childhood would become stronger and stronger. After all, small children do not know very much about most places to make any really informed judgment about them (48), but as they grow older, and share roughly the same streams of information, the strengthening preference signals should 'crystallize out'. I expected to get rather nice S-shaped learning curves, and in the south of Sweden I found some evidence for them (119). All the indices of spatial preference rose nicely, and then levelled off from about 18 years old onwards.

The only problem was that the scatter around the learning curve was enormous (118), and, once again, the Northerners were refusing to fit. I was getting a rather jaundiced view of northern Swedes by this time, until I remembered that as a real scientist I had to conduct my research in a totally unemotional and objective way. Even so, those damned Northerners were messing everything up. No nice sensible and rational learning curves, but a miserable flat mess all over the place (120), and it did not matter what age the wretches were, they did not seem to agree about anything. However, when the indices were plotted on a map, an extraordinarily regular trend appeared in *geographic* space (121)! This was quite uncanny, totally unexpected, and not the sort of thing that could possibly have been hypothesized in any ritualistic way before the research started. The degree of agreement in a group of people for the residential desirability of other places did not seem to vary consistently with age, but only with relative geographic location. I submit that only a geographer, and only an unleashed empirical geographer at that, could have brought this fact to light. Economists, sociologists, psychologists, and other human scientists, just do not *think* to investigate in these ways and directions.

But the next question was *why?* Frankly, I am not really sure why to this day, but I think the answer probably lies somewhere in that tricky, difficult-to-measure business of *information*. If people share to a very high degree the same sets of information, then we would expect people to transform them into roughly similar likes and dislikes. If a raw and simple measure of information is highly predictable from location, it seems perfectly reasonable to expect that Northerners will share a set of quite homogeneous information, even though the actual content may be different from the set of information shared by Southerners. So both the Southerners and Northerners, with their own quite homogeneous sets of information, *should* have preference 'signals' of roughly similar strength. But they did not. That extraordinarily regular change of the agreement indices over geographic space pointed to something else at work. The homogeneity of the information sets shared by groups of people at a place must vary in some very regular way with location. *Why?*

Perhaps it is because we acquire geographic information in basically two different ways: we can either sit there and let the information come to us, or move about and learn about places through our travels. The more we choose *not* to be prisoners of our location, *not* to let Them transmit what they choose to us, the less our own quite personal preferences will resemble those of others immediately around us.

So how do people travel and move around the country, acquiring in the process fresh information that differs from the transmitted information shared by the stay-at-homes? At this point, something geographically very deep seems to emerge, something we still have not really clarified as geographers. People, as a rule, visit and interact with other people – visits to relatives, friends, and so on. So where there are many people, we would expect the visits of many travellers. Conversely, in areas of few people, we would expect few travellers.[3] So how the people of a country are distributed will strongly influence how people travel, and so influence, in turn, the degree of homogeneity of their information which they form into their own, quite personal, geographic preferences. Just by sheer luck (for I had no inkling at the beginning that the information would ultimately be used in this way), I had asked the adults to tell me on the map-questionnaire what places and regions they had visited for a week or more. This seemed a reasonable length of time for a person to acquire some familiarity with a region, while cutting out those that were just traversed quickly by car or train.

When these visits were plotted on a map (126–136), some striking differences emerged. People in the South had made very few visits to the North, and over 90 per cent of them had confined their information-enriching travels to their own half of the country. Since this southern part already generated most of the transmitted information, these relatively local visits only reinforced their already strong homogeneous viewpoints. In marked contrast, people in the North had divided their information-acquiring travels about half and half between the North and South, so that in a well-defined sense they were much less parochial on the average than their southern peers. As a result, they had much more heterogeneous information sets, and these were reflected in the much lower agreement indices of their spatial preferences.

Emerging Problems and Linkages

Out of this empirically based programme of research, some provocative glimpses of more coherent, perhaps proto-theoretic, ideas were seen, and these glimpses still continue to brighten. At the macro-scale, the travel patterns influencing information and preference were perhaps nothing more than William Warntz's population potentials (Warntz, 1964). Even deeper was the fact that although the information was quite strongly predictable from simple gravity model ideas, the estimates of the 'friction of distance' were anything but consistent (100). At the same time, they displayed, once again, extraordinary regularity over *geographic* space. What we had was the Curry Effect (Curry, 1972), in which the pattern of the interacting population was inextricably entwined with the estimates of the distance effect (102–106). Numbers purportedly measuring the average effect of distance on human behaviour were doing nothing of the sort. They were simply reflecting (in the literal sense of being a quadratic function of) relative location. But Curry's 'pattern of interacting population' was the autocorrelation function of the population map, and this really measured some deep *structural* properties of the distribution, properties that we have not come to the bottom of yet.

One of the rewarding things about carrying on empirical research is that sometimes the unexpected things that turn up do connect with ideas that have emerged from more theoretical perspectives. Some people would assert that this is back to front: it is the theory that should guide the empirical research. Happily, this is not how scientific research always and *actually* takes place, but only how logicians, who never do any research themselves, say it should take place (Hempel, 1965). In fact, it is a mixture of the two, the theoretical and the empirical, and a discipline, and even a person, may swing from one viewpoint to the other. Any time a theorist gets too conceited, just point out that there is nothing in all those deductions that was not contained in the original definitions. It is 'just' a matter of grinding out the consequences – a merely mechanical task. Which says, of course, that theory is really grounded on fruitful definitions, not the relatively trivial binary operations of logic which follow. Even a computer can do these, if it has been properly trained, i.e. programmed.

On the other hand, any time an empiricist gets too uppity, and sneers at all that abstract theoretical stuff, just point out that without systematic, coherent, and connected ideas and concepts, all our 'facts' will remain unstructured heaps, like untidy hayricks scattered around an intellectual landscape. This means that to see all the possibilities of your research, to bring these to light, you must try very hard to keep your own thinking open for the unexpected things that might emerge from the empirical realm, and also try to see how these might fit in, or perhaps even reshape, the theoretical frameworks that are currently available. To do research that genuinely illuminates requires a lust for both the theoretical and the empirical. One is useless without the other, in the sense that one unconnected to the other has no *meaning*. There is simply no point in carrying out theoretical work unless its ultimate purpose is to illuminate a concrete aspect of our world, and equally no point in carrying out empirical work if its ultimate purpose is to throw up another factual hayrick. The problem is that the theorist may become so enchanted with the formal logical operations that the *geographic* purpose is forgotten. Equally, the empiricist may become so enchanted with the factual details – another hayrick for the collection – that, once again, the *geographic* purpose passes beyond recall. As a geographer you must learn to ride two horses, and if they decide to diverge, and split you up the middle . . . well, surgeons can do wonders these days.

However, if you can become highly aware and sensitive to theoretical problems confronting geographers *before* you enter an area of empirical research, you obviously enhance your capacity for seeing connections between the *concrete* things emerging from the substantive topic you have chosen, and the more *abstract* concepts that may deepen your understanding and enhance your appreciation for the difficulties involved. Sometimes these difficulties turn out to be methodological, again in the literal sense of finding an appropriate way towards knowledge. Several appeared during the research, including a couple of mathematical questions that no one had ever solved, although they were tractable with Monte Carlo methods (118, 150–151). But let me point towards one particular difficulty that is especially geographic, even if we get into rather deep technical, and even philosophical, waters.

You would think that after 2500 years, and a century in the university, that geographers would know how to compare maps, and be able to tell you if one map was 'significantly different' from another. Let me try to convince you that we are not very good at this apparently simple, usually totally taken-for-granted, task.[4] First, why would we want to compare maps? In this context, we might want to know if the spatial preferences of men were different from those of women. Or whether those of well-educated people were different from those less well-educated. Or whether young adults look at things differently compared to more elderly people, and so on. An obvious way of comparing two sets of numerical values distributed over the same map is to subtract one map from the other to highlight the differences. If the differences are small, and randomly scattered, we might be tempted to say that there was no significant difference between them. The small differences are just due to 'random noise' – whatever we mean by that.

But suppose all the positive differences form 'distinct clusters', by which we presumably mean clusters of areas (regions) on the map that were *not* random? As geographers, and indeed as human beings, our eyes are drawn towards patterns formed by distinctive blobs. Which raises the question of what we mean by 'distinctive blobs'. Presumably we mean blobs that are unlikely to occur just by a chance, random assignment, of, say, positive differences to the map – shown, to keep things simple, as black, rather than white, regions. But some blobs *will* form just by chance on a map, just from a random assignment, depending upon how the regions *are connected together*. In other words, blobbing also depends on the underlying contiguity structure of the map. But a contiguity matrix is a relation on a set, and this allows us to make the cartographic structure explicit as a simplicial complex of zero obstruction (Atkin, 1974). The assignment of positive differences constitutes a mapping that fragments the complex and raises the values in the obstruction vector (Johnson, 1983). What obstruction values should we expect? It depends upon the number of differences, n, we assign, i.e. the mapping $\Delta_i : \kappa_1 \rightarrow \kappa_2$. We know little about these mappings now, and I knew nothing of them then, although extensive Monte Carlo simulations (143) gave me an idea of what to expect. But even these did not solve the problem, because, once again, the generation of such a statistical 'text' from the purely technical perspective did not solve the interpretive task of the hermeneutic (Gould, 1985a). It was the old question of statistical significance as opposed to geographic meaning. Blobs of a certain size might occur quite often as a result of random assignments, and from a purely statistical point of view these would be dismissed as insignificant. But if these blobs happen to fall *meaningfully*

around the major urban areas of Sweden, no geographer in her right
mind would dismiss them as insignificant.

So how *do* we compare maps? Meaningfully . . . only meaningfully.
Which means the use of rhetoric – linguistic, graphic, and algebraic –
to persuade a reader that the story is true. Geographic research, like any
other scientific research, is story telling. Only do not tell the 'scientists'
– they are such intellectual prudes that they get frightfully embarrassed
by being thus exposed.

Geographic Structures

For nearly three decades now, various pieces of theoretical and empirical
research have been pointing towards the fundamental implications of the
structure of geographic space, and these are going to be found at a
variety of scales and times. At the macro-scale, both information and
preference are conditioned by by the distribution of population that
constitutes the source of human interaction. This is summarized in the
autocorrelation function that enters, and distorts, any estimate of the
effect of distance on human behavior, and this idea has now been
confirmed and extended (Fotheringham, 1981). At the meso-scale, the
actual structure of the transport network comes into play, shaping the
way in which the information surfaces of children 'emerge' in highly
regular and predictable ways (79, 93). At this scale, there are often clear
corridors of travel, or perhaps warped probability fields, shaped by the
way geographic space is structured for human purposes. Hägerstrand,
for example, has put forward the idea that these 'structural channels'
may be extraordinarily stable, influencing the spread of innovations and
diseases in very consistent ways over long historical periods (Hägerstrand,
1966). Again, confirmation comes from two studies of historical
epidemiology (Pyle, 1969; Pyle and Patterson, 1984), but we still know
very little about the way the geographic structure of one time influences
and shapes another. Indeed, we really do not know very much about
geographic structure at all: how it maintains its form and influence, how
structures at one scale aggregate, or disaggregate, at other scales (Couclelis,
1982), how societies maintain their geographic structures, and are shaped
by them in turn (Gregory, 1984; Pred, 1982). In fact, we are not very
good yet at making our strongly intuitive notions of *structure* actually and
concretely operational (Atkin, 1977; Johnson, 1983; Gould, 1980;
Beaumont and Gatrell, 1982). Yet it is clear that in a newer perspective
and terminology trying to grasp these difficulties, the connectivity
and dimensionality of the structural backcloth always have important
consequences for the traffic that exists upon it and is transmitted over
it. It is only by seeing these different things in the context of common

structural concern that apparently disparate and unconnected pieces of geographic research begin to connect up, and we can begin to limn the still fragile, but gradually strengthening, fabric that *is* human geography (Gould, 1985b). As one who has been called, you must attempt, in every waking (and even dreaming) moment of your professional life, to see the connections that make up the structure of geography. Otherwise, things fall apart . . . because the center cannot hold. As the poet Yeats well knew. But then, poets have that capacity to expose themselves for Truth, rather than Sooth, saying.

Notes

1   The extraordinary insight that all places are unique, because no place is located where any other place is located, is one that we owe to Professor Herman Krick (1962), quoted in Gould (1985b, p. 19).
2   There is simply not room here to include large numbers of tables, maps and graphs. These are found in *People in Information Space* (Gould, 1975), one of the *Lund Studies in Geography, Series B*, which you should really have alongside you as you read. All page references in this section refer to this monograph.
3   Although we recognize that places of outstanding beauty may attract sightseers, even though there may be few people actually living there.
4   The problem crops up everywhere. For example, when does a dot map of a particular surname differ significantly from one that is simply a result of sampling from the general population? This might have genetic implications (Lasker, 1985).

References

Abler, R., Adams, J. and Gould, P. (1972) *Spatial Organization: The Geographer's View of the World*. Prentice-Hall, Englewood Cliffs.
Atkin, R. (1974) *Mathematical Structure in Human Affairs*. Heinemann Educational Books, London.
Atkin, R. (1977) *Combinatorial Connectivities in Social Systems*. Birkhauser, Basel.
Beaumont, J. and Gatrell, A. (1982) *An Introduction to Q-analysis*. Catmog Series No. 34, Norwich.
Berry, B. (1968) Approaches to regional analysis: a synthesis. In B. Berry and D. Marble (eds), *Spatial Analysis: A Reader in Statistical Geography*, 24–34. Prentice-Hall, Englewood Cliffs.
Billinge, M., Gregory, D. and Martin, R. (1984) *Recollections of a Revolution: Geography as Spatial Science*. Macmillan, London.
Cattell, R. (1966) The data box: its ordering of total resources in terms of possible relational systems. In R. Cattell (ed.), *Handbook of Multivariate Psychology*, 67–128. Rand McNally, Chicago.
Couclelis, H. (1982) Philosophy in the construction of geographic reality. In P.

Gould and G. Olsson (eds), *A Search for Common Ground*, 105–38. Pion, London.

Curry, L. (1972) A spatial analysis of gravity flows, *Regional Studies*, 6, 131–47.

Fotheringham, A. (1981) Spatial structure and distance decay parameters, *Annals of the Association of American Geographers*, 71, 425–36.

Gould, P. (1975) *People in Information Space*. C. W. K. Gleerup, Lund.

Gould, P. (1980) Q-analysis or a language of structure, *International Journal of Man–Machine Studies*, 12, 169–99.

Gould, P. (1985a) Will geographic self-reflection make you blind? In R. Johnston (ed.), *The Future of Geography*, 276–90. Methuen, London.

Gould, P. (1985b) *The Geographer at Work*. Routledge & Kegan Paul, London.

Gould, P. and Ola, D. (1970) The perception of residential desirability in the western region of Nigeria, *Environment and Planning A*, 2, 73–87.

Gould, P. and White, R. (1968) The mental maps of British school leavers, *Regional Studies*, 2, 161–82.

Gould, P. and White, R. (1986) *Mental Maps*. George Allen & Unwin, London.

Gregory, D. (1984) People places and practices: the future of human geography. Address to the Geographical Association, London.

Hempel, C. (1965) *Aspects of Scientific Explanation*. Free Press, New York.

Hägerstrand, T. (1966) Aspects of spatial structure of social communication and the diffusion of information, *Papers and Proceedings of the Regional Science Association*, 16, 27–42.

Johnson, J. (1983) Q-analysis: a theory of stars, *Environment and Planning B*, 10, 457–69.

Krick, H. (1962) The geography of willow creek, *Geography*, 1, 18–21.

Lasker, G. (1985) *Surnames and Genetic Structure*, Cambridge University Press, Cambridge.

Medawar, P. (1963) Is the scientific paper a fraud?, *The Listener*, 70, 377–8.

Pred, A. (1982) Social reproduction and the time-geography of everyday life. In P. Gould and G. Olsson (eds), *A Search for Common Ground*, 157–86. Pion, London.

Pyle, G. (1969) Diffusion of cholera in the United States, *Geographical Analysis*, 1, 59–75.

Pyle, G. and Patterson, K. (1984) Influenza diffusion in European history. *Ecology of Disease*, 2, 173–84.

Warntz, W. (1964) A new map of the surface of population potentials for the United States 1960, *Geographical Review*, 54, 170–84.

Warntz, W. (1966) The topology of a socio-economic terrain and spatial flows, *Papers and Proceedings of the Regional Science Association*, 17, 47–61.

3

Research and the Private Sector: Assessing the Socio-economic Impacts of a New Coal Mine

Barry J. Garner

Some years ago, at the end of 1978 to be precise, I received a telephone call from a person called Ties (it's a Dutch name) whom I'd met the previous year when we were both serving on the Council of the New South Wales Geographical Society. After graduating with an Honours Degree in Geography, Ties started work with a well-known international firm of environmental consultants which specialized particularly in the field of environmental engineering and related areas. Ties was at the time a project manager in the firm's Sydney office and he clearly had a problem.

As a result of the telephone call and subsequent meetings, I agreed to help Ties out and was hired as a sub-consultant to work on a project of which he was then in charge. What follows is an account of the work undertaken as part of that project, of the experiences gained from what was then my very first foray into the world of consulting and 'doing research' for the private sector – the coal industry, and how this led to a proposal for a piece of more academically oriented research that was eventually funded by the Australian Research Grants Scheme.

Setting the Stage

Ties' firm had been awarded a contract to prepare an Environmental Impact Statement (EIS) for a proposed new open-cut coal mine in the Hunter Valley – a region that is about three hours drive to the north and west of Sydney, in New South Wales (NSW). You can easily locate it on a good map of Australia; it's the region behind the iron and steel port of Newcastle. Look for a town up the valley called Singleton and then about 30 km up another called Muswellbrook. The proposed coal mine was to be developed on a lease located between these two small country towns. When fully operational it was expected to employ 410–420 workers and produce 3.5 million tonnes of coal a year.

Although Ties' firm (and Ties himself for that matter) had much experience and a widely respected reputation in preparing EISs this particular one was a different matter. The State Government had just changed the rules by which the game was to be played by introducing a new set of guidelines for the preparation of an EIS for a surface coal mine. To understand the significance of this, and subsequent developments, it is helpful to know something of the context within which what was to follow took place.

The coalfields in the Upper Hunter Valley contain NSW's largest coal reserves. Coal mining had been an important part of the economy of the region for over 60 years – albeit on a relatively small scale. Since the mid-1970s, however, the scale and pace of coal and coal-related developments had accelerated remarkably. By June 1979, 17 coal mines – mostly open-cut – were operating in the region – concentrated mainly in an area of about 1000 km^2 referred to by the locals as the Singleton–Muswellbrook–Denman triangle. An estimated 2400 workers were directly employed in the industry there and production totalled some 15.4 million tonnes in 1978–79, almost half of which was exported through the port of Newcastle, mainly to Japanese steel mills and power stations.

The cost effects of the second oil crisis were beginning to bite at about this time so there was a rush to get into coal as a cheaper alternative source of energy and what was widely believed to be Australia's second mining boom began – short-lived as it eventually turned out to be. Spurred on by the bonanza of what was perceived by the coal industry to be unlimited markets globally for fossil fuels, intentions were announced by coal companies and international consortia – in which incidentally the major oil companies and Japanese interests were well represented – to develop a further 18–24 new coal mines (principally open-cut) in the area in the six years to 1985. At the same time many of the already existing mines planned to expand their operations. Production was forecast to double to between 35 and 45 million tonnes in the six years to 1986, by which time an additional 3700 workers were expected to be directly employed in the proposed new mines. Together with their spin-off effects the new and enlarged coal developments were confidently predicted to create additional jobs for about 5500 people in the Hunter Valley. It was an exciting scenario indeed.

The State Government, and especially the Premier, were elated, for only a short time before an important report had been released by the Hunter Region Planning Committee in which a very gloomy outlook was presented of the region's future (HRPC, 1977). The report – colloquially referred to as the Pumpkin Report on account of the shocking colour of its covers – claimed that as a result of structural changes in the regional economy there was a need to create an additional 20,000 new jobs in the Hunter region by 1982 if massive outmigration was to be avoided, unemployment eliminated and deterioration of the social infrastructure prevented. The picture was clearly not a very favourable one politically for the State Government, and promised to be even worse in human terms for those living there. All the indicators pointed to one conclusion – the Hunter region looked like becoming Australia's very first Depressed Area. It was feared that the 'Lucky Country', as Australia was then fondly thought of, might now at long last be about to run out of luck! (Horne, 1977).

The anticipated boom in coal mining, while helping to solve the problems of the ailing regional economy, of course presented a set of entirely new problems for the State Government – those associated with planning for the rapid large-scale growth in the region. Not only was it expected that there would be considerable impacts on the natural environment in the area as a result of coal developments but, more significantly, it was clear that the existing infrastructure in the area was inadequate to accommodate the anticipated inflow of new workers and their families. There would inevitably be significant and substantial socio-economic impacts in the region, particularly on the small towns of Singleton and Muswellbrook and at the villages in their rural hinterlands.

At this time, before the new planning legislation embodied in the 1979 Environmental Planning and Assessment Act came into effect, the role of evaluating the adequacy of EISs as a basis for granting development consent (permission to start a project) was the responsibility of the NSW State Pollution Control Commission (SPCC). The dominant emphasis in the preparation of an EIS for coal mines in NSW, as in other States, at the time was essentially the concern with the impact of proposals on the natural environment, particularly with regard to satisfying the requirements of the State's pollution control legislation (*viz.* the Clean Air, Clean Water and Noise Acts). In the absence of comparable legislation, the effects of proposals on the human environment typically had only received cursory treatment in EISs.

To cope with the new situation, the SPCC had issued early in 1978 a revised set of guidelines for the preparation of an EIS for a 'typical' surface coal mine proposal. A key feature in the contents brief of these new guidelines was that the effects of proposals on the socio-economic environment must henceforth be explicitly addressed and, moreover, that regard must be paid to the cumulative impacts of proposals at all stages on the changing regional environment. For the first time, therefore, there was a clear directive to the coal industry in NSW to include and emphasize in an EIS the likely impacts and effects (both adverse and beneficial) of new coal mines on all significant aspects of what was loosely termed the 'regional socio-economic environment' – a requirement that incidentally has been made mandatory in the current legislation.

On Becoming a Consultant

Ties' problem was that no-one on his staff at that time was qualified to provide the information required about the socio-economic impacts which now had to be included as part of the EIS he was charged with preparing for the new mine. That's why he came to me and that's how I became involved in consulting and doing research for the private sector.

Geographers, with their particular skills and ways of looking at the world, have a long tradition of being engaged as consultants. The experiences and challenges of consulting are often immensely rewarding – not least of all from a pecuniary viewpoint. The occasional forays from the normal routine of university teaching and research have a refreshing, even rejuvenating, effect for most academics. Teaching is often valuably enhanced by the 'case studies' and first-hand experiences that are gained from consulting and, importantly, 'in many areas of geography students seem to have more confidence in teachers who sometimes practise what they preach' (Gould, 1985, p. 174).

For me this was the primary factor behind my decision to become involved in Ties' project. I had moved to Australia just two years before, to take up the second Chair of Geography at the University of New South Wales in Sydney. Unlike most universities in Commonwealth countries geography's situation at that university is unique in one important respect. Geography is not placed in the Faculty of Arts or Science or Social Science, as it typically is elsewhere, but in the Faculty of Applied Science where its charter was to promote and develop courses in Applied Geography. Its programmes were to be vocationally oriented, designed to educate and train geographers for careers in the public sector (but not school-teaching) and in business, commerce and industry, and over the years the school has been very successful in fulfilling this goal.

In my new position, then, I was confronted with a different set of practical and intellectual challenges than had been the case in the other geography departments I had worked. This for me was a new 'ballgame', one for which my experiences and academic interests in urban geography seemed to be sadly deficient and somehow not quite appropriate. How could I preach what I practised to all those young, aspiring applied geographers if I had no practical experience? So this was an opportunity too good to miss. I now have quite a lot of experience in what may be loosely termed applied geography, but to be honest I am still rather uncertain about what is really meant by that term notwithstanding the considerable literature on the subject that has appeared in the past decade (for example, see Sant, 1982).

And So It Came To Be . . .

My formal involvement in the project began with a flying visit to Brisbane, where the proposers of the new mine were headquartered, for a day's discussion with the team of mining engineers, accountants and managers who were responsible for getting the project off the ground. I recall that they were not too impressed with the fact that I was a geographer – they seemed to think that an economist would have been a better choice on Ties' part to do the job. I can vaguely recall the excitement of the flight up to Brisbane but will never forget the feelings of self-doubt, inadequacy and fear of what I'd let myself in for which I felt on the way back later that evening. I had to admit that I knew very little about the Hunter Valley and the coal industry at the time, virtually nothing about the preparation of an EIS, or for that matter the way the business world really worked. The couple of pages summary of what I'd planned to do was clearly not what was required – too academic they said.

I learned a lot during the course of the meeting. First, this was big business with much at stake. The mine involved an investment of about A$75 million, a tidy sum in those days. Some A$5 million had already been spent in surveying the coal deposit and preparing the mine feasibility study, a necessary prerequisite for embarking on the preparation of the EIS and, importantly, raising capital in the money market. Second was the sense of urgency in getting the project off the ground; time was money and schedules were all-important. But then there were good reasons for that – interest payments on borrowed capital had to be repaid regardless of whether income was being generated or not. Contracts with the Japanese to deliver coal had already been entered into. In addition the winds of change were blowing in the form of new planning legislation which, it was feared, would specify more stringent guidelines for the preparation of the EIS, causing delays in obtaining development consent and certainly increasing costs. The third was that the preparation of the EIS was to cost the minimum possible in order to satisfy the legal requirements – in the end it cost about A$2 million – and that I was indeed fully answerable to my new masters. I was about to be introduced to what others had perhaps learned about research ethics a long time before, namely that 'when researchers function as consultants they often face conflict between their scholarly inclinations to understand the totality of a problem and their sponsor's right to delimit what aspects of the problem researchers study' (Mitchell and Draper, 1982, pp. 70–1). Mining, they told me rather arrogantly, was about digging coal. It was not about people – they were the planners' problem, so all that stuff about socio-economic impacts should be kept in proper perspective, which I think meant that whatever I came up with should present the proposed development in the most favourable light possible.

There was, however, another dimension to the whole affair which I quickly came to appreciate. The firm of consultants itself was in the business of making money, and of course had a vested interest in the success of this particular venture which was the first of the new wave of coal mine developments in the region. They wanted to produce the model EIS in order to demonstrate clearly their capabilities in the field of environmental consulting, thereby maximizing their chances of obtaining further contracts to prepare EISs for the many other new coal mines that were to follow. By now I felt very much like the meat in the sandwich; serving two masters with completely different expectations and aspirations. And I had about six months at most to deliver the goods to the satisfaction of both, which in the end I managed to do successfully, but not without a lot of blood, sweat and tears and much burning of the midnight oil.

The EIS was eventually submitted more or less on schedule, development consent was granted and the mine is now operational – although at a smaller scale than was originally planned owing to the changed demand for coal. Ties' firm did, I think, produce a model EIS and it went on to win contracts to prepare similar statements for many of the other coal mines to be developed in the region. My contribution on the mine's impact on the socio-economic environment received very favourable coverage in the region's local press and the following year I was asked to present the keynote address at the 'Singleton Coal Day' – an annual get-together of representatives of the coal industry and local residents aimed at informing the public about the ramifications of the coal boom for the community. In addition I prepared several papers for publication (see Garner *et al.*, 1981) and presentation at conferences, although I must admit that I could have used the experiences I gained to better advantage.

Getting Started

In formulating any research project two basic questions have to be addressed: What is it I am setting out to do?, and how am I going to accomplish it? The first question pertains to the bounds and scope of the project – to its content, its aims and objectives, the hypotheses to be tested, its theoretical or practical context, rigorous definition of the problem and so on. The second question, which of course is in large part inevitably dictated by the first, relates to practicalities – the data required, how they are to be obtained, the conceptual framework, methods of analysis and so on. Inevitably the success or failure of any research project depends very much on the 'how' of research, on the way one goes about bringing it to its logical conclusion. In this regard experience usually turns out to be the best teacher; one learns from one's own mistakes!

In my case, as is typical in most consulting, the bounds of the problem, scope and content of the research were effectively dictated by the guidelines issued by the SPCC for the preparation of an EIS for a surface coal mine, although these were expressed in rather broad and imprecise terms. Thus the socio-economic environment was to be interpreted as including all the features of the 'man-made' (sic) landscape in the region that are likely to be affected by the proposal. These were to include existing land-use patterns, population and demographic characteristics, employment, occupation and labour force profiles, all relevant infrastructure (both physical and social) and especially transport facilities. In addition the social impacts on local communities, as well as the economic and revenue-generating effects of the proposal, were to be considered. The guidelines went on to stress that a clear distinction should be drawn between the short-term and long-term impacts of a permanent nature, for example, the effects of the construction phase of a project compared to its effects when fully operational.

From the outset, therefore, the focus was on the 'how of research' – how to measure and assess the ways in which the new coal mine would impact the various components of the socio-economic environment. In this regard it is important to recognize that an EIS is a statement about futures; the emphasis is thus primarily on prediction and forecasting – murky waters for geographers given their predominantly retrospective as opposed to prospective orientation. I certainly didn't feel at all comfortable about this, but was heartened by the fact that the only certain thing about the future is its *uncertainty* and the knowledge that because of this better minds than mine had found it enormously difficult, if not at times impossible, to make definitive statements about the future (see McKern and Lowenthall, 1985).

A logical place to begin any research project, once the problem has been identified and the tasks defined, is to take a critical look at the ways other researchers have approached similar problems: What frameworks were used? What assumptions had they made? Which kinds of methods were employed? What conclusions were reached? Did these seem reasonable in the overall context of the research? and so on. So I too began by looking at the many EISs that had previously been prepared for coal mines in the region – an exercise which in this case wasn't particularly helpful in large part because they had been prepared to satisfy a less stringent set of EIS requirements than those specified in my brief. Discussion of socio-economic impacts in the earlier EISs was typically restricted to a few pages of, well, descriptive regional geography:

a little on settlement, somewhat more on transport, a table or two showing population and employment figures (mostly outdated), and a couple of maps for decoration. Statements specifically about impacts were clearly the exception rather than the rule. They could hardly be considered as prediction or forecasting but rather were vague, imprecise and essentially uninformed guesswork – for example:

It is expected that labour will be drawn from rural areas and the centres of Singleton and Cessnock although the availability is not known. Many new employees recruited outside of Singleton Shire are likely to elect to reside in the township to reduce travelling distances and time.

Extending the search to comparable overseas literature – there being little available locally – didn't help very much either. And of course the pressures of meeting deadlines for completing the task meant that time was not available to undertake an exhaustive literature search as would typically be the case in the more open-ended environment of an academically oriented research project. But nevertheless the exercise proved to be a very useful one in building up my knowledge of the region and in giving me a more critical understanding of the myths and realities of EISs which formed the basis later for a paper I presented at a conference and which should now perhaps be updated (Garner, 1983).

The pressing task was to devise a framework within which the research could proceed – one which unified into a coherent whole the various aspects of the socio-economic environment specified in the SPCC guidelines and which showed the interrelationships between them. Importantly I felt that the framework should explicitly recognize the logical chain of causal linkages through which the various impacts of the coal mine would be expressed. The framework, admittedly incomplete in many respects, which finally emerged, is shown in figure 3.1. Actually it took quite a while to develop. The first thing to note is that it is constructed in the form of an elementary flow diagram, the starting point in which is at the top – the existing regional environment into which the coal mine was to be introduced. Thereafter the diagram attempted to describe in a structured way the chain of sequenced events by which the process of change unfolds to result, at the bottom of the diagram, in the 'altered regional environment' brought about by the impacts of the new mine. In the context of assessing the cumulative impacts of expanded coal mining this would then become the new regional environment and starting point for evaluating the impacts of the next additional coal mines in the area. In reality, of course, the pace of expansion of the coal industry in the region was such that the cumulative impacts were being expressed in a simultaneous rather than the sequential fashion implied in figure 3.1. Note also that the timing of events is implied but not explicitly stated in the figure. The objective was to

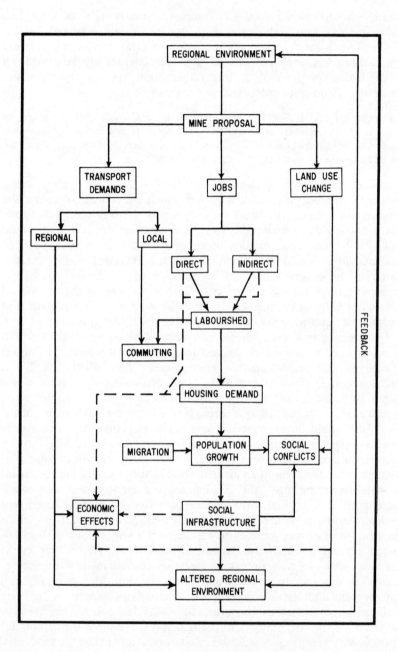

Figure 3.1 A conceptual framework for assessing the socio-economic impacts of a new coal mine.

identify in what ways and where the impacts would be felt, rather than when they would take place.

The timing of events was, however, critical in another and more practical context; namely the scheduling of the work involved which itself needed to be undertaken simultaneously for the most part rather than sequentially. Despite one's good intentions the timetables for much academic research have a nasty tendency to become open-ended. In the world of consulting, however, timetables and schedules are rigidly imposed to ensure that jobs are completed on time. To programme work and to monitor progress it is customary therefore to prepare a work schedule that formally sets out in diagram form the goals to be achieved by critical dates for the duration of the project. This was a new experience for me too, for time in my life has a habit of being peculiarly elastic! To be honest I'm not particularly reliable when it comes to meeting deadlines in my own research. I'm considerably better now than I used to be, however, and I can thank Ties for that because I now pay very much more attention to this necessary prerequisite for doing research than before. So you should too, whether it be planning an essay, preparing a report or writing a dissertation. The conceptual framework in figure 3.1 thus became the organizational framework shown in figure 3.2 for scheduling the work to meet successfully the various deadlines for meetings, progress reports and the preparation of the final documents.

Doing the Work

Apart from the pressure-cooker environment I had to work in for the best part of the following six months, doing the actual research turned out to be a lot of fun and, once I got into it, a lot less difficult in many respects than I had anticipated as my confidence in what I was trying to achieve, and my own ability to succeed, strengthened. Most of the basic data required were available from published sources, for example publications of the Australian Bureau of Statistics and reports from various government departments and agencies. Admittedly much of this was already dated – a fact recognized and accepted by the SPCC and the coal industry generally. It wasn't necessary therefore to do a lot of survey work to collect new data, although it was essential for some of the technical aspects of the research and I recall spending many hours interviewing key people in the coal industry, government and in the Hunter region as part of the background information and data gathering process. I was of course also able to call upon the experiences and utilize the resources of Ties' firm, and had direct access to the knowledge, views, expertise, data and information of the specialists assigned to the project within the coal company itself.

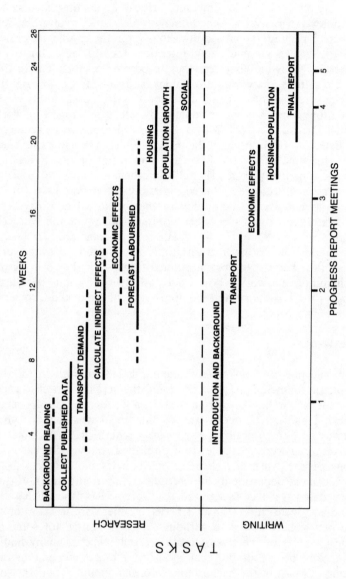

Figure 3.2 The organizational framework for completing the research project.

The latter turned out to be especially valuable in so many respects, and especially in obtaining much of the critical data required which was not publicly available – nor likely to become so. Just as coal miners themselves tend to form cohesive and mutually supportive social communities, coal mining too is a tightly organized and mutually supportive industry, and one which in a sense I was now formally recognized as belonging to in my role as consultant. I quickly became a member of the family so-to-speak. Doors were thus opened which I am certain would have remained firmly closed had I been engaged in the same exercise purely as a piece of independent academic research, for the simple reason that much of the data and background information I needed was highly sensitive and confidential – especially that relating to corporate planning, investment and finance and the politics of industrial strategy vis-à-vis the government. And these open doors were not restricted to the coal industry alone, but also to the various key departments of the State Government had by then established to coordinate the planning efforts across its own departmental boundaries to cope with the coal boom. One of the most important of the Task Forces was the small group of top aides in the Premier's Department itself who were charged with formulating government policies for the NSW coal industry in general and the Hunter region in particular. And of course because my entrée was right to the top in most instances, it wasn't just sensitive data that I acquired but, much more importantly, it was an inside understanding of the political and industrial context within which the facts were placed, gleaned from the many informal meetings during which discussions were often 'off the record'. I learned a lot from this practical experience about the issues relating to research ethics, especially the importance of trust and confidentiality that are discussed at length in an excellent book by Mitchell and Draper (1982) which every aspiring young researcher should read.

Time does not permit a detailed account of all aspects of the research that subsequently followed – much of it in any case was a reasonably straightforward task of piecing together information, interpreting trends in data and understanding them, making informed judgements about what impacts might arise and writing progress reports typical of any research project. Most of it was not particularly exciting nor intellectually demanding, but for the most part merely a case of plodding on. For example, estimating the impact of the new mine on the existing railway system was a straightforward task. Since the coal was to be marketed overseas it would need to be railed from the mine to the coal loader in the port of Newcastle. When fully operational a maximum movement of 3.5 million tonnes would be involved. The main question therefore was whether this could be accommodated within the existing system. A visit to the Public Transport Commission offices in Newcastle quickly provided the answers. The rail link from the mine south to a town called Maitland consisted of double track, increasing to four tracks from Maitland to Newcastle. The largest unit coal train at that time consisted of twenty-two 100-tonne wagons with a carrying capacity of 76 tonnes each, giving a total train capacity of 1680 tonnes. The track capacity on the railway line was estimated from this to be 23 million tonnes per annum. At that time only about 11 million tonnes of coal were being moved along the line annually; hence the capacity was more than sufficient to handle the additional output expected from the new coal mine.

Two specific components of the work, however, were not quite as straightforward as this, and deserve a more detailed discussion. These were the problems of forecasting the indirect jobs likely to be created by the proposal and predicting the labourshed for the new coal mine workforce (see figure 3.1). In both cases I was determined to use a more quantitative, model-based approach to assess the socio-economic impacts which had not been attempted in preparing an EIS previously in NSW, or for that matter Australia.

Forecasting Indirect Employment

Besides the employment created directly by expansion of an existing enterprise or the establishment of a new one, for example the 410–420 workers to be employed in the new coal mine, additional jobs will normally be created as a result of spin-offs to other sectors in the economy. These additional jobs may be disaggregated into two components: (a) the jobs created in linked or ancillary activities (e.g. transport, maintenance and suppliers of materials) and (b) those jobs created as a result of the monetary expenditures in the community or region by those directly employed at the mine. These are known as the *indirect* and *induced* employment effects respectively, and are collectively referred to as the employment multiplier in economic geography and regional science (Jensen *et al.*, 1979).

One of my initial tasks was to calculate the numerical value of the employment multiplier as a basis for forecasting the number of indirect jobs that could reasonably be expected to be generated by the new coal mine. There was considerable interest in this matter at the time, particularly in government circles, because not very much was known about the size of the multiplier effects of coal mining in the Hunter region and the political boasters wanted to capitalize on the coal boom by stressing the size of the total number of new jobs that would result from it.

Calculating multipliers is a highly technical and tricky business. Normally one would use the methods of input–output analysis (Miernyk, 1967). However, the data needed for this approach were unavailable at the time for the Hunter region, although after my research was completed two different input–output tables for the Hunter were independently prepared, which were subsequently used to measure employment as well as income and output multipliers (HVRF, 1979 and Unisearch Ltd 1980). In the absence of the right kind of data, therefore, how did I overcome the problem? Well the concept of the multiplier is well established in Keynesian economics and most advanced textbooks in that subject treat it adequately. First thing, then, was to do some more reading! Fortunately I was supervising a postgraduate student at the time who, for his Masters thesis, was trying to solve a similar problem but in a different context – namely predicting the job losses in a small country town in NSW which were likely to result if it was bypassed as part of a major upgrading of the main highway between Sydney and Melbourne on which it acted as a major service centre for passing traffic. By this stage of his research he had a very good grasp of how the Keynesian multiplier worked, and so I relied very much on his help. Together we were able to operationalize the Keynesian model to calculate the employment multiplier. The big problem was that of providing the best possible estimates – for that is all they could be – of the numerical values for the different terms in what at first sight is a pretty forbidding equation:

$$E_i = E_a + \left[(E_d w_d + E_a w_a) C r^n + (E_d + E_a) Y \right] \times \frac{1}{1 - w_x C_r \text{n} + Y}$$

where: E_i = indirect employment
E_a = ancillary employment
E_d = direct employment
w_d = average disposable income of direct employees
w_a = average disposable income of ancillary employees
C_r = proportion of disposable income that is expended within the region
n = reciprocal of the average amount of consumption expenditure needed to support one worker in the distributive trades
Y = ratio of public sector to private sector employment
w_x = weighted average of wages in the distributive and public sectors.

This aspect of the research took a lot of effort, and in the end took a lot longer than I had planned to complete. It involved building up a fairly detailed understanding and knowledge of tax and wage rates in the industry, the amount of disposable income expended in the region, the relationship between consumption expenditure and employment and so on through the terms of the equation. Much of the data needed to operationalize the model was available from government statistics – but again these were out of date; the rest was obtained from discussions with government statisticians and representatives from various industry groups. It was also necessary to undertake some sample surveys in local communities to collect primary data which were unavailable in published sources. These various items of data were then used to calculate as best we could what the required values were.

For example take the term C_r in the model – the proportion of disposable income that is expended within the region. This was unknown since no-one had studied it before. We were able to come up with a reasonable estimate of this, however, by extrapolating from the 1975–76 National Household Expenditure Survey for urban regions, recognizing however that the official statistics may not be completely reliable because our region was essentially rural in character, and supplementing this with the results of a small sample survey of expenditure patterns by local residents specifically undertaken for the research. Our estimate was that 62 per cent of disposable income was spent in the region.

I must admit to being quite worried about making these calculations, because to be really effective the model required precise values for its different terms, and more importantly because I was straying far away from the subject-matter areas in which I felt most at home. But I took comfort from the knowledge that we were doing our best and believed that the estimates used were the best possible under the circumstances – a very necessary attitude to have in applied research.

There was one critical assumption, however, that had to be made if the model was to predict at all accurately – namely about the origins of the workforce to be employed at the mine. Where were they going to come from geographically? The widespread belief at the time amongst planning circles in the region was that a large proportion of the new jobs in the new coal mines would be filled by migrants to the region and not by locals. This I found rather strange, given the high unemployment rates in the region discussed earlier in the chapter. Although I did not really believe they were correct in their assumption, the 'experts' were the experts, and I bowed to their infinitely better wisdom in such matters. So we followed their lead and finally calculated the value of the employment multiplier from the model on the assumption that only 10 per cent of the mine workforce would be recruited locally and 90 per cent would be filled by migrants to the region. My unease at the unrealistically high figure for the latter was confirmed later on, and it turned out that we were quite, quite wrong in that assumption! It turned out that as new jobs became available in coal mining a very high proportion were filled by local residents, not from the unemployed but as the result of workers switching jobs.

It was in this way that we calculated the value of the employment multiplier to be 1.4. This is interpreted to mean that for every one new job created directly in our coal mine, 0.4 of a job would be created indirectly somewhere else, or two new jobs would be created indirectly for every five jobs at the mine. Given that the mine planned to employ 410–420 workers when fully operational, the net additional increase in employment as a result of the multiplier could be expected to be about 166 (between 164 and 168) and hence the total employment impact of the mine would be of the order of 580 jobs. The careful work put into estimating the values of the terms in the model using inappropriate data at times, and certainly a fair measure of guesswork, seemed to have paid off. Later when the more reliable input–output method was used to calculate the employment multiplier for coal mining in the region the value for the so-called Type I multiplier, which practitioners in that field consider indicates the *most likely* impact of new coal mine investment, was calculated to be 1.44, a figure virtually identical to ours and which thereafter became the 'official' figure for planning purposes by the State Government. I recall getting into a slanging match with the proponents when we told them what the value of the employment multiplier we had calculated was . . . the industry firmly believed that it was at least 5 . . . now they knew the facts!

Forecasting the Mine's Labourshed

It will be recalled at the beginning of this story that the expansion of coal mining in the Hunter region focused on a relatively small area bounded by the towns of Muswellbrook and Singleton and the village of Denman – the so-called Muswellbrook–Singleton–Denman triangle. It was here that the socio-economic impacts of the new mine were likely to be felt most acutely. Because of this it was important that the EIS dealt specifically with the situation in this area, which in turn meant that any spatial forecasting should be at the sub-regional rather than the regional scale. It is a well-documented fact that the more specific one attempts to be in forecasting, the more difficult the task becomes and the greater the likelihood of error. Fully aware of this, and the difficulties it presented, I nevertheless felt that an honest contribution demanded that I firmly grasp the nettle in this respect. After all we'd already calculated a reasonable value for the employment multiplier – even though we didn't know its accuracy at the time – and my confidence was buoyant. So I believed that it was possible to make realistic forecasts of the labourshed for the new mine. By comparison this was a much easier technical task anyway.

The delimitation of the labourshed for a new coal mine, as shown in figure 3.1, is obviously an important first step in forecasting the magnitudes and location of the demand for housing, population growth, infrastructural needs and ultimately where social conflicts might occur. Superficially it might appear that identification of the employment catchment area for a new coal mine is relatively straightforward; surely it will generally be similar to that of an already existing neighbouring mine. The problem with that line of argument, which others had followed, was that at the time there was a critical shortage of housing and land for development in the sub-region. Potential residential land at Muswellbrook had effectively been 'frozen' because the town was situated on top of the coal measures, and until the economic value of the coal reserves around the town had been determined by the Department of Mineral Resources no further developments were permitted. Singleton was not on the coal field but adjacent to the floodplain of the Hunter River, and stringent zoning regulations seriously constrained residential development there. Moreover surrounding villages were not viewed as becoming potential 'dormitory suburbs' in the growth strategies laid down in the Hunter Regional Plan which had been released some months before. The Regional Plan did, however, specify that in the longer term the expansion expected to result from the coal boom should be concentrated at Muswellbrook and Singleton, which were envisaged as the major growth centres. Both were gearing themselves up for this, particularly Singleton where the Shire Council had already embarked on land banking and an ambitious plan to service land for residential and industrial development. It should be borne in mind too that the mine itself would not have an impact on the area until 4–5 years later, by which time it was believed the housing situation would have improved substantially as a result of investments to be made during the intervening period.

Table 3.1 Forecasts of the labourshed for the coal mine

Settlement	Case 1		Case 2		Case 3	
	No.	Percentage	No.	Percentage	No.	Percentage
Muswellbrook	246	58.6	211	50.2	171	40.7
Singleton	75	17.9	121	28.8	150	35.7
Aberdeen	17	4.0	17	4.0	19	4.5
Denman	8	1.9	7	1.7	10	2.4
Scone	22	5.2	21	5.0	23	5.5
Cessnock	24	5.7	20	4.8	21	5.0
Maitland	21	5.0	20	4.8	22	5.2
Branxton/Greta	7	1.7	3	0.7	4	1.0
Totals	420	100.0	420	100.0	420	100.0

The problem I faced was how to allocate spatially the workers at the new mine by place of residence – one about which I thought I knew more than estimating employment multipliers. After all there was a substantial body of literature in the discipline on problems of this sort (see Wilson, 1974, for a good coverage). The methods developed by Professor Wilson, the so-called entropy-maximization models, seemed to be appropriate in this context. So once again it was back to the textbooks to brush up my understanding of the specific details, and with the help of a mathematician friend I proceeded to forecast the mine's labourshed using variations of an entropy-maximizing gravity model, the results of which are presented in table 3.1.

Three variations of the basic model were used. In the first of these (Case 1), the model was specified as:

$$C_{im} = P_i E_m Y_m e^{-dD_{im}}$$

with:

$$Y_m = \frac{1}{\sum_i P_i e^{-dD_{im}}}$$

where:
C_{im} = residents of place i working at the mine
P_i = population of place i
E_m = jobs available at the mine (420)
D_{im} = commuting distances (in kilometres) from place i to the mine
d = the Lagrangian parameter measuring the frictional effect of distance

In this model it is assumed that workers would be allocated to place of residence on the basis of distance to the mine and in proportion to the then existing population size of towns and villages in the sub-region – typical first assumptions in this kind of modelling process. Unrealistically, perhaps, it was further assumed that in the long run there would be no housing shortages at any of the settlements, and that they were adequately provided with infrastructure; that the different occupational status of the mine workers had identical residential preferences; and that the future employees would not have any abnormal personal ties with a particular location. The limited data requirements of the model were readily satisfied, hence the main difficulty in making it operational was to determine the numerical value of the parameter d, measuring the frictional effect of distance. This is done by calibrating the model for the region using data for a known situation (Foot, 1981). Fortunately a small coal mine was operating on land adjacent to the proposed new mine, and it was possible to obtain the residential addresses of its 75 employees from the mine manager for this purpose. Using this data set it was then a fairly straightforward arithmetic task to find the value of d, which was calculated as 0.43.

Using these assumptions, the calculated value for d and inserting in the equation the other values, the results in table 3.1 showed that the greatest proportion (58.6 per cent) of the mine's projected workforce was forecast to live in Muswellbrook, the town closest to the mine site. Singleton could be expected to take the major part of the overspill, and other settlements in the region the remainder of the workforce. What was questionable about this pattern, however, was that it didn't take into account the known shortage of housing in the sub-region. Indeed it was specifically assumed as a starting point that there would not be any shortage of housing at the various settlements in the future. Clearly this was somewhat unrealistic, given what everyone knew about the problems existing at the time. In view of this the model was modified to take this into account by including an additional term in the equation measuring the availability of housing at Muswellbrook and Singleton.

It was then possible to rerun the model by inserting hypothetical values of housing availability – thereby altering the relative attractiveness of the two settlements over and above that due to their population size and resulting from the frictional effect of distance – a surrogate for travel times really. In this way different scenarios of the seriousness of the housing problem at the two main centres could be used to simulate alternative allocation of the mine workforce as shown in Cases 2 and 3 in table 3.1 by way of example. The allocation in the former is based on the assumption that a smaller proportion of the total number of new home sites would be available at Muswellbrook than at Singleton; in the latter case it is assumed that there would be a serious shortage of housing at Muswellbrook – a situation which of course would arise if it was decided to reserve land there for coal extraction, thereby inhibiting town expansion. These results then became the key for estimating population growth at the various places and to identify social infrastructure needs at them, the details of which I'll save for another time.

By now I had really stuck my neck out! The approach I had adopted was sustantially different from that others had used before – recall the example I quoted earlier in the piece. To be honest I had cold feet by this time, and remember going to discuss the results with the chief planner in Singleton, an engineer who could at least understand what it was I was attempting to do. Unlike the calculation of the employment multiplier there was no way of checking the accuracy or reliability of the results I had obtained. That could only be done later by empirically monitoring events as they unfolded – but the EIS had to be submitted long before that was possible; indeed, until the EIS had been submitted and development consent approved there could be no events to monitor! Discussions with the chief planner, I recall, were most reassuring. He seemed to think that the general picture matched his own views of what was likely to happen, and strongly encouraged me to continue down that track. In fact long before the EIS was submitted, the results in table 3.1, together with those from other runs of the model, were being used as one of the bases for developing the Strategic Plan for the town of Singleton.

A New Research Project

Some years later, in 1983, after my consulting had ended and the EIS had been submitted and approved, I was invited back to Singleton to attend another Coal Discussion Day. By then the global recession was beginning to affect developments in the region as the demand for coal in world markets began to fall. Many of the planned new coal mines proposed some years earlier had been reduced in size, some were postponed until the economy improved; a few were even abandoned altogether. It was clear then to many that the assumptions I had made in my work no longer applied. The theme for the discussion that day was 'Coping with the Downturn'. I remember that the new chief planner at Singleton used the contents of the keynote address I had given at a similar gathering a few years previously as the basis for his own presentation, which was particularly gratifying to me.

My interest was, however, awakened particularly by the presentation by the mine manager of one of the coal mines that had started production just about the time Ties' EIS was submitted. By now they had a couple of years' operating experience and the talk was essentially about this. The mine manager devoted a good part of his talk to the problems of recruiting labour to work at the mine, and in this connection quoted from their records that 57 per cent of the workforce had been recruited from other jobs in the region. In the general discussion which followed, the effects of 'job switching' were dealt with at length because many of the firms in other sectors that were losing workers, attracted to coal mining by considerably higher wages and better working conditions, and were experiencing difficulties in finding suitable replacements. The general feeling amongst those present was that the proportion of job switchers had been running at around 50–60 per cent during the previous years. As a 'guesstimate', it was believed that between 500 and 600 workers at least had switched jobs locally to enter the coal industry during the previous three years. This, you will recall, was not at all in agreement with the prediction of the 'experts' that most of the jobs would not be filled by local residents but by newcomers to the region resulting from migration. Clearly there was, and had been, considerable ignorance about the way the regional labour markets functioned. It was all very puzzling, I thought.

Back in my office a few weeks later I was reading an article by two Swedish geographers, Öberg and Oscarsson (1979) in connection with a lecture I was preparing. The article was about matching jobs and individuals in local labour markets, and at one point very brief mention was made of vacancies in the stock of jobs in the region which the authors had studied. Interestingly, reference was made to a book on opportunity chains by White (1970), who is an expert in the field of organizational behaviour. Still puzzled by the 'job switching' process that had been going on in the Hunter region, I borrowed the book from the library and it turned out to be fascinating reading, even if it was largely concerned with the way in which promotion occurs within large organizations. It clearly had nothing to do with geography at all. Much of its content was concerned with the concept of vacancy chains, which I knew from my general reading had been extensively applied in a somewhat different way in studies of housing markets. I also knew that, since the pioneering work of Holt and David (1966), vacancies have been viewed as one of the key elements in the 'stocks and flows' concept underlying research into labour market dynamics and accounts. But this wasn't an area that I had been especially interested in or, for that matter, knew very much about at all.

However, I began to realize that the 'job switching' explicit in the expansion of the coal industry in the Hunter Valley was not completely unrelated to these ideas. Obviously, each time a worker moved from a job locally to fill one in the coal industry, a vacancy is created at the previous place of employment which – if it is to be filled – becomes a new employment opportunity for someone else. In this context the chaining effect created by the successive filling of vacancies would seem to be important. In a sense it gave rise to what may by analogy be thought of as a game of musical chairs in the labour market. Thus the relatively high level of 'job switching' in the Hunter region must obviously give rise to vacancy chains in the local labour markets there – chains which were directly attributable to the expansion of coal mining and which, once started, resulted in a casual sequence of spatial moves into and out of jobs.

And so my thoughts gradually developed, and the ideas for a new research project related to the coal developments in the Hunter region began to take shape. Why not investigate the 'job switching' process in an analogous way to Maher's (1979) analysis of vacancy chains in the Melbourne housing market which I'd recently looked at. I still had good contacts in the coal industry, so could obtain information from mine managers about their new workers as a starting point. All I needed was

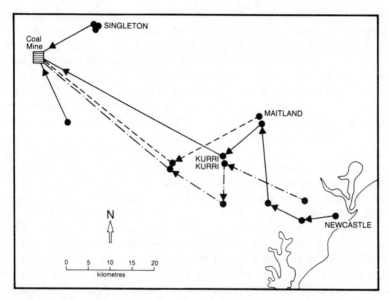

Figure 3.3 Hypothetical vacancy chains in the Hunter Valley, NSW, Australia.

the money to pay for research assistance to trace the chains back through time and to collect the data. What jobs were being affected? In which kinds and types of firms? How long did vacancies remain unfilled? Which jobs disappeared altogether? Were males being replaced by females? Were the unemployed presented with new opportunities for work by filling vacancies? Which considerations motivated a move from one job to another? Did the process relate to upward mobility in the labour market? and so on. Done rigorously, and in a systematic way, I felt that I would be able to provide some very interesting and valuable information for the planners and others in the region while at the same time making a valuable contribution to our understanding of the way labour markets actually work. Publications would most certainly result, and my University Masters might even be impressed with my diligence.

There was still, however, something missing from the ideas as they were then formulated. What could I really say about the geographical behaviour of the labour market? This kept nagging me and I tossed the problem round and round in my mind and then – the brainwave! Think of the vacancies; conceptually they can be thought of as moving from job to job sequentially to create the chain. More importantly, the vacancies must also move from place to place through the chain, which because of this had a spatial expression. Vacancy chains could be mapped, as shown hypothetically in figure 3.3. The significance of the patterns created would depend on the geographical configuration of the chains themselves, which in turn depends on the number of vacancies (i.e. links) in a chain and their relative location. A given chain ends when a particular vacancy is filled by an 'outsider', for example a migrant to the region or a person who previously was not in the labour force, or alternatively if management decided not to fill the vacancy at all (the job disappears). Thus some chains would be short, perhaps involving only one link, whereas others would be much longer as the 'job switching' process continued to unfold geographically.

But this was the clever bit! If the vacancies created directly and indirectly by the coal industry are thought of not as opportunities but rather as 'innovations', and the workers who fill the vacancies as 'adoptors', then in aggregate vacancy chains can be considered as a special class of innovation diffusion, and potentially could perhaps be modelled as a spatial diffusion process (Brown, 1981). The pattern of diffusion will be determined by the configuration of the chains of varying length; the rate of diffusion by the duration of the vacancies, which in turn will be dictated in part by the 'coupling constraints' implicit in the notion of the 'attractiveness of jobs for workers and the appropriateness of workers for jobs'. It is in that way that the barrier effects explicit in most diffusion processes could be incorporated. Perhaps most important of all, when viewed as a diffusion process, vacancy chains thus became a key mechanism by which the impact of expanding employment in coal mining is transmitted through space to create spread effects similar to those postulated, for example, in growth pole models (see Moseley, 1973). The problem had never been thought of conceptually in this way before, and an entirely new dimension was introduced to the discussion of the impacts of the coal boom in the region. Well, as you can imagine, I had little difficulty in obtaining a substantial research grant under the Australian Research Grants Scheme in 1984 to develop the ideas and undertake the research which is currently under way. If I'm asked again to contribute to another volume on doing research, this project would, I'm sure, make just as interesting a story.

Afterword

You don't always have to be particularly clever to do research, but you do have to be well organized, think out your ideas clearly, be able to express them concisely and precisely, and understand the methods that are appropriate for the job. You have to learn to accept that things have a habit of going wrong, usually when least expected – that is what coping is all about. Importantly don't be afraid to be adventurous in the 'doing of research' and, when you believe you are right, then stick to your guns because you most probably are!

References

Brown, L. A. (1981) *Innovation Diffusion: A New Perspective*. Methuen, London.
Foot, D. (1981) *Operational Urban Models: An Introduction*. Methuen, London.
Garner, B. (1983) Socio-economic Impacts of Coal Developments in the Upper Hunter Valley: Myths and Realities in Environmental Impact Statements. Mimeographed.
Garner, B. J., Holsman, A., Phibbs, P. and van Kempen, T. (1981) Assessing the socio-economic effects of coal mine developments with special reference to the Upper Hunter, NSW. In J. C. Hannan (ed.), *Environmental Controls for Coal Mining*. The Australian Coal Association, Sydney.
Gould, P. (1985) *The Geographer at Work*. Routledge & Kegan Paul, London.
Holt, C. and David, M. (1966) The concept of job vacancies in a dynamic theory of the labour market. In *The Measurement and Interpretation of Job Vacancies*. National Bureau of Economic Research, Washington, DC.
Horne, D. (1977) *The Lucky Country*. Penguin Books, Harmondsworth.
HRPC (1977) *The Hunter Region: Problems and Proposals*. Hunter Region Planning Committee, Newcastle, NSW.
HVRF (1979) New input–output tables for the Hunter Region, *Hunter Valley Research Foundation, Newcastle, NSW, Working Paper* 5.
Jensen, R. C., Manderville, T. D. and Karunaratne, N. D. (1979) *Regional Economic Planning*. Croom Helm, London.
McKern, R. B. and Lowenthall, G. C. (1985) *Limits to Prediction*. Australian Professional Publications, Sydney.
Maher, C. (1979) Private housing construction and household turnover: a study of vacancy chains in Melbourne's housing market, *Monash University, Department of Geography, Publications in Geography 22*.
Miernyk, W. H. (1967) *The Elements of Input–output Analysis*. Random House, New York.
Mitchell, B. and Draper, D. (1982) *Relevance and Ethics in Geography*. Longman, London.
Moseley, M. J. (1973) The impact of growth centres in rural regions. I: An analysis of spatial patterns in Brittany; II: An analysis of spatial flows in East Anglia, *Regional Studies*, 7, 57–75, 77–94.
Öberg, S. and Oscarsson, G. (1979) Regional policy and interregional migration – matching jobs and individuals in local labour markets, *Regional Studies*, 13, 1–14.
Sant, M. E. C. (1982) *Applied Geography: Practice, Problems and Prospects*. Longman, London.
Unisearch Ltd (1980) *Hunter Valley Input–output Study*. University of New South Wales, Kensington, NSW.
White, H. C. (1970) *Chains of Opportunity*. Harvard University Press, Cambridge, Mass.
Wilson, A. G. (1974) *Urban and Regional Models in Geography and Planning*. John Wiley & Sons, London.

4

Policy-oriented Research in Industrial Location

J. B. Goddard

Introduction

Human geographers have always had an uneasy relationship with public policy-makers. On the one hand they have felt a desire to be 'relevant' and on the other have recognized the dangers of sacrificing their independence. The dilemmas can be sharpened when policy-makers request supporting evidence for the propositions arising from academic research whilst at the same time either retaining control over vital secondary data or only providing financial resources in the form of research contracts for primary data collection on their own terms. Such situations arise in many social sciences; nevertheless human geography has probably progressed less far in developing a mutually beneficial dialogue with policy-makers than many other disciplines.

Drawing from my own research on office location and regional aspects of technological change, and my experience in establishing a multi-disciplinary urban and regional research centre, I hope to suggest how applied research can contribute both to the evolution of public policy and further the understanding of processes of urban and regional development. I hope the chapter will also indicate how contract research can be used as a means of obtaining data that might not otherwise be available, and how traditions of empirical research in geography can be built upon in order to operationalize concepts that are widely used in other social sciences, particularly economics – an operationalization that is essential in a public policy context.

The study of industrial locations does illustrate a number of the possible interconnections between theory and practice in human geography. On the academic side there is a well-developed body of theory about the location of industry which has its roots in economics and in which the concept of overcoming the cost of distance is central. However, this body of theory has been lacking on a number of counts. In relation to my own work it has focused on the location of manufacturing industry, while in reality non-manufacturing, particularly office-based activities, have come to dominate most advanced economies. For such activities the transfer of information rather than material goods is a major consideration. Next, and following a well-established tradition in economics, industrial location theory has not explicitly considered the disequilibrating role of technological change in creating new industries, displacing the products of older industries and changing the way in which established goods are produced and delivered. This is a particular problem for the study of the location of office activities where advances in telecommunications would *a priori* seem to indicate a marked reduction in the friction of distance as an influence on the location of information exchange activities.

Such considerations have important bearings on public policy; the connection here is provided by another strand of theory, namely that concerned with the development of areas as distinct from the individual enterprises which tend to be the focus of industrial location studies. Policy-makers are interested in areas because of a concern with economic opportunities, particularly the tendency for the persistence of shortfalls in jobs relatively to labour demand in some areas resulting in high levels of unemployment, and a more buoyant demand in other areas leading to labour shortages and other congestion costs to the economy as a whole. So policy-makers need to know not only about the factors influencing the location of industrial enterprises, but the broad range of considerations that determine the development of the economic base of an area in the round; such knowledge is necessary in order to identify initiatives to overcome the structural problems of localities – such as improving the economic milieu through the provision of communications infrastructure and the stock of skills.

The Communications Factor in Office Location

I began my PhD research at the London School of Economics in 1965, just after the election of a Labour Government. One of the major issues on the Government's agenda was speculative office development in London, which was perceived to be not only creating excess profits for property speculators, but also adding to the congestion of the capital. Previous spatial policy had been concerned with controlling industrial development, but it was readily apparent that the main growth of London had not been within the manufacturing sector but in office activities. The new Government therefore introduced a ban on new office building in 1964, and the Location of Offices Bureau was bolstered to encourage office dispersal from London; however a key problem for policy-makers was which office activities could and should be dispersed.

The initial focus of my thesis topic was in the area-based tradition of urban geography, and concerned with understanding the growth of the

central business district of London. However, in the context of the
emerging public policy debate I soon decided to focus on the question
of the nature of the links that tied offices to the city centre. There had
been some academic writing on this subject, particularly by economists
in the United States, but little policy orientated research in the UK.

The literature suggested three possible ways into the problem, two
indirect and one direct. The first was to examine the locational association
between different types of offices using a very detailed disaggregation of
'nature of business' on the supposition that activities with strong
functional links would exhibit a spatial association within the centre
because of the importance of interpersonal contacts in maintaining those
links. The second approach was directly to measure the links in terms
of personal contacts between activities using survey techniques. The
third alternative was to look at physical movement within and between
districts in the city centre with different mixes of office types as a
surrogate of functional dependencies.

However, the possibility of one individual researcher pursuing any of
these approaches in an office centre employing 1.1 million people in over
30,000 office establishments was severely limited. There was some data
on these establishments which could be utilized for analysis of spatial
association. These data were collected as a by-product of Health and
Safety at Work legislation, but access was constrained by confidentiality.
In any case the resources required locationally to code and classify the
data were beyond one individual.

Then came one of those lucky breaks of being in the right place at
the right time, on which most successful research depends. The City of
London Corporation had commissioned a team of consultants to undertake
an economic study of the City of London, partly to support their case
against a Labour Government intent in controlling the growth of the
City (Dunning and Morgan, 1971). The consultants required data on the
nature and structure of office employment in the City, and through a
contact made by my supervisor, Peter Hall, I was able to draw attention
to records that were available in the City Medical Officer's Department;
I was subsequently engaged to advise on data collection and analysis.

The year 1968 marked the heyday of the quantitative revolution, and
geographers were making extensive use of the technique of factor analysis,
but primarily in the study of urban social structure. I decided to use
this technique in an economic geography context to identify sets
of spatially associated office activities; these corresponded well with
descriptions of the functioning of the City of London produced by
institutional economists (Goddard, 1968). The extent to which the results
subsequently proved relevant to identifying the sorts of activities that
had a special case for remaining in the City, and therefore influenced
the issue of Office Development Permits, is not clear. Nevertheless the

research work did provide important insights into the nature of the internal structure of the central business district.

However, the City of London was only a small part of the London central area. I was fortunately able to extend the work into the remainder of the central area using firstly physical movement data as a further surrogate for functional linkage, and also through the direct measurement of interpersonal contacts. The first of these extensions involved the analysis of data on taxi flows made available as part of a Home Office enquiry into the operation of the London taxi-cab trade, chaired by a member of staff at the London School of Economics and on which I also acted as an adviser. Analysis of these data identified a number of functional regions within the central area (Goddard, 1970).

More significant in policy terms was the analysis of direct interpersonal contacts made possible by a research grant from the Department of the Environment on behalf of the newly established South-East Economic Council, of which Peter Hall was a member. The Council was concerned with the strategic planning of the South-East region, and recognized that central London played a key role in this wider region. The Planning Council, and also the Greater London Council in its first Development Plan, were both concerned to identify essential activities for the central area as a background to their advice to government on office development permits and local planning permissions. The Department of the Environment financed an extension of the City of London work on office location patterns to the entire central area and also supported a direct survey of interpersonal contacts between different office activities. These contact studies were much influenced by Swedish geographers and economists who had begun to identify information flows as a location factor (Tornqvist, 1970; Thorngren, 1970). The studies involved measuring the quality as well as quantity of information transacted in personal contacts, and applying another classification technique (latent profile analysis) in order to identify the strength of the links tying different functions to the city centre (Goddard, 1973, 1982).

One of the chief shortcomings of this analysis was that it did not prove that a strong functional tie bore any relationship to actual or potential mobility, because there were clearly a wide range of other factors influencing office location. I was therefore able to persuade the Location of Offices Bureau, whose role was to encourage dispersal from London, to fund a survey of offices that had relocated different distances from the capital and compare them with another sample which was about to move and a further group that had considered relocation but had rejected it. The analysis of contact patterns in these three groups of offices revealed the expected differences between them, and confirmed the importance of communication factors in mobility; it was largely the less communication-intensive firms which had moved or were about to move, and those with diverse or highly specific links which had remained (Goddard and Morris, 1976).

The comparison of central London and decentralized offices revealed that on relocation firms changed their organization – contact data suggested a considerable degree of adjustment to the changed situation. In attempting to explain this I was forced to look to organization theory; the behavioural approach was just entering into industrial geography, and confronting this with my empirical work it became apparent that my own and other studies of office location had generally divorced the office from its organizational context (Goddard, 1976).

This insight proved to be valuable in the next phase of my work on office dispersal, namely the likely contribution of advances in telecommunications in supporting relocation (Goddard and Pye, 1977). An enterprising architect had established the Communications Studies Group in University College London to undertake research sponsored by the Long Range Studies Division of the then Post Office and the Civil Service Department into the question of telecommunications substitution for face-to-face contact in business and government. The Post Office was concerned with the impact on the demand for telephone services, and the Civil Service Department with the dispersal of government work to the regions. I was extensively engaged with the Group in a long-running debate about the fallacy of a substitution approach; this was based on psychology experiments on the performance of different tasks in the office, and large-scale surveys of contacts events generally divorced from their organizational context.

With the benefits of hindsight this early phase of my research had one major shortcoming in relation to how the results could be implemented by the sponsoring policy-makers. I had succeeded in identifying different office activities that might or might not be relocated. However, the policy instruments available were far less refined in their ability to differentiate activities – the only means of control was over the provision of office space, and not over the nature of the occupiers of that space. It was only when the client had direct control, as in the case of the Civil Service, that it was possible to draw a direct link between the research and the policy outcome. The next phase of my work contains examples of better linkages between research and policy implementation.

New Technology and Regional Development

In 1975 I practised what I had preached and decentralized myself from London to Newcastle-upon-Tyne. In arriving in a 'peripheral' region it was apparent that it was necessary to look at the question of office development and the role of communications technology from the other end of the telescope. A corollary of office concentration in London was an impoverishment of information-based activities in the regions, with wide-ranging implications for their long-term development. Such interconnections had only been weakly made in policy terms where the emphasis had been on office dispersal from London itself, with little regard to the final destinations, or to the role of such activities in the broader development of regional economies (see, for example, Goddard, 1978a).

The introduction of the 'Rothchild' principle in government-sponsored research had ensured that funds were earmarked for long-term strategic investigations; the Department of the Environment decided to use these funds to sponsor a number of major studies on the impact of telecommunications on the environment. I was therefore fortunate to obtain support for a study of the potential role of telecommunications in supporting office activity in the Northern Region – a study which could build upon my earlier work in London. This funding enabled me to investigate more fully a number of major academic issues about the influence of corporate organization on the location of office functions within industry, and build stronger bridges between the office location and industrial location research communities, lines of research which had previously been separate (Goddard, 1978b). A series of largely academic papers spun off from the research; for example, the studies revealed the importance of ownership in shaping the distribution of office jobs between work places and regions (Marshall, 1979) and revealed wide-ranging implications arising from the growing external ownership of industry in the northern region (Goddard and Smith, 1978; Smith, 1978) confirming findings from other regions, notably Scotland (Firn, 1975).

As a piece of longer-term research this study was not intended to have immediate impacts on policy-makers. Moreover, the main potential policy levers were the responsibility of departments other than the Department of the Environment (e.g. the Department of Trade and Industry, the Monopolies and Merger Commission and British Telecommunications). Indeed in relation to telecommunications policy the detailed studies of inter- and intra-organizational information flows that were undertaken for the project using diary and business travel techniques suggested that, far from providing the basis for sustaining office development in northern England, the more widespread use of telecommunications could further the 'remote control' of economic activity in the region from headquarters based in London or elsewhere. This was hardly a finding likely to be welcomed by policy-makers looking for quick-and-easy technological solutions to the regional problem (Goddard, 1980; Goddard and Thwaites, 1980).

Notwithstanding such negative conclusions the research did contribute to a newly emerging body of academic and policy thinking about the problems of economic development in declining industrial areas. Up until the mid-1970s it was generally accepted that the answer to decline in staple industries was to use financial incentives to attract new firms from outside the region in different sectors of production. Industrial diversification was the principal objective of policy. However, it was becoming increasingly apparent after the first oil price shock that there was insufficient mobile investment available to replace the jobs lost in traditional industries, like coal, steel and mechanical engineering. In such circumstances areas would have to rely more on their indigenous enterprises to generate additional employment (Segal, 1980). One of the key findings of the research on office communications was the dependence of indigenously owned enterprises in the Northern Region on the immediate locality for sources of information that could be vital to their long-term survival (Marshall, 1979). Similar findings were produced from studies in Scotland and the South-East of England (McDermott, 1976) with the important caveat that the local environment in the South-East contained many more significant information sources.

As the results of the office communication research were becoming available the Northern Region Strategy Team, sponsored by central government, local government and the Northern Economic Planning Council (of which I was a member), and led by development economists with World Bank experience, was preparing an economic strategy for the region. The Team's final report placed greater emphasis than hitherto on a range of policies designed to promote the development of industries indigenous to the region rather than on the attraction of branch factories (Northern Region Strategy Team, 1977).

A central contention of the Strategy Team's report was that industry in the region was declining partly as a result of a failure to introduce new products and processes; in a competitive world economy witnessing an accelerating rate of technical change firms which did not innovate were clearly at the risk of losing out in national and international markets. I was fortunate at this stage to team up with an economist, Alfred Thwaites, who had been studying the role of technological innovation in industrial entrepreneurship. He had a fund of research ideas based on the literature in the economics of innovation. His reading of this literature suggested that regions such as the North had an economic environment that was not conducive to innovation; moreover, policies designed to attract mobile investment, in so far as this involved the production of goods at the later stage of their product life cycle and the setting up of establishments lacking research and development functions, would not contribute to developing the technological capacity of such regions (Thwaites, 1978). We put the propositions to the Department of Trade and Industry – which was responsible for regional industrial policy – that there were regional variations in rates of industrial innovation in

Britain. Our propositions were rejected partly because we had no empirical evidence, but also because mainstream economic theory tended to treat technology as an exogenous factor of production ubiquitously available to all enterprises. We were, however, fortunate to persuade the Department of the Environment, which had a responsibility for regional economic planning research, to support a detailed empirical study of product and process innovation in manufacturing industry in Britain from a geographical perspective. The unsubstantiated propositions of the Northern Regional Strategy Team provided the peg on which to hang this research.

The success of the study we undertook stemmed from a number of key features in the design and analysis. First it was the selection of three industries which had a proven record of innovation and which were represented in all the regions of Britain; this was necessary in order to highlight potential regional differences in rates of innovation. Second was the need to produce an operational definition of innovation which could be the focus of the survey. We decided to concentrate on what firms themselves regarded as the most significant (if any) new or improved product or process introduced in a five-year period, and then subject these to technological adjudication by a panel of industry experts. This enabled us to handle the spectrum of technological innovation from fundamental new products to the incremental improvement of existing products. Third, we were able to make use of a technique, logit analysis, for isolating the non-spatial influences, such as size of establishment, sector and ownership, in order to focus on the specifically geographical differences in the incidence of innovation.

The results of the research (reported extensively elsewhere) were timely in the sense that they became available as a number of commentators were pointing to the economic and social implications of an accelerating rate of technological change associated with the widespread adoption of microelectronics (Goddard, Thwaites and Gibbs, 1986). The research revealed significantly lower rates of technological innovation in the old industrial regions of the UK, particularly amongst smaller firms, a situation largely attributable to a lack of commitment to research and development. While larger firms did exhibit a higher rate of innovation this was generally the result of products being transferred to the area from research centres in the South-East of England and elsewhere, and thus not contributing to the stock of technological knowledge within the locality.

We subsequently went on to study the diffusion of manufacturing innovations, an area which had been previously examined by economists, but not in a spatial context (e.g. Mansfield, 1968). The bulk of the geographical literature on innovation diffusion has hitherto been concerned with agricultural innovations: our approach was similar, namely to identify a set of potential adopters of a range of production technologies and to survey these in order to identify whether they had adopted and if so when. Parallel studies were undertaken by collaborators in the United States and Germany (Rees, Briggs and Oakey, 1984; Kleine, 1982). These international comparisons revealed stronger differences between rather than within countries, confirming our earlier findings about the limited extent of regional variations in process innovations.

The American and German studies formed part of a growing international interest in regional aspects of technological change. Researchers in the Netherlands (e.g. Lambooy, 1984; Molle, 1983; Nijkamp, 1986), France (Aydalot, 1986), Italy (Camagni, Cappelin and Garafoli, 1984) and Switzerland (Maillat, 1982) began to address these issues from a similar perspective. However, the impact of our research on national policy within the UK was limited. With the election of a Conservative Government in 1979 less committed to the reduction of regional inequalities, the findings of the research were not deemed to be relevant to the sponsoring department. However, the research did find an audience in the European Commission in Brussels. Through the International Institute of Management in Berlin the Commission sponsored a review of the factors influencing the indigenous development of the less-favoured regions of Europe; we were responsible for covering the situation in Britain. As we had the only hard evidence on regional patterns of industrial innovation our findings had a considerable influence on the policy recommendations emerging from the overall project. These recommendations were subsequently incorporated into revised regulations for the European Regional Development Fund (House of Lords, 1984) which now contains several budget lines to support policies designed to promote technological innovation in small and medium-sized enterprises indigenous to the less-favoured regions of the community.

There was also a positive response to our studies amongst local authorities in the North-East of England eager to promote the development of their local economies and to fill the policy vacuum created by the decline of central government interest. We have been closely involved in one such initiative in Newcastle, namely the establishment of the Newcastle Technology Centre, which is attached to the University and Polytechnic. The origins of the Technology Centre can be traced back to the naïve view that every area of a country could participate in technological advance, and that one way to achieve this was to develop science parks attached to universities in order to accommodate the spin-off of new enterprises from academia (Goddard and Thwaites, 1983). Not surprisingly Newcastle City Council thought that the city should have a science park, but it could not find a large enough site adjacent to the university. However, our research and that of others had indicated that there are dangers of being mesmerized by high technology and new firms at the possible expense of the introduction of new processes and the incremental improvement of existing products in established firms. We had found many small firms in the North-East utilizing their limited R&D resources to tackle technical problems which had already been resolved elsewhere, and rediscovering solutions that were often well known to the scientific community. We therefore developed a plan for a technology transfer centre which eventually surplanted the idea of a science park, and which was designed to link local enterprises to the body of technological expertise in the university and polytechnic (Thwaites, 1983). The Newcastle Technology Centre has now been established under the joint sponsorship of the university, polytechnic and local authorities. The functional specification for the Centre had its roots in studies of information flows in relation to technological development in a spatial context, and more specifically in the notion that information is not a ubiquitous resource but is highly constrained in its availability by spatial as well as institutional factors.

A key conclusion of our research on technological change which has both academic and policy relevance has been the identification of powerful bottlenecks to industrial innovation operating at the local level, which may in the long run constrain the transformation of the national economy. This conclusion links into theories of technological change in national economic development propounded by economists such as Freeman, who follow the pioneering work of Schumpeter (Freeman, 1986). Thus Freeman draws attention to a range of institutional constraints holding back the widespread diffusion of microelectronics, a diffusion which, he argues, could herald a major upswing in the economies of advanced industrial nations. Amongst other considerations Freeman points to the vital importance of the general availability of appropriate telecommunications infrastructure. This network-based infrastructure is inherently geographical, and thus provides one of the many interfaces between our work and that of students of technological change in economics who are not specifically concerned with spatial issues.

Studies of Information and Communications Technologies

The latest phase of my research retains a focus on information, but in the wider context of the emerging information economy. As a result of the convergence of telecommunications and computing a vital transformation is in progress in the way in which information is handled in the economy (Goddard and Gillespie, 1986; Hepworth, 1986). At the time of undertaking my research on telecommunications and office location in the Northern Region in the late 1970s there were still severe technical limitations on the ability to transmit large volumes of information 'over the wire'. Subsequent developments in fibre-optic transmission and digital switching have transformed the telecommunications infrastructure and dramatically reduced the costs of information transfer between locations. This has impacted on organizations not by the substitution of telecommunications for high-level face-to-face meeting, as was envisaged 10 years ago, but by the way in which routine information can be distributed within organizations and by creating the possibility to commodify knowledge previously transacted informally between organizations and now trading this at a price on public markets. The emergence of global information markets has facilitated the development and growth of international corporations in the service sector, and poses a threat as well as opportunities for economic development in lagging regions. The privatization of British Telecommunications, designed in part to speed up the development of information markets, could also create problems for regional development in terms of undermining the uniformity of provision of advanced telecommunication services throughout the country.

The development of this line of research has been much influenced by a new co-worker, Mark Hepworth, who has recently moved from Toronto to Newcastle. His study of the growth of computer networks in Canadian firms has clearly shown the growing influence of American multinationals on the distribution of information occupation. The subordination of the Canadian economy to the United States has been a powerful influence on the agenda of applied research in that country, and has contributed to a community of North American researchers investigating the political economy of communications (e.g. Schiller, 1984). The changing regulatory environment for telecommunications in the United States has been identified as being one of the many factors posing real challenges for different social groups and different regions of the United States (e.g. Langdale, 1983).

We have begun to develop a programme of policy-related research on these issues, again working closely with the European Commission and local authorities in the North-East of England and also with the support of the Economic and Social Research Council. The Commission, concerned with the widening technological gap between Europe and the United States, has been attempting to simulate the development of a European information and communications manufacturing industry through support for R&D. The Regional Policy Directorate, charged with examining the regional consequences of other community policies, asked us to review the likely consequences of such a strategy for the less-favoured regions of Europe not only in terms of the location of information technology production but also in relation to the more widespread utilization of telecommunications in business.

Our review led to the conclusion that, far from reducing regional disparities, present tendencies were likely to reinforce existing differences

(Gillespie *et al.*, 1985; Goddard *et al.*, 1985). Many of the less-favoured regions lacked the necessary telecommunication infrastructure, and others with that infrastructure were not making effective use of the opportunities. Our review directly resulted in a £800 million programme, the Special Telecommunications Action for Regions, being laid before the Council of Ministers. This includes support for bringing forward the modernization of telecommunications in selected less-favoured regions of the Community, coupled with appropriate demand-stimulation measures. The programme therefore clearly recognizes the danger of only improving 'electronic highways' which could simply become one-way streets enabling information providers in more-favoured areas to undermine services based on traditional means of transaction in the less-favoured areas. We have therefore worked with local authorities and a computer software house linked to the University of Newcastle-upon-Tyne in developing value-added network services to support sectors such as tourism and offshore engineering in the Northern Region.

On the academic side we have been fortunate to be selected as one of a network of Centres to be supported by the Economic and Social Research Council to study the implications of advances in information and communications technology. Our research will examine the nature of threats and opportunities for different localities of technological change in the manufacturing sector, the support of the research council will be of vital importance in developing more basic work which can underpin policy-oriented investigations.

Conclusion

The reader will have noticed a switch to the first person plural some way through this chapter. This change coincides with my decision to establish the Centre for Urban and Regional Development Studies (CURDS) in the University of Newcastle-upon-Tyne in 1977, and the resultant emphasis on collective research. On my arrival in Newcastle, to a chair where I was expected to initiate a programme of applied research in regional development studies, it was soon apparent that this was a problem needing contributions from disciplines in addition to geography. It was also clear that significant contributions could not be made by an individual working on his own. CURDS was established within the Geography Department, but with links to a wide range of social science departments in the expectation that academics in these departments would contribute to a team enterprise. As it has turned out the research has developed as much from the spin-offs from initial projects and the efforts of the research staff from different disciplines recruited to work on those projects as from established academics working in other departments. At the time of writing CURDS has 23 full-time research staff working on a range of projects supported by the Economic and Social Research Council, government departments and the European Commission.

In the Centre we have sought to maintain a wide spectrum of research from the purely academic to the heavily applied, with each reinforcing and/or challenging the other. The development of a team of full-time researchers with adequate support has made it possible to react swiftly to the requirements of policy-makers and deliver high-quality research products on schedule. At the same time the existence of a core of three, recently increased to four, tenured academic staff and core-funds from the Economic and Social Research Council as one of their Designated Research Centres, has made it possible to undertake some longer-term work, which has succeeded in setting the agenda within which policy-makers commission more specific pieces of applied work.

The achievement of policy impact which is well grounded in empirical and theoretical investigations requires a long-term view and consistency of research endeavour. Soundly based applied research tends to be incremental in nature, with each research project leading on to new enquiries that build on previous theoretical insights and empirical foundations. These are of course dangers that this leads to a conservatism and a loss of originality, and in this respect the criticisms of outside academics are of vital importance. With such inputs it has been possible to develop a challenging interchange between policy-makers and researchers from different disciplinary and theoretical backgrounds (see for example Amin and Goddard, 1986).

I will conclude this chapter by reminding geographers who desire to have influence on public policy, at least in the British context, of the need for patience and persistence. This can be illustrated by my last example, namely the establishment by the University of Newcastle of a Regional Industrial Research Unit attached to CURDS and sponsored by three government departments (Environment, Trade and Industry, Manpower Services) and the English Industrial Estates Corporation. On numerous public and private occasions over the past 10 years I have complained of a lack of coordination of the activities of central government departments in the Northern Region, and of the generally short-term approach to dealing with the long-term and deep-seated structural problems of the regional economy. After negotiations which have taken several years to complete the departments have agreed to finance a unit which will provide a research foundation for their activities relating to the regeneration of the economy of the region. The unit will have its own director and management committee, composed of policy-makers from the sponsoring departments and the director and deputy director of CURDS. It will undertake studies which seek to identify the strengths and weaknesses of different sectors in the region, of skills and training requirements in local labour markets and deficiencies in the physical infrastructure. The unit will draw upon the intellectual resources of CURDS and the wider academic community as and where appropriate. However, the unit will be at arms' length from CURDS, having been established by the university as a company limited by guarantee partly in order to protect the independence of the Centre. The unit will disseminate the findings of its research and hopefully contribute to the creation of a body of economic development expertise in the sponsoring departments through in-depth briefings of officers. In this way it is hoped that research will contribute to policy coordination by helping those working in particular spheres to understand the broader context for their activities.

The unit has been established in the belief that the chief contribution of a university to the local community can come through the mobilization of its intellectual resources. Academics have the advantage of working in a global community, but although they live *in* a particular locality they seldom are part *of* that place. There are numerous ways by which such contributions can be made other than in the particular spheres of industrial location described in this essay. Nevertheless, geographers, because of their understanding of places in a national and international context, can play a leading role in linking their institutions to the local community. Such links can take different forms in different localities, and may necessitate some adjustments of individual research interests in order to maximize the opportunity for the development of a synergetic relationship between the global and the local community. Given the speed with which geographers seem to change their research orientation and priorities such adjustment should not be too tall an order.

References

Amin, A. and Goddard, J. B. (eds) (1986) *Technological Change, Industrial Restructuring and Regional Development*. Allen & Unwin, Hemel Hempstead.

Aydalot, P. (1986) *Milieux Innovateurs en Europe*. Gremi, Paris.

Camagni, R., Cappelin, R. and Garafoli, G. (eds) (1984) *Cambiamento Tecnologica e Diffusione Territoriale*. Franco Angeli, Milano.

Dunning, J. H. and Morgan, E. V. (1971) *An Economic Study of the City of London*. Allen & Unwin, London.

Firn, J. (1975) External control and regional development, *Environment and Planning*, A(7), 393–414.

Freeman, C. (1986) The role of technical change in national economic development. In Amin and Goddard (1986).

Gillespie, A. E., Goddard, J. B., Robinson, J. F. and Thwaites, A. J. (1985) *The Effects of New Information Technology on the Less Favoured Regions of the Community*. Commission of the European Communities Studies Collection,

Regional Policy Series No. 23. Commission of the European Communities, Brussels.

Goddard, J. B. (1968) Multivariate analysis of the office location patterns in the city centre: a London example, *Regional Studies*, 2, 67–85.

Goddard, J. B. (1970) Functional regions in the city centre: a study by factor analysis of taxi flows in Central London, *Transactions and Papers, Institute of British Geographers*, 49, 161–82.

Goddard, J. B. (1973) *Office Linkages and Location*. Pergamon Press, Oxford.

Goddard, B. J. (1976) Organisational information flows and the urban system, *Economie Appliquée*. Special issue edited by J.-R. Boudeville and F. Perroux (Paris).

Goddard, J. B. and Pye, R. (1977) Telecommunications and office location, *Regional Studies*, 11, 19–30.

Goddard, J. B. (1978a) Office development and urban and regional development in Britain. In P. W. Daniels (ed.), *Spatial Patterns of Office Growth and Location*. Wiley, Chichester.

Goddard, J. B. (1978b) Urban and regional systems, *Progress in Human Geography*, 1, 309–17.

Goddard, J. B. (1980) Technology forecasting in a spatial context, *Futures*, 12, 90–105.

Goddard, J. B. (1982) Movement systems, functional linkages and office location in the city centre. In L. S. Bourne (ed.), *Internal Structure of the City*. Oxford University Press, Oxford.

Goddard, J. B., Gillespie, A. E., Robinson, J. F. and Thwaites, A. J. (1985) New information technology and urban and regional development. In A. T. Thwaites and R. Oakey (eds), *Technological Change and Regional Development*. Frances Pinter, London.

Goddard, J. B. and Gillespie, A. E. (1986) Advanced telecommunications and regional economic development, *Geographical Journal*, 152, 383–97.

Goddard, J. B. and Marshall, J. N. (1983) The future for offices in the city centre. In R. L. Davies and A. G. Champion (eds), *The Future of the City Centre*. Academic Press, London.

Goddard, J. B. and Morris, D. (1976) *The Communication Factor in Office Decentralisation*. Pergamon Press, Oxford.

Goddard, J. B. and Smith, I. J. (1978) Changes in corporate control in the British urban system 1972–77, *Environment and Planning A*, 10, 1073–84.

Goddard, J. B. and Thwaites, A. T. (1980) *Technological Change and the Inner City*. Social Science Research Council, London.

Goddard, J. B. and Thwaites, A. T. (1983) Science parks and national and regional and local technological policy, *The Planner*, 69, 36–7.

Goddard, J. B., Thwaites, A. T. and Gibbs, D. (1986) The regional dimension to technological change in Great Britain. In Amin and Goddard (1986).

Hepworth, M. E. (1986) The geography of technological change in the information economy, *Regional Studies*, 20, 407–24.

House of Lords (1984) *European Regional Development Fund*, Select Committee on the European Communities 23rd Report. HMSO, London.

Kleine, J. (1982) Location, firm size and innovativeness. In Maillat (1982).

Lambooy, J. G. (1984) The regional economy of technological change. In J. G.

Lambooy (ed.), *New Spatial Dynamics in Economic Crisis*. Finn Publishers, Helsinki.

Langdale, J. (1983) Competition in the United States' long distance telecommunications industry, *Regional Studies*, 17, 393–409.

Maillat, D. (ed.) (1982) *Technology: A Key Factor for Regional Development*. Saint-Saphrin, Garogi, Bern.

Marshall, J. N. (1979) Ownership, organisation and industrial linkage: a case study of the Northern Region of England, *Regional Studies*, 13, 531–57.

Mansfield, E. (1968) *The Economics of Technical Change*. Longmans, London.

McDermott, P. J. (1976) Ownership, organisational and regional dependence in the Scottish electronics industry, *Regional Studies*, 10, 319–35.

Melody, W. N. (1985) Implications of the information and communications technology: the role of policy research, *Policy Studies*, 6. Policy Studies Institute, London.

Molle, W. (1983) *Industrial Change, Innovation and Location*. OECD, Paris.

Nijkamp, P. (ed.) (1986) *Technological Change, Employment and Spatial Dynamics*. Springer, Berlin.

Northern Region Strategy Team (1977) *Strategic Plan for the Northern Region*. HMSO, London.

Rees, J., Briggs, R. and Oakey, R. (1984) The adoption of new technology in American machinery industry, *Regional Studies*, 18, 489–504.

Schiller, D. (1984) Business users and the telecommunications network, *Journal of Communications*, 32, 84–96.

Segal, N. S. (1980) The limits and means of 'self-reliant' regional economic growth. In D. MacLennan and B. Parr (eds), *Regional Policy: Past Experiences and New Directions*. Martin Robertson, Oxford.

Smith, I. J. (1978) The effects of external takeovers and manufacturing employment change in the Northern Region', *Regional Studies*, 13, 421–37.

Thorngren, B. (1970) How do contact systems effect regional development?, *Environment and Planning A*, 2, 409–27.

Thwaites, A. T. (1978) Technological change, mobile plants and regional development, *Regional Studies*, 12, 445–61.

Thwaites, A. T. (1981) Some evidence of regional variations in the introduction and diffusion of industrial products and processes within British manufacturing industry, *Regional Studies*, 16, 371–81.

Thwaites, A. T. (1983) Regional Technological Change Centre, Discussion Paper No. 47, Centre for Urban and Regional Development Studies, University of Newcastle-upon-Tyne.

Tornqvist, G. (1970) *Contact Systems and Regional Development*. Lund Studies in Geography (B), No. 35, Department of Geography, University of Lund, Sweden.

5

Planning for SADCC's Future

Phil O'Keefe and Richard Peet

Universities are feeling the effects of world economic recession through cutbacks in funding and increased demands for research which is 'pragmatic' in the narrow sense of the word. Geographers, especially those committed to radical analysis and change, are equally, if not more, under pressure. Debate about social change tends to be stifled by fiscal crisis, while students seek to amass immediately 'sellable' skills and technical expertise at the expense of a more general understanding of social structures and relationships. Bearing this political context in mind, we report here on our involvement with energy and development planning that seeks to utilize an understanding both of political economy in general and technical skills in particular, to draw broad future scenarios for the southern Africa frontline states' regional development group – SADCC.

SADCC

SADCC, the Southern African Development Coordinating Conference, was formally founded at a summit conference in Lusaka in April 1980, between the member countries Angola, Botswana, Lesotho, Malawi, Mozambique, Swaziland, Tanzania, Zambia and Zimbabwe. The founding declaration, entitled *Southern Africa: Toward Economic Liberation*, outlines four conference objectives:[1]

1. reduction of economic dependence particularly, but not exclusively, on the Republic of South Africa;
2. the forging of links to create a genuine and equitable regional integration;
3. the mobilization of resources to promote the implementation of national and regional policies;
4. concerted action to secure international cooperation within the framework of a strategy for economic liberation.

This constellation of states is the most important regional initiative to emerge in Africa during the past decade. Economic integration, to which it aims, is a difficult process judged by the record of past failures, and given the widely divergent political systems and levels of economic development of the member countries. The organization is not inherently socialist in character, reflecting rather the popular struggles for national independence that have dominated the recent history of southern Africa. It seeks to break the stranglehold that imperialism, acting through South Africa, has on African development. This task is all the more urgent given current efforts by South Africa to destabilize regional economic activity.

The first SADCC conference was held in Arusha, Tanzania, in July 1979.[2] At this conference, studies were requested dealing with the following areas of potential regional cooperation: transport and communications, agriculture, forestry and fisheries, energy, water and minerals, trade and industry, and employment. Angola was given responsibility for energy development and conservation. Working with the Beijer Institute (Royal Swedish Academy of Sciences), we became involved with document preparation for the energy sector. This essentially involved compiling a national energy budget for each member state with projection to the year 2000. These were accumulated to provide a review of all sectoral requirements across the region. In addition, we helped draft individual national energy policy papers for presentation by member governments.

Why Energy? Why Geographers?

Energy[3] expenditures dominate the capital and current accounts of the SADCC member countries. The capital account is dominated by the electricity sector. Substantial capital outlays are made on dams, generators and turbines, and a host of downstream distribution systems and end-use appliances. Most member states do not presently have the means to manufacture light bulbs and electric cookers, let alone switching stations. Therefore the great bulk of production and consumption equipment is imported, with a consequent drain on foreign exchange.

The current account, in contrast, is dominated by the purchase of liquid hydrocarbons. Oil imports account for between 18 and 42 per cent of the member countries' total imports by value. Also many countries, with the exception of Angola, receive their petroleum products imports either directly from South Africa, or along routes that can effectively be destabilized by South Africa. Clearly energy issues are of central economic and political importance to the SADCC countries.

But why use geographers of radical persuasion? The emphasis that radical geographers, and more particularly environmentalists, bring to energy planning has grown out of their opposition to nuclear power, their concern for the ecological impacts of energy policies, and their support for conservation initiatives. In broad political terms there has been increasing evidence of self-supporting relationships between military and civil programmes, paralleled by increased opposition to the siting of nuclear facilities and the transport and location of nuclear wastes. Furthermore, serious questions have been raised about the relative contribution of electricity to the overall energy balance, especially as a fuel for low-grade applications. In contrast to highly centralized, conventional generation patterns there have been calls by geographers for decentralized initiatives using renewable technologies, while regional planners have emphasized the employment-generating potential of conservation programmes. In terms of energy studies this political–economic movement led to the development of end-use energy accounting.

End-use Energy Accounting

All too often national energy accounts have been calculated on a highly aggregated basis. That is, they have been available for total requirements of the major commercial fuel forms – coal, petroleum products, electricity and natural gas. Such accounts have generally been developed from a supply side orientation, since the major institutions for planning, administration, production, distribution, import and export have been in place for many years and have procedures for keeping good statistics.

   A major problem emerging from this experience is that, for the commercial fuels themselves, detail is often available on the supply side (e.g. different forms of electricity generation or different petroleum products). However, this detail is not matched on the demand side. That is, the final destination of each specific commercial fuel type within society, by sector, subsector and process or end-use, is not adequately known. A second problem is the almost complete neglect of quantitative information, on both the supply and demand sides, for traditional fuels (i.e. fuelwood; crop and animal wastes). These are used primarily in the large rural sectors of the developing societies in the SADCC region.

   In the rural sector itself it has been widely noted that its stability and growing productive output is a vital component of overall economic and social development. The income it generates, the output it provides, and the goods and services it requires articulate with activities in the rest of the economy, and help spur economic growth. The difficulty in obtaining sufficient fuelwood and the impending problems of 'deforestation' can undermine the physical and economic basis of continued rural development.

Planning for overall national development thus entails planning for the basic energy requirements for productive activities in all sectors of society. *And* planning requires a forward look if such basic needs are to be provided without major physical or economic bottlenecks. Thus, energy planning must be based upon comprehensive, accurate, and detailed forecasts of energy requirements.

Knowledge of current energy use in the aggregate for only commercial fuel forms is not an adequate foundation for such forecasts. On this basis one can merely extrapolate historic trends or, at best, build the forecasts on new projections of overall economic and demographic growth. The inadequacy of this approach is quite clear. In fact, in the industrialized world itself, e.g. the United States, such procedures and related approaches have failed dramatically.

A detailed end-use approach to baseline forecasts of energy requirements is essential to provide an adequate basis for planning. Different sectors and subsectors within society are likely to grow at different rates, and since each, in turn, has its own specific end-uses or processes which require energy in amounts and in fuel forms specific to that activity, the overall growth in the demand for various fuels will depend upon the detailed growth and changing fuel mix within each sector, subsector and end-use. For example, increasing urbanization and income shifts will likely result in more rapid growth in commercial fuels of various types than in fuelwood demand. Differential growth in the various industrial subsectors could result in a changing mix of oil, coal and electricity use over time.

Shifts in transportation modes within transportation subsectors can lead to changes in the amounts and types of fuels used in these activities, and so on. Thus accurate forecasts of future requirements for various energy forms require:

1. detailed end-use account of current fuel use,
2. projections of the growth in the sector/subsector and end-use activities for which energy is required,
3. projections of equipment, physical stock and associated fuel mix associated with the end-use activities.

Establishing such a base case (or baseline) scenario of future energy requirements under the assumptions of smooth evolution of current demographic, economic, technical and policy conditions is just the first step in energy planning. The end-use approach can then provide a detailed basis for the identification of potential emerging problems and opportunities with regard to energy supply and demand. It thus becomes possible to create a programme which embodies a mix of initiatives with regard to policies and regulations, and with regard to technologies, fuels, pricing, land-use etc. Such a programme would be designed to ensure that the type, timing, magnitude, and cost of energy supplies is appropriate to evolving energy needs. End-use energy accounting, like end-use accounting for water, requires substantial consumer surveys.

Early attempts to apply end-use accounting to developing countries revealed that household consumption dominated the energy budget, while detailed fieldwork showed that it was wood from outside the forests that dominated biomass supply. The development of supply options thus required careful consideration of land-uses and involved land-use planning (a traditional geographic technique) to ensure future energy sources. To this end a group of geographers and physicists set out to establish a system that would incorporate land-use as a critical variable in energy accounting. This was completed within the context of ongoing fieldwork in Africa.[4]

The SADCC Energy Budget

The derivation of the SADCC regional energy budget, which involved utilizing the end-use energy budgeting model and extensive fieldwork,[5] produced political and technical findings. The largest part of energy consumed within the SADCC region comes from biomass (vegetation in general), with 79 per cent being accounted for by woodfuel, followed by petroleum, coal and electricity (table 5.1). The importance of biomass fuels reflects the rural characters of most of the SADCC countries as well as the critical role of biomass in the provision of basic energy for most subsistence populations. Regretfully, this is the area to which least research and governmental resources are committed.

Due to an increased rate of household formation biomass utilization is expected to grow by some 70 per cent by 2000 (figure 5.1). Consumption of commercial fuels will increase more quickly because of industrial development and increased rural to urban migration. Electricity consumption will increase by 150 per cent, coal consumption by 120 per cent, and petroleum consumption by over 100 per cent. When all these figures are projected to 2000, on a 'business-as-usual', basis that assumes no policy intervention to alter energy programmes, total energy consumption increases by some 80 per cent.

The SADCC region, as a whole, has an abundance of existing exploitable energy resources. Table 5.2 shows the energy surplus, given current production and expansion in demand, in 1990. The central problem in regional energy questions, we concluded, is the transport and distribution system, not the production system.

Three particular issues have been isolated, which demonstrate the political importance of energy analysis, and our alternative approach to southern African energy issues.

Table 5.1   1980 Final energy consumption (PJ)[a] and average annual growth rate 1980–2000 (percentage/year)

Country	Grand total	Commercial fuels[b]				Traditional fuels
		Total	Electricity	Coal	Petroleum	
Angola						
PJ*	105.5	23.8	2.3	0.0	21.6	81.6
percentage/year	2.6	4.3	6.3	0.0	4.1	2.0
Botswana						
PJ	22.1	9.7	1.7	3.7	4.4	12.4
percentage/year	3.3	4.0	4.3	3.6	4.1	2.8
Lesotho						
PJ	24.2	5.2	0.3	1.9	2.9	19.0
percentage/year	2.4	4.2	6.4	5.1	3.2	1.8
Malawi						
PJ	165.2	9.4	1.3	1.4	6.7	155.8
percentage/year	1.8	3.8	5.9	3.2	3.4	1.7
Mozambique						
PJ	281.7	30.6	2.5	5.8	22.3	251.1
percentage/year	2.6	3.9	7.2	3.0	3.7	2.4
Swaziland						
PJ	24.0	9.6	1.6	3.3	4.7	14.4
percentage/year	3.5	3.9	4.4	4.7	2.9	3.2
Tanzania						
PJ	438.9	37.5	2.3	0.2	35.0	401.4
percentage/year	3.4	4.1	7.7	3.0	3.8	3.3
Zambia						
PJ	150.8	62.8	20.4	11.2	31.3	87.9
percentage/year	2.8	3.9	4.1	3.5	3.9	1.9
Zimbabwe						
PJ	244.1	117.2	24.9	65.8	26.4	126.9
percentage/year	3.4	3.9	4.4	4.1	3.2	2.8
SADCC						
PJ	1456.3	305.9	57.3	93.3	155.2	1150.5
percentage/year	3.0	4.0	4.7	4.0	3.7	2.6

[a] One PJ (peta-joule) = 0.034 million tonnes coal equivalent = 0.022 million tonnes oil equivalent.
[b] Final consumption only (e.g. coal figures do not include coal used for electricity generation).

Expanded Utilization of Energy Accounts

Part of the problem for development planners in the SADCC region is the assumption that 'plans' are merely summaries or lists of approved

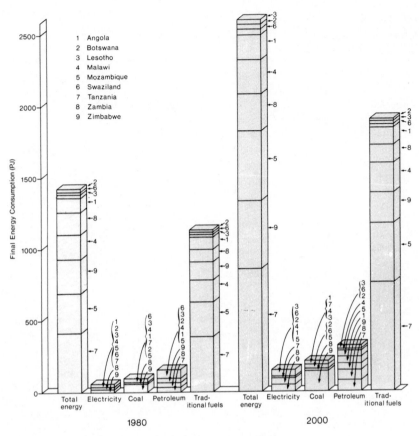

Figure 5.1 SADCC Growth in final energy consumption

Table 5.2 1990 SADCC-wide energy surpluses (PJ/year)

	Requirements	Production	Surplus
Electricity	98.5	215.2[a]	116.7
Coal	208.4	478.9	270.5
Refined oil	232.3	233.2	0.9
Crude oil	245.0	458.2	213.2

[a]Maximum output of all hydro and coal facilities.
One Pj = 10^{15} joules = 0.022 million tonnes = 0.034 million tonnes oil equivalent = 277.7 GWh (gigaWatt-hours)

projects. In the past decade a particular form of project appraisal, approved by the World Bank, has come to dominate planning in Third World countries. While not rejecting the value of some kind of benefit–cost appraisal, we argue that current methods approved by the Bank do little except provide an assured return to capital, *as capital*. Current methods, in addition, do not allow the location of any particular project within an overall planning effort. Energy accounts, by comparison, particularly if completed at a detailed sectoral level, allow the production of a formative plan, utilizing physical rather than monetary units, for the whole economy. This replaces the accountant mentality of project appraisal with strategic, political planning. Within such strategic, political plans there is, of course, value to benefit–cost comparisons, but the narrow project focus is redressed and broad considerations re-emerge. An additional benefit is that the short term in energy planning (5–10 years) is long term in capital planning. Energy planning therefore can be used as a total physical framework within which capital planning takes place.

Biomass as Energy

While stressing the importance of wood as the primary energy source of rural households, we are critical of conventional notions of forestry which generally focus on production for industrial plantations and expatriate gardens. An emphasis on biomass also brings to the fore the critical role of women in the procurement, management and maintenance of the energy system. This central role contrasts with the absence of female political and economic power even in socialist countries. Such analysis suggests that the answer to the problem, and the concomitant problem of land degradation, will be found by moving 'within farm' with policies that ensure a demand-driven, participatory afforestation initiative in which local people control local resources.

Energy Forecasting

Most energy forecasting is still carried out from the supply side. The demand analysis, completed during this SADCC work, provides an interesting contrast. Our estimates (table 5.2) suggest that there is already capacity to meet short- and medium-term energy requirements. These estimates are lower by a factor of three than estimates provided by conventional engineering consultants. This is not simply a matter of technical disagreement; it results, rather, from a fundamentally different world-view. Engineering consultants used the opportunity of SADCC energy planning to point out a 'need' for the establishment of a new programme of electrical generation. We argued the case for the sufficiency of existing resources, most notably the Caborra Bassa electricity supply, but the need to distribute it more effectively. The latter programme promotes regional integration while involving minimal investment costs.

The political dimensions of our planning initiatives, allied to technical competence, provided for an alternative view of such additional issues as energy security, environmental degradation through offtake, and energy requirements in war situations. Energy planning, for us and for SADCC member states, is a critical issue of political economy.

Industry and Energy Demand

The emphasis on biomass did not preclude work on commercial energy demand, however. Even in a region characterized by the highly uneven but generally low development of the productive forces, industry accounts for 25 per cent of total energy consumption (and 4 per cent of this commercial consumption is from biomass).

It was therefore important that we provide an accurate conception of the overall economic future of the southern African region to guide more detailed energy forecasting. In providing projections of the economic basis of energy demand, accuracy is difficult to achieve, especially in that much of the structure of the economic life of the region is determined externally. The region's future is still very much being made, and could immediately take several quite different courses – it will not be merely a linear extension of the past. An attempt was therefore made to capture the dialectic of the future through composing scenarios of alternative economic futures, using several existing studies developed by institutions and individuals within competing political perspectives. These largely qualitative statements about the future of economic sectors were converted into quantitative growth rates and applied to a data set consisting of national gross domestic products (GDPs), sectoral contributions to GDPs, and GDP growth rates between 1965 and 1980.[6]

Two simple linear extensions of the past were constructed in which economic growth rates were assumed to be lower than the growth rate of 3.9 per cent a year estimated for the GDP of the region in the years 1965–80. We called these Historical I Scenario (2.6 per cent growth rate) and Historical II Scenario (3.8 per cent). Projections, based on further scenarios, were then developed from two entirely different political perspectives presently playing a contending role in shaping consciousness in the region: the World Bank Report[7] and recent papers written essentially from a socialist position by Ann Seidman, Chairperson of the Department of Economics at the University of Zimbabwe.[8,9] We made a detailed analysis of the theoretical arguments behind these proposals to bring out the essentially different political stance adopted by their authors.

The World Bank Scenario

The World Bank attributes slow growth in the region to a set of internal constraints on development, such as shortages of trained manpower, military conflict, the institutional heritage, physical environmental and locational problems and high population growth rates, operating in the context of external relations which also have been increasingly negative, i.e. shifting terms of trade following a five-fold increase in the price of oil, and declining primary exports. Behind the apparently miscellaneous nature of these constraints (so miscellaneous as to be practically useless as a guide to a focused regional planning response) lies a political position based in conventional, even conservative, economic theory: the constraint idea is essentially that a set of obstacles prevents regional economic growth which would otherwise occur 'naturally' through contact with the world capitalist system. The report therefore favours a development strategy based on increasing the traditional ('natural') exports of the region (subtropical foods, agricultural raw materials, minerals) in a policy climate of reduced governmental intervention, especially in the areas of exchange rates and industrial subsidization. A scenario of future development was constructed assuming the adoption of these recommendations – this involved quantifying what were often very generally stated, qualitative proposals. Generously interpreted, it was calculated that the World Bank proposals, *if successful*, would yield a growth rate in GDP for the region of 4.3 per cent a year between 1980 and 2000 – the accelerated growth the World Bank was seeking. Realizing this rate, however, would depend on economic growth in the world capitalist system, expressed especially in terms of steady or rising prices for the region's staple exports.

Even as the World Bank report was being written, however, these prices were dropping rapidly with the onset of world recession in the late 1970s and early 1980s. This soon forced a revision in the Bank's opinion about the rate of growth in the world system and its regions.[10] The World Bank came to have a particularly bleak prognosis for the future of sub-Saharan Africa. This later prognosis was used in two further World Bank scenarios which we estimated would yield regional growth rates of 2.5 and 3.1 per cent a year. The World Bank's proposals would intensify the regional connection with an increasingly precarious world capitalist economy – a wide range of possible economic growth rates was the inevitable conclusion.

The Seidman Scenario

Seidman argues that economic development has been prevented by the imposition, during both colonial and post-colonial periods, of a certain set of institutions on the region. Within this institutional framework a partial economic development has occurred, focused on mining and plantation agriculture. The institutional structure also acts to channel the locally produced investable surplus out of the region. Even in the post-independence period, amounts estimated at between 25 and 40 per cent of the GDPs of the various countries have been withdrawn as profit, interest, dividends, and expatriate salaries, or drained by manipulation of the terms of trade.

This outflow has made necessary huge foreign loans even to provide infrastructure for extended transnational corporate operations which would, in turn, increase the outflow. Seidman therefore predicates her regional development proposals on the state taking control of the 'commanding heights' of various national economies. This, she argues, would enable the surplus to be invested in a more balanced, integrated pattern of development to meet basic needs. A regional investable surplus of $4 billion (in 1975 dollars) is sufficient to form the financial basis for long-term, planned development, using the twin spatial strategies of decentralized, need-oriented industries and regional pole-of-growth industries of a basic type.

Seidman's proposals suggest a protracted period of political struggle, followed by a development path characterized especially by investment in, and the rapid growth of, manufacturing industry. In our 'Seidman scenario', therefore quantitative assumptions were made in accord with this understanding – 10 years of intense class struggle followed by sectoral growth rates similar to those of the 1965–80 period except in manufacturing, which was assumed to grow at 150–200 per cent of the historical rate. This produced a growth rate in regional GDP of 4.1 per cent a year between 1980 and 2000. More revealing is the economic structure produced, in comparison with our projections from the World Bank proposals (table 5.3). However, we criticize the Seidman argument in terms of its lack of specificity on the actual nature (amount and form) of the investable surplus, which she estimates at 25 per cent of GDP, and for a lack of discussion of the reaction by the outside world to the seizing of the commanding heights of the national economies.

'Composite Scenario'
The future is made from the collision and intersection of a number of historical tendencies. Our own forecast of commercial energy demand was based on a 'composite scenario' which essentially said that the future of Southern Africa will be composed of a version of the historical trend and aspects the two main alternatives posed from competing ideologies.[11] That is, the regional economy will grow more slowly than in the recent past; some countries will react by specializing all the more on mining and agricultural commodities for the world market (World Bank proposals), while others will react to crisis through socialist transformation

Table 5.3 Projections of sectoral structure of SADCC regional economy, 2000, under World Bank and "Seidman" scenario

	World Bank scenario (% GDP)	Seidman scenario (% GDP)
Agriculture	22.5	17.3
Manufacturing	11.6	22.6
Mining	17.8	13.8
Other	48.1	46.3
GDP	100.0	100.0

and a more autonomous pattern of economic growth (Seidman proposals). Synthesizing the World Bank's original proposal with the Seidman proposal and the two historical scenarios yielded a regional growth rate of 3.6 per cent per annum, with national rates varying around this figure. *Based on detailed proposals available at the time*, this was the most realistic appraisal of the economic future that could be made to guide energy planning in the region. (Long-term recession, however, would yield a regional growth rate in the range of 2.5–3.1 per cent a year proposed by the World Bank.)

We argue further that this growth rate could be increased in the long run only through raising labour productivity through the use of improved means of production. 'Heavy manufacturing' is the source of these improved means. Yet the 'heavy' variety makes up only 34 per cent of the region's total manufacturing compared with 55 per cent of that of all 'developing' countries, and 66 per cent of that in the 'developed market economies'. We advocate that priority be given to means of production manufacturing in the region. Our work ends with an estimate of the future composition of manufacturing based on the achievement, by 2000, of a heavy manufacturing component more in line with that of the norm for the rest of the 'developing' world. The result of adopting this proposal would be to greatly increase the industrial demand for energy. Using Zimbabwean figures, we calculate that for a given value of output heavy manufacturing uses four times the energy used by light manufacturing, with coal assuming an increasing percentage of energy used at the expense of oil.

Industry and Energy

Industry is slowly responding to the changing conditions of the world energy market. As SADCC's share of world manufacturing rises so will energy requirements, in absolute and relative terms. Oil is currently the preferred source of commercial and industrial energy, but a major transition to coal will begin to occur over the next 20 years. An industrial policy which favours increasing the local processing of raw materials, output mix, the location of production facilities and technology will change in response to the energy-input costs.

Rises in SADCC energy prices, compared to price increases of other inputs, have changed the economics of industrial processing. However, the transition in output mix, location and technology is slow because the adjustment is to changes in relative price. The reasons for this slow adjustment include:

1. The national economies of SADCC member countries, for a variety of reasons, respond slowly to changes in relative prices.
2. The sharp rises in crude oil prices have not been fully charged on final oil product prices, so that industrial management has not felt the full impact of increases.
3. The importance of commercial fuel consumption in the household sector (kerosene and gas) limits a policy formulation which would severely restrict imported commercial fuels; consequently, industrial management assumes a somewhat similar energy-input mix in the next decade.

An industrial policy which seeks to expand the production of the means of production, focuses attention on heavy industry. From historical experience it seems that the share of heavy industry in manufacturing output rises as industrialization proceeds. As this occurs, the manufacturing sector becomes more energy-intensive. Although the use of energy is becoming more efficient, the energy requirements of SADCC member countries will rise as this structural change occurs.

Emphasis on energy conservation is of critical importance in the next decade: it is better to conserve than produce an additional unit of energy. However, efforts to promote conservation measures must be tempered by an understanding of the problems of industrialization in SADCC member countries. Conservation measures are unlikely to offset consumption increases – conservation is only a partial solution. Additionally, competition for capital investment, particularly for scarce foreign exchange, between the conflicting claims of national sectors will not allow rapid replacement of energy-inefficient technologies or rerouting of industrial processing chains. For successful implementation of energy conservation, detailed audits of industrial processes will be necessary, to identify cost-effective pathways that will decrease the burden of recurrent expenditures. That remains a pressing task for the future.

The Struggle Continues

The line of research briefly described above is far from concluded. Work continues on a detailed study of energy in Zimbabwe, and the implementation of prior work in Kenya. A team visited Grenada in July–August 1983. Although the research was completed it remains to be seen whether the results will be used by whatever regime emerges.

Our work indicates that the radical tradition yields different research methodologies and brings different policy and planning conclusions than does conventional social science. These are particularly significant in energy planning, which otherwise is dominated by research institutions and methodologies with a vested interest in certain (expensive) outcomes – i.e. the building of products involving heavy capital outlays and extensive importing of expertise and equipment. If these kinds of investments are to be made, they should occur in manufacturing industry; specifically in means of production manufacturing. We conclude in general that there remains a need for research and planning from a number of alternative political positions, including those on the left. In terms of education the radical aim at discovering the economic and social roots of issues and problems remains pragmatically relevant. A time of crisis should promote the renewed search for the most basic truths.

Notes and References

1 For the general background to SADCC see A. J. Nsekela (ed.) (1981) *Southern Africa: toward economic liberation*, Rex Collings, London; A. Kgarebe (ed.) (1981) *SADCC 2 – Maputo*, SADCC Liaison Committee, London; R. Leys and A. Tostenson (1982) Regional co-operation in Southern African Development Co-ordination Conference, *Review of African Political Economy*, 23.

2 A. Tostenson (1982) *Dependence and Collective Self-Reliance in Southern Africa*. Research Report No. 62. Scandinavian Institute of African Studies, Uppsala.

3 Barry Munslow and Phil O'Keefe (1984) Energy and the southern African regional confrontation, *Third World Quarterly*, 6(1).

4 For an example of this work see Phil O'Keefe *et al.* (1984) *Energy and Development in Kenya: opportunities and constraints*. Scandinavian Institute of African Studies, Uppsala.

5 Barry Munslow, Phil O'Keefe and Paul Raskin, *SADCC: Energy and Development to 2000*. Scandinavian Institute of African Studies, Uppsala, 1984.

6 Richard Peet, *Manufacturing Industry and Economic Development in the SADCC Countries*. Scandinavian Institute of African Studies, Uppsala, 1984.

7 World Bank. *Accelerated Development in Sub-Saharan Africa: An Agenda for Action*. Washington, 1981.

8   Seidman, A. (1980) Towards integrated regional development in southern Africa. Unpublished paper, Department of Economics, University of Zimbabwe, Harare, Zimbabwe.
9   Seidman, A. (1982) A development strategy for Zimbabwe. Unpublished paper, Department of Economics, University of Zimbabwe, Harare, Zimbabwe.
10   World Bank (1982) *World Development Report 1982*. Oxford University Press, New York.
11   Richard Peet (1984) Alternative trajectories for economic development in southern Africa, *Antipode*, 15(3), 37–44.

6

Towards a Geography of the Common People in South Africa

C. M. Rogerson and K. S. O. Beavon

Introduction

For the past seven years our research has centred on the activities of the casual poor of Johannesburg and Soweto. The actors are the petty commodity producers who engage in such seemingly trivial pursuits as the hawking of fruit, vegetables, live chickens, cups of tea and coffee, sandwiches, flowers or liquor in an effort to eke out an existence in the so-called 'informal sector' of Johannesburg's economy. This focus is in sharp contrast to that of our earlier research activities which were informed by and spurred on by the models, paradigms, and methods of Anglo-American geography, and which in retrospect had no social relevance to the society in which we found ourselves. In this chapter we shall seek to trace the steps which led towards the writing of geographies of the common people in South Africa. This task will be pursued initially by directing attention to the changing complexion of South African human geography during the 1970s and 1980s. Thereafter, the focus shifts to chronicle the circumstances behind the transition from a research programme which was at first confined to an exploration of the characteristics and organization of street traders in contemporary Johannesburg and developed into a broadening project encompassing both historical and contemporary investigations of the spectrum of economic activities pursued by the city's common people. Included in the discussion will be a critical evaluation of the changing methodologies of the research and a consideration of its perceived successes and limitations.

The Changing Face of Human Geography in Apartheid South Africa

Looking back to the early 1970s the nature of research in South African human geography was very different from that of today. At the risk of simplification it might best be described as a 'colonized' form of human geography because it was dominated or, perhaps more correctly, obsessed by the thinking and predominant models of Anglo-American human geography (Crush, Reitsma and Rogerson, 1982). When the quantitative tide was in full surge in our part of the world a decade ago, human geographers were mesmerized by the delights of delineating the nature and characteristics of work and business places, fascinated by central place theory and the search for continua or hierarchies (Rogerson and Browett, 1986). In addition, they were inexorably committed to diffusionist notions of development which asserted that by operationalizing growth poles, and promoting industrial decentralization, one would achieve a magical hierarchical spread of development from the affluent 'core' regions of 'White' South Africa into the poverty-stricken, 'backward' peripheral areas, then styled derogatorily as the 'Bantu Homelands' (Beavon and Rogerson, 1981). The major preoccupation of the community of human geographers in South Africa was of retaining an academic respectability, defined by the standards and current bandwagons rolling in North America and Western Europe. Reinforcing this belief that we must endeavour to keep up with the latest trends in what was seen as the discipline's academic heartland, were the frequent visits by overseas scholars to monitor the 'progress' of human geography at this peripheral outpost of Anglo-American geography. (Notwithstanding this comment, the authors are forever in debt to a number of visiting geographers from abroad who have encouraged us in the type of research reported here.) In short, the dominant thrust of research in the early 1970s was towards the testing and refining of a variety of models and theories deriving from Western Europe and North America or to 'fitting' our empirical findings on South Africa into these imported models. Typically our own research concerns in the early 1970s involved investigating the validity of the dual-population hypothesis of industrial movement to the South African situation (Rogerson, 1975a,b), and to revising and refining the classical location theories of Christaller and Lösch (Beavon, 1974, 1975, 1977). In retrospect it is hard to imagine a combination of research interests less 'relevant' to the circumstances of apartheid South Africa of the 1970s.

Nonetheless, it is evident that two significant sets of problems arose from this situation of academic colonialism, the ultimate recognition of which would propel our own research in dramatically different directions. First, the hegemony of Anglo-American geography caused an almost total neglect of the conditions prevailing in the areas of Black South Africa. The latest imported fashionable techniques and models – principal components analysis, factorial ecology or trend-surface analysis – were readily absorbed by South African geographers but could only be applied to those areas with readily accessible data sets, usually from census material. Since the most reliable and comprehensive data sources related to the circumstances of 'White' South Africa, our efforts to keep up with the fads of Anglo-American geography blinkered us from pursuing investigations on the worsening conditions of 'Black' South Africa and, more importantly, of the world of Black South Africans. The second, and perhaps more worrisome, consequence of the development of a colonized form of human geography was that the imported European and American theories and models, in combination with the deployment of the latest 'scientific' techniques of quantitative analysis, lent themselves conveniently to a general legitimization of the political *status quo* in South Africa; in other words, to an uncritical acceptance of apartheid. For example, interpretations of poverty and inequality in South Africa rooted upon diffusionist models of a dual economy could 'explain' the poverty of Black South Africa in terms of the 'backwardness' of certain cultures, their lack of entrepreneurship, inability to farm and so forth. In addition, our new kitbag of quantitative techniques furnished us with a basis not only for modelling the regional and urban system but also for 'predicting' strategies to improve its efficiency. Critics of all things South African might easily attribute the traits of local human geography to the belief that because most geographers in South Africa are White (and by definition automatically racist) they callously chose to ignore the 'inhuman' geography of the Black communities. Nevertheless, we would argue that a major share of the blame for this situation must be laid squarely at the doors of those 'gatekeepers' of academic geography who forged and continued to encourage the subordination of South African human geography to the dominance of Anglo-American geography.

The dramatic transformations that overtook and refashioned human geography in South Africa during the 1970s and 1980s were partially a reaction to the consciousness-raising of political events in the sub-continent, and partially also a response to the appearance outside human geography of a new revisionist literature in South African studies (Beavon and Rogerson, 1981; Crush and Rogerson, 1983; Rogerson and Browett, 1986). The early 1970s saw the independence of Mozambique and Angola, with the successful liberation struggles which brought to power regimes committed to new political programmes, previously unheard of (and, to a large extent, unmentionable) in South Africa (albeit at least, by most geographers), namely those of socialist development. Further reinforcing the relevance of reading Marx and Lenin to understanding southern Africa in the 1970s was the parallel transition which began in Zimbabwe. Undoubtedly these dramatic events on the political stage of southern Africa precipitated a rising awareness of, and interest in, more radical and critical forms of social enquiry. In terms, however, of shifting our own personal situation, the most significant watershed in human geography for us undoubtedly was 16 June 1976, the day that Soweto erupted in fire and violence. Suddenly, we were confronted by a host of questions which pitifully we were unable to answer: what was everyday life like in the townships?, how did those angry people on our television screens make a living?, and how had the situation emerged of the existence of segregated townships about which we knew virtually nothing? On that sad day our silence concerning the uprising in the Black townships stood as stark testament to the poverty of South African human geography in the 1970s. We could say little on the tragedy then taking place in Soweto because the Black townships hitherto had been *terra incognita* for urban geographers (Beavon, 1982). Out of our sight, the extent of the neglect of these areas by local geographers is revealed by the sombre fact that during the first 50 years of the appearance of the *South African Geographical Journal*, only one article on Soweto (or indeed on any Black township) was ever published. To add further insult to geographical injury, that single article was the product not of geographical endeavour but of the Manager of the Non-European Affairs Branch of the City of Johannesburg! Research on the themes of the historical making and contemporary existence in these Black townships, and more generally on the world of Black South Africans, was imperative in a redirection of human geographical enquiry in South Africa (Beavon and Rogerson, 1981). It appeared that this new research frontier within South Africa must be explored even at a cost of potentially losing our credentials in relation to Anglo-American human geography. Confirming our faith in this new direction for research was the glare of the international spotlight upon the continuing rebellion in the townships which culminated in the declaration of a repressive national state of emergency both in July 1985 and June 1986 (Rogerson, 1986a). Of significance also was the perceived need to begin a re-alignment of our teaching programme in recognition of the fact that South African universities are quintessentially a part not of the 'First World' but of the 'Third World' generally, and developing Africa in particular.

Alongside the stimulus provided by the turbulent political currents of southern Africa, an equally vital influence upon the remaking of South African geography was the appearance and strengthening of a 'new school' in South African studies (Johnstone, 1982; Crush and Rogerson, 1983; Mabin, 1986). This new school was of a neo-Marxist historiography led by the writings of a group of political scientists, historians and sociologists, the most notable being Charles van Onselen (1976, 1982), Belinda Bozzoli (1979, 1983), Shula Marks and associates (Marks and Atmore, 1980; Marks and Rathbone, 1982), and Frederick Johnstone (1976, 1978, 1982). The focus of these writers was on explaining South African society not in terms of simple considerations of race but of developing a sensitive form of analysis, informed by historical materialism, on the themes of class, capitalism, racial domination and the institutions of labour repression. The roles of the compound, the Native reserve, and the migrant worker hostels were revealed as crucial both as institutions for social control and in terms of their contributions towards capitalist profits.

The importance of this literature was three-fold. First, it undercut the theoretical base of much contemporary work in South African studies, not least in human geography. Illustratively, it demolished the myths of a dual economy and correlatively of that whole school of interpretations of Black poverty whose emphasis lay upon understanding the significance of the characteristics of traditional, backward economies and societies. The new wave of South African historiography instead directed our attention to the relentless pursuit of profits and the mechanics of labour coercion under capitalism, and especially under its specific manifestations in South Africa, apartheid. Second, the literature of the new school forced us to look seriously for the first time (if events in Soweto were not trigger enough) at the conditions and lifestyles of the mass of South Africa's population. It contributed greatly therefore to the de-whitening of South African human geography and to a growing feeling that we should not try and 'fit' South Africa into North American-based models and theories (Rogerson and Browett, 1986). Rather, what occurred was a tentative examination of the prospects for developing indigenous 'theory' and the greater application of lessons rooted in Third World research to South African conditions. The third major influence of the new wave writings in historiography was its deep involvement in historical analysis. It was emphasized that contemporary situations of poverty and underdevelopment could not be divorced from the historical processes of underdevelopment and capitalist exploitation of the Black reserves. In addition, it was significant that social historians were moving away from writing histories dealing with themes of modernization and the individuals or 'great men' responsible for forging a 'modern' city. Against the writing of commemorative volumes and epic sagas on the works of the mineowners, van Onselen lambasted those historians of Johannesburg who prefer 'peering into the homes and lifestyles of the "Randlords", attempting to put a romantic gloss on the ceaseless pursuit of wealth at a time when, elsewhere in the city, the dusty streets were bursting at the seams with a seething mass of struggling humanity' (van Onselen, 1982, vol. 1, p. xv). In sum, what emerged in South African studies has been the influence of popular history – the history of the common folk, ordinary people, the histories of common men (and women), the histories of peasants and proletarians – upon historical geography and human geography as a whole (Crush and Rogerson, 1983; Crush, 1986; Mabin, 1986).

From the middle-1970s, and continuing into the 1980s, we felt that human geographers in South Africa should cast off the shackles imposed by the links with Anglo-American geography and instead begin to forge closer ties with the new school of South African studies, and especially to take cognizance of the trends which were reshaping historical enquiry. In relation to geographical research, the new wave African historiography fostered a great resurgence of interest in historical geography. This new historical geography, however, is not an historical geography which examines White settlement and frontier expansion in terms of Turner's frontier thesis. Instead, it is a 'people's historical geography' (Crush, 1986) which, for the first time, examines the conditions of existence and the world of the common peoples of South Africa. This project forms an integral part of the broader contours of a newly emergent South African human geography, or perhaps more appositely 'inhuman geography of apartheid' (Rogerson, 1985a, 1986a), which is coming to grips with critical investigations of the conditions of South Africa's oppressed and exploited peoples.

Towards a Geography of the Common People

The beginnings of our work on the common people and their activities in the South African city were inspired through the somewhat late 'discovery' by South African social scientists of the concept of the 'informal sector' (Rogerson and Beavon, 1980). The writings of Terry McGee (1974, 1976), in particular, struck a familiar chord in South Africa, for here on the pavements of the apartheid city, tucked away from the imposing tower blocks of steel and glass, was a whole world of urban economic activity which we had formerly eschewed. This 'world' appeared to us to have much in common to that which McGee had been studying in the setting of South-East Asia. Believing, as many before us have done, that dirty boots begets wisdom (McGee, 1978) we set out to explore on the ground some of the dimensions of the 'informal sector' of Johannesburg. In this we were not alone, as the Johannesburg City Planning Office was also commencing a study of hawkers with a view to improving their lot. To both groups of investigators it soon became clear that there was no ready source of data that would inform us of how many hawkers were operating on the streets of the city, where they were located and why they were operating as hawkers. A field survey that would provide us with some quantifiable information seemed an appropriate first step in our quest to research what, at that time, might simply have been termed the geography of hawking in Johannesburg.

The First Tentative Steps

At the outset of field work it was clear that conventional sample survey and questionnaire techniques would have to be dropped, or at the very least severely modified, if we were to collect any useful data. This realization applied even to the collection of information concerning seemingly mundane items such as age, home address, types of commodities sold, days on which commodities were sold and time of selling, nature of the journey to work, numbers of years in hawking, and previous occupations. From observation of the hawkers operating at their 'pitches' it had become evident that the street hawkers were chary of strangers, that not all hawkers were regular attendees at their 'pitches', and few hawkers were proficient in English. The apparent reticence of hawkers to communicate with strangers sprang from the fact that municipal officials attached to the traffic and health departments were actively attempting to reduce the number of hawkers operating on the streets of Johannesburg. As we were to discover, there exists a veritable arsenal of regulations, legislation, by-laws, and controls that made it relatively easy for officialdom to clamp down on hawking activities when and if they so desired (Beavon and Rogerson, 1982, 1984; Rogerson and Beavon, 1985). For example, hawkers are not allowed to sell on the streets without a licence, and even with a licence they are not permitted to sell in a large part of the Central Business District that is proclaimed a 'restricted area'. Licensed hawkers outside of the restricted area had at the time to move their 'pitch', together with their goods, 25 metres every 20 minutes. Failure to adhere to these 'move-on' regulations could render them liable to arrest, confiscation of their goods, and a sizeable fine. Little wonder then that they were not inclined to talk about their businesses with White strangers!

Thus it was that, during the first haltering stages of this research, we continued to visit the main hawking areas in the city for several months, frequently accompanied by a Black friend or associate, in order to establish a friendly presence. Only then, with the aid of our Black interpreters, did we begin to ask any questions. In the first instance these took the form of simple exchanges of greeting, an indication of who we were and where we worked, and then an enquiry of how long they had been hawking in the area, how often they came to hawk, and whether they experienced harassment by municipal officialdom. From information gleaned in this informal manner it became possible to construct a more formal questionnaire that would assist us in collecting data for what we then regarded as our hawker study. The type of information we were interested in was that which would allow us to understand something of the nature of the persistence of hawking as an activity, the costs and efforts involved, the nature of the commodities sold in different parts of the city, the extent to which hawking could be regarded as the basis for a 'living', and what possible steps could be taken to ease their plight. Questions necessarily had to be framed in a very simple and direct form if they were to be understood by our 'target' group. In addition, questions would have to be translated in the field by assistants so that they could be put with (hopefully) equal clarity to Zulu speakers as well as to hawkers who spoke Southern Sotho, Northern Sotho, or Xhosa. Obviously, we were in no position to draw a random sample of hawkers who would be interviewed, and had no reasonable prospect of obtaining a statistically acceptable sample. Furthermore, given their precarious position in terror of the law, we recognized a need to respect the fact that many hawkers might shy away from answering specific questions, or from answering any questions at all. If this meant that we would be unable to draw any inferences at conventional statistical levels of confidence then so be it. In the event we interviewed some one hundred hawkers in the downtown area of the city. Despite problems, we felt reasonably satisfied with the results obtained from our explorations of the 'informal economy' of Johannesburg. Indeed, we were so much encouraged by our findings that it was decided to embark upon a similar venture deploying comparable research methods in the more demanding surroundings of the townships of Soweto. The results of these investigations were eventually written up in a series of reports and a clutch of scholarly papers (Biesheuvel, 1979; Beavon, 1981; Beavon and Rogerson, 1982, 1984; Rogerson and Beavon, 1980, 1982).

Discovering the Past

In the early forays into establishing the complexion and geography of hawking on the streets of Johannesburg our research was very similar to that which had been pioneered by McGee in South-East Asia and by Bromley (1978a,b, 1981, 1982) in Latin America. This parallel was hardly surprising, for these innovative geographical works had acted as a considerable stimulus in the selection of hawking as an activity worthy of study within the context of creating a more socially relevant geography in South Africa. From these first tottering steps in a new research world, however, arose a host of unanswered questions prompted partly by the continuing flow of international literature on the 'informal sector' but more importantly by the ongoing work of colleagues at the University of the Witwatersrand who were engaged in researching the region's popular history (Bozzoli, 1979, 1983; van Onselen, 1982). Our fortuitous 'discovery' of the past 'informal sector' on the Witwatersrand was to re-orient the direction of the whole research programme and to lead to a considerable divergence in our research methodologies and objectives to the studies undertaken by Bromley, McGee or later by Forbes (1978, 1979, 1981a,b,c) and Rimmer (1978, 1982). The most critical realization was that research on the South African 'informal sector', as elsewhere, had largely by-passed historical investigations (Rogerson, 1983, 1985b). This neglect was somewhat surprising in view of the situation of the 'informal sector' as a central issue in development studies, a field of research which increasingly was turning, through dependency and neo-Marxist writings, towards historical explanations for present-day underdevelopment. It was clear that even if the concept of the 'informal sector' had only been discovered in the early 1970s, the people involved in its activities did not suddenly spring into it overnight; rather they had been operating in such income niches long before Keith Hart (1973) drew attention to their existence. Given the absence of historical work in the field of 'informal sector' studies our research on the geography of hawking in Johannesburg and Soweto experienced a dramatic metamorphosis, broadening in focus to become a longitudinal-based research programme which would seek to investigate the changing actors and activities of the city's 'informal sector' as part of a new project to reclaim the lost geographies of the city's common people. To chart the events precipitating this transformation in the research on hawking in Johannesburg attention now turns.

The starting point for the metamorphosis in our research may be traced back to events taking place on the streets of Johannesburg at the time of the hawker survey. More specifically, our survey was threatened by arms of the local authority which were active in their attempts to clear hawkers from the streets. Although we feared that these repressive actions had been precipitated by publicity accorded our research activity, we were soon to discover that the policing was simply part of a long-standing cycle of repressive actions taken against 'informal sector' activities. Investigation of the newspaper reportage on the harassment of the hawker community indicated that such attempts had a long ancestry in Johannesburg (see Rogerson and Beavon, 1985; Beavon and Rogerson, 1986a). This finding prompted us to examine the historical clippings files of local newspapers, and it was here that we found the first clues to a rich vein of material that recorded aspects of the history of hawking in Johannesburg over a period of 60 years or more. From a perusal of newspaper files it became apparent that not only had street sellers been operative on the streets of Johannesburg for many years, but the dominant forms of street selling had changed with the passage of time (Beavon and Rogerson, 1980). Examination of the files of newspaper photographs, and thereafter other collections of old photographs, showed that at the turn of the century street sellers had operated with barrows, vending a much greater variety of goods and wares than now appeared to be the case. The photographic records hinted tantalizingly that small hand-pushed refreshment barrows or kiosks had been characteristic features of the 1940s, and larger kiosks at which a variety of refreshments were obtainable had been located semi-permanently on the pavements of the industrial areas of the city in the 1950s. Captions to photographs, and items in the clippings collection, gave us leads to the possible existence of other historical source material dealing with the activities of street sellers and policies of the municipal authorities.

As most of the actions against the street sellers appeared to have taken place under the aegis of the city health department we now attempted to secure access to the health records of Johannesburg. Whereas our earlier sally into the collections of the city's newspapers revealed a vein of historical material, the archives of the city's Medical Officer of Health were the veritable mother lode. Here were reports of health inspectors commenting on street sellers at specific locations and times, copies of periodic surveys recording numbers of hawkers at different sites, and even detailed inventories of goods being sold at each stand, barrow or kiosk. Here also were copies of summary reports revealing, *inter alia*, how many licences had been issued in particular years, how many hawkers had been prosecuted for disobeying the by-laws, which by-laws were most frequently invoked in prosecutions, and comments by officials and councillors on how by-laws might be changed to achieve a desired result. In addition, there were annotated extracts from the minutes of council meetings that afforded pointers to the way in which the 'hawker problem' was perceived throughout the city's history. The archival material confirmed our suspicions based upon photographic evidence that the single major activity of the street traders in Johannesburg during the 1930s through to the early 1960s was the selling of refreshments from an array of 'carts' (later kiosks) known as coffee-carts or 'café-de-move-ons'. The volume of official correspondence, reports and surveys on coffee-carts appeared to exceed anything on any other category of hawking. Furthermore, the files of the city health department furnished many references and rich insights into the historical patterns of hawking in the formative stages of the emerging Black townships on the south-western side of Johannesburg, now known collectively as Soweto. Newly armed with 'hard data' from the clippings files, the photographic records, and the substantial primary material from the city health archive we were in the fortunate position of being able to contemplate the pursuit of a far more substantial study of street trading in Johannesburg and Soweto than originally envisaged.

By 1979–80, after two years of research, however, it was time to take stock of our position. Reassessment was imperative, especially as the directions of the planned research programme on the geography of hawking were veering markedly away from contemporary issues to detailed historical analysis. Consideration was given now to the prospects of mounting an historical study on the dynamics of street trading in Johannesburg, in particular focusing upon the rise and fall of the coffee-cart traders. Any hesitation that such a study would not constitute a worthwhile research venture was dispelled at a meeting with Charles van Onselen, now to our considerable good fortune the Director of the African Studies Institute at Wits. He was then involved in reconstructing the social and economic history of the Witwatersrand between 1886 and 1920. The writings and research conducted by van Onselen were a critical influence upon the re-orientation of our own research programme, for they belied the notion of the 'informal sector' as a novel or new economic form. For the early days of Johannesburg as a throbbing mining camp van Onselen documented an important area of the economy which offered a considerable segment of the city's populace a living outside of the working class. Although his writings did not explicitly consider theoretical issues relating to the 'informal sector', it was evident that van Onselen's research foci, viz. the world of the riksha puller, cab driver, washerman, liquor seller, prostitute, and common criminal, constituted the original manifestations of an 'informal sector' in Johannesburg (van Onselen, 1982; Rogerson, 1983, 1986b).

Exploring Past Worlds

As a consequence of the fortuity of close contacts with a social historian actively engaged in reconstructing histories of the 'ordinary people', we found ourselves in the unusual situation of having two comparative 'snapshots' of the Witwatersrand 'informal sector', the one furnishing a detailed portrait of life and existence at the turn of the twentieth century, the other providing a picture of the 'informal economy' in the latterday apartheid city (Rogerson and Beavon, 1980, 1982; Beavon and Rogerson, 1982). A comparison of these two very different pictures of the 'informal' economy on the Witwatersrand provoked new sets of research questions which, once more, would re-direct our work towards explorations of the past.

It was apparent that explanations must be sought for the overall existence and persistence of an 'informal sector' as a fabric of the economic landscape. In part these explanations were already encompassed within the historical writings of the new school in South African studies. From a continuing exposure and reading of this literature we began to appreciate the significance of turning our attention to a set of deeply rooted structural considerations surrounding the uneven march of proletarianization processes, the creation of a situation of structural unemployment and the existence of 'poverty-in-employment' under the circumstances of South Africa's labour-coercive economy (Beavon and Rogerson, 1982; Rogerson, 1983). Any account for the persistence of an 'informal' economy on the Witwatersrand would have to embody research relating to these broad themes of South African political economy.

Beyond questions surrounding the enduring nature of the 'informal' economy, a further set of challenges now appeared in respect of reconstructing the shifting historical matrix of life and existence in the 'informal sector'. Seeking to trace the changing contours of Johannesburg's 'informal sector' over a century, Kenneth King's (1974) metaphor of the 'moving frontier' best appeared to encapsulate the kaleidoscopic elements of change in the city's economic nooks and crannies, which now had become our research focus. In racial terms we had to account for the progressively darkening hue of the actors on Johannesburg's 'informal sector' stage, for while van Onselen (1982) had documented the vital participation of 'poor Whites' as liquor sellers, pimps or transport riders in the early years of the mining camp, our concern in modern Johannesburg was with an almost exclusively Black drama of struggle for survival in the brutal context of apartheid. Equally compelling was the challenge of unravelling the saga of women's changing involvement in the city's 'informal' fabric. Alongside a suite of economic spheres, child care, prostitution, home dressmaking and most importantly, brewing and shebeening, in which women's domination remained unchallenged, were other income niches, such as washing or coffee-cart trading, exhibiting a change in the sexual composition of their participants.

Finally, we confronted the prospect of reconstructing the overall changing mix of occupational categories in which the casual poor of Johannesburg sought out a livelihood. In this regard we could discern a category of income opportunities in street trading, crime or liquor production/selling which had an unbroken record of existence in the city since its genesis as mining camp. The thread of historical continuity was evident also in the appearance of a clutch of newer income niches spawned by new innovations or technologies. Illustratively, the motor-car generated fresh 'informal' income opportunities in the guises variously of the driving of pirate taxis or the repair of vehicles in backyards. Nevertheless, the appearance of new income opportunities was paralleled by the demise of others. Most notable in the Johannesburg context was the need to account for the emergence and subsequent decline of the spheres of washing and coffee-cart trading. It was clear now that our chance discovery of the past worlds of the 'informal sector' was the crucial pivot in redirecting us towards explorations of the everyday lives of the common people of Johannesburg.

The research work undertaken since 1980 has sought to investigate, through a series of micro-level longitudinal studies, the several economic spaces occupied by the casual poor of Johannesburg (Rogerson, 1986b). Archival sources and the collection of oral histories furnished the necessary base for reconstructing the emergence and decline of the coffee-cart traders and the vacillating fortunes of the community of Indian flower-sellers (Rogerson, 1983; Tomaselli, 1983a,b; Rogerson, 1985c, 1986c; Beavon and Rogerson, 1986a; Tomaselli and Beavon, 1986). Similarly, a combination of archival research, the investigation of newspaper records, government commissions, and informal interviews with participants facilitated investigation of the world of the shebeeners, the illicit brewers or sellers of liquor in Black Johannesburg (Rogerson and Hart, 1986). New horizons were opened, however, in the study of shebeens with the recognition of creative literature as a potentially valuable medium for illuminating the hidden experiential world of those struggling for existence in the 'informal sector' (Hart and Rogerson, 1987).

Throughout the course of these ventures into the life of the common people recourse was made to the broader theoretical debates raised by the literature of 'informal sector' studies (see Rogerson, 1985b). Early in our exposure to this literature we were convinced of the rich insights to be reaped through the conceptualization of the urban economic landscape as constituted by the articulation of a dominant capitalist mode of production with a series of petty commodity forms of production (cf. Forbes, 1981a,b,c). Exploration of this literature suggested the particular value that might derive from researching the changing balance of forces favouring the conservation as opposed to the dissolution of specific income niches of the casual poor (Rogerson, 1983, 1985b, 1986b; Rogerson and Hart, 1986). Nevertheless, shortcomings of petty commodity production analysis were revealed by our study of women's changing involvement in the matrix of 'informal sector' activities (Beavon and Rogerson, 1986b). In particular, the gender-blind nature of petty commodity production analysis compelled us to turn to feminist writings for adequate interpretations on the theme of 'women's work' and the 'informal sector'. Accordingly, in weaving a pathway through the maze of economic spaces occupied by the Johannesburg casual poor the original conceptual apparatus of an 'informal sector' was modified successively by various theoretical infusions from the Marxian-based literature on petty commodity production, humanist writings, and feminist analysis.

Reflections

A decade after the Soweto uprising it is evident that apartheid geography is in a state of considerable flux, and that an insurrection, if not a revolution, is occurring to re-shape South African human geography. No longer is South Africa viewed as a mere dumping ground for Anglo-American theories and models (Rogerson and Browett, 1986). The major directions are towards a more de-whitened, de-colonized, and critical human geography with a strong emphasis on historically based research. The strengthening of this homespun genre of human geography with close ties to a distinguished literature of social history is a trend that we have consciously sought to promote, and wish to advance in future.

In 1986 we as geographers do have a much greater appreciation of the conditions of oppression and suffering daily endured by Black South

Africans, an understanding gained by looking through the 'window' of the past and by having mingled in the world of the common people. Nonetheless, we accept the criticism of our detractors (Wellings and McCarthy, 1983) that in Nero-like fashion we may be 'fiddling' while Soweto and other Black South African townships continue to burn. Clearly the contemporary imperative in South Africa is to end Black suffering, rather than to simply understand and report its manifestations, past or present. If progress in South African human geography is to be gauged merely by contributions towards the direct overthrow of the White minority regime then we have singularly failed. As we struggle towards a post-apartheid society, however, a more positive evaluation of the research programme reported here might be offered in light of the discarding of the Anglo-American teaching mould of human geography at South African universities. In the past decade a host of young geographers have been weaned on an intellectual diet more in keeping with the development of critical faculties for detecting and removing the evils of a racist oppressive society. Hopefully then our students are better equipped to bring about the necessary changes to the structures of South African life, either through direct manipulation working within the system or increasingly, and sadly but inevitably, by direct confrontation with the apartheid state apparatus.

References

Beavon, K. S. O. (1974) Interpreting Lösch on an intra-urban scale, *South African Geographical Journal*, 56, 36–59.

Beavon, K. S. O. (1975) Christaller's central place theory: reviewed, revealed, revised, *Environmental Studies*, University of the Witwatersrand, Johannesburg, Department of Geography and Environmental Studies, Occasional Paper 15.

Beavon, K. S. O. (1977) *Central Place Theory: A Reinterpretation*. Longman, London.

Beavon, K. S. O. (1981) From hypermarkets to hawkers: changing foci of concern for human geographers, *Environmental Studies*, University of the Witwatersrand, Johannesburg, Department of Geography and Environmental Studies, Occasional Paper 23.

Beavon, K. S. O. (1982) Black townships in South Africa: *terra incognita* for urban geographers, *South African Geographical Journal*, 64, 3–20.

Beavon, K. S. O. and Rogerson, C. M. (1980) The persistence of the casual poor in Johannesburg, *Contree: Journal for South African Urban and Regional History*, 7, 15–21.

Beavon, K. S. O. and Rogerson, C. M. (1981) Trekking on: recent trends in the human geography of southern Africa, *Progress in Human Geography*, 5, 159–89.

Beavon, K. S. O. and Rogerson, C. M. (1982) The informal sector of the apartheid city: the pavement people of Johannesburg. In D. M. Smith (ed.),

Living Under Apartheid. George Allen & Unwin, London, pp. 106–23.

Beavon, K. S. O. and Rogerson, C. M. (1984) Aspects of hawking in the Johannesburg central business district, *Proceedings of the Geographical Association of Zimbabwe*, 15, 31–45.

Beavon, K. S. O. and Rogerson, C. M. (1986a) The council vs the common people: the case of street trading in Johannesburg, *Geoforum*, 17, 201–16.

Beavon, K. S. O. and Rogerson, C. M. (1986b) The changing role of women in the urban informal sector of Johannesburg. In D. W. Drakakis-Smith (ed.), *Urbanization in the Developing World*. Croom-Helm, Beckenham, pp. 205–20.

Biesheuvel, S. (1979) Planning for the informal sector: hawking in Johannesburg. Unpublished M.Sc. (TRP) dissertation, Department of Town and Regional Planning, University of the Witwatersrand, Johannesburg.

Bozzoli, B. (ed.) (1979) *Labour, Townships, and Protest*. Ravan, Johannesburg.

Bozzoli, B. (ed.) (1983) *Town and Countryside in the Transvaal*. Ravan, Johannesburg.

Bromley, R. (1978a) Organization, regulation and exploitation in the so-called 'urban informal sector': the street traders of Cali, *World Development*, 6, 1161–71.

Bromley, R. (1978b) The locational behaviour of Colombian urban street traders: observations and hypotheses. In W. M. Denevan (ed.), *The Role of Geographical Research in Latin America*. Conference of Latin American Geographers Publication No. 7, Muncie, pp. 41–51.

Bromley, R. (1981) Begging in Cali: image, reality and policy, *International Social Work*, 24(2), 22–40.

Bromley, R. (1982) Working in the streets: survival strategy, necessity or unavoidable evil? In A. Gilbert, J. Hardoy and R. Ramirez (eds), *Urbanization in Contemporary Latin America*. John Wiley, Chichester, pp. 59–77.

Crush, J. S. (1986) Towards a people's historical geography for South Africa, *Journal of Historical Geography*, 12, 2–3.

Crush, J. S., Reitsma, H. and Rogerson, C. M. (1982) Decolonizing the human geography of Southern Africa, *Tijdschrift voor Economische en Sociale Geografie*, 73, 197–8.

Crush, J. S. and Rogerson, C. M. (1983) New wave historiography and African historical geography, *Progress in Human Geography*, 7, 203–31.

Forbes, D. K. (1978) Urban–rural interdependence: the trishaw riders of Ujung Pandang. In P. J. Rimmer, D. W. Drakakis-Smith and T. G. McGee (eds), *Food, Shelter and Transport in Southeast Asia and the Pacific*. Australian National University Press, Canberra, pp. 219–35.

Forbes, D. K. (1979) The pedlars of Ujung Pandang, Monash University Melbourne, Centre for Southeast Asian Studies, Working Paper 17.

Forbes, D. K. (1981a) Beyond the geography of development, *Singapore Journal of Tropical Geography*, 2, 68–80.

Forbes, D. K. (1981b) Petty commodity production and underdevelopment: the case of pedlars and trishaw riders in Ujung Pandang, Indonesia, *Progress in Planning*, 16, 105–78.

Forbes, D. K. (1981c) Production, reproduction and underdevelopment: petty commodity producers in Ujung Pandang, Indonesia, *Environment and Planning, A*, 13, 841–56.

Hart, D. M. and Rogerson, C. M. (1987) Literary geography and the informal sector, *Geography Research Forum*, 8, 15–29.

Hart, K. (1973) Informal income opportunities and urban employment in Ghana, *Journal of Modern African Studies*, 11, 61–89.

Johnstone, F. A. (1976) *Class, Race and Gold*. Routledge & Kegan Paul, London.

Johnstone, F. A. (1978) The labour history of the Witwatersrand in the context of South African studies, and with reflections on the new school, *Africa Perspective*, 9, 27–36.

Johnstone, F. A. (1982) 'Most painful to our hearts': South Africa through the eyes of the new school, *Canadian Journal of African Studies*, 16, 5–26.

King, K. J. (1974) Kenya's informal machine-makers: a study of small-scale industry in Kenya's emergent artisan society, *World Development*, 2(4 & 5), 9–28.

Mabin, A. S. (1986) At the cutting edge: the new African history and its implications for African historical geography, *Journal of Historical Geography*, 12, 74–80.

McGee, T. G. (1974) *Hawkers in Hong Kong: a Study of Policy and Planning in the Third World City*. Centre of Asian Studies, University of Hong Kong, Hong Kong.

McGee, T. G. (1976) The persistence of the proto-proletariat: occupational structures and planning of the future of Third World cities, *Progress in Geography*, 9, 1–38.

McGee, T. G. (1978) Western geography and the Third World, *American Behavioral Scientist*, 22, 93–114.

Marks, S. and Atmore, A. (eds) (1980) *Economy and Society in Pre-Industrial South Africa*. Longman, Cape Town

Marks, S. and Rathbone, R. (eds) (1982) *Industrialization and Social Change in South Africa*. Longman, London.

Rimmer, P. J. (1978) The future of trishaw enterprises in Penang. In P. J. Rimmer, D. W. Drakakis-Smith and T. G. McGee (eds), *Food, Shelter and Transport in Southeast Asia and the Pacific*. Australian National University Press, Canberra, pp. 195–217.

Rimmer, P. J. (1982) Theories and techniques in Third World settings: trishaw pedlars and *towkays* in Georgetown, Malaysia, *Australian Geographer*, 15, 147–59.

Rogerson, C. M. (1975a) Some aspects of industrial movement from Johannesburg, 1960–1972, *South African Geographical Journal*, 57, 3–16.

Rogerson, C. M. (1975b) Industrial movement in an industrializing economy, *South African Geographical Journal*, 57, 88–103.

Rogerson, C. M. (1983) The casual poor of Johannesburg, South Africa: the rise and fall of coffee-cart trading. Unpublished Ph.D. thesis, Department of Geography, Queens University, Ontario.

Rogerson, C. M. (1985a) Censorship and apartheid geography, *Environment and Planning, A*, 17, 723–8.

Rogerson, C. M. (1985b) The first decade of informal sector studies: review and synthesis, *Environmental Studies* University of the Witwatersrand,

Johannesburg, Department of Geography and Environmental Studies, Occasional Paper 25.

Rogerson, C. M. (1985c) From coffee cart to industrial canteen: feeding Johannesburg's Black workers 1945–1965. Unpublished paper presented to the African Studies Seminar, African Studies Institute, University of the Witwatersrand, Johannesburg.

Rogerson, C. M. (1986a) South Africa: geography in a state of emergency, *GeoJournal*, 12, 127–8.

Rogerson, C. M. (1986b) Johannesburg's informal sector: historical continuity and change, *African Urban Quarterly*, 1, 139–51.

Rogerson, C. M. (1986c) Feeding the common people of Johannesburg, 1930–1962, *Journal of Historical Geography*, 12, 56–73.

Rogerson, C. M. and Beavon, K. S. O. (1980) The awakening of 'informal sector' studies in Southern Africa, *South African Geographical Journal*, 62, 175–90.

Rogerson, C. M. and Beavon, K. S. O. (1982) Getting by in the 'informal sector' of Soweto, *Tijdschrift voor Economische en Socialie Geografie*, 73, 250–65.

Rogerson, C. M. and Beavon, K. S. O. (1985) A tradition of repression: the street traders of Johannesburg. In R. Bromley (ed.), *Planning for Small Enterprises in Third World Cities*. Pergamon, Oxford, pp. 233–45.

Rogerson, C. M. and Browett, J. G. (1986) Social geography under apartheid. In J. Eyles (ed.), *Social Geography in International Perspective*. Croom Helm, Beckenham, pp. 221–50.

Rogerson, C. M. and Hart, D. M. (1986) The survival of the 'informal sector': the shebeens of Black Johannesburg. *GeoJournal*, 12, 153–66.

Tomaselli, R. E. (1983a) Indian flower sellers of Johannesburg: a history of people on the street. In B. Bozzoli (ed.), *Town and Countryside in the Transvaal*. Ravan, Johannesburg, pp. 215–39.

Tomaselli, R. E. (1983b) The Indian flower sellers of Johannesburg. Unpublished M.A. dissertation, Department of Geography and Environmental Studies, University of the Witwatersrand, Johannesburg.

Tomaselli, R. E. and Beavon, K. S. O. (1986) Johannesburg's Indian flower sellers: class and circumstance, *GeoJournal*, 12, 181–9.

van Onselen, C. (1976) *Chibaro: African Mine Labour in Southern Rhodesia, 1900–1933*. Pluto, London.

van Onselen, C. (1982) *Studies in the Social and Economic History of the Witwatersrand 1886–1914*, 2 vols. Ravan, Johannesburg.

Wellings, P. A. and McCarthy, J. J. (1983) Whither southern African human geography? *Area*, 15, 337–45.

7

Getting By in Indonesia: Research in a Foreign Land

Dean Forbes

Narékko mupakalebbi tauwé alémutu mupakalebbi. (Wajonese proverb – if you respect others then you respect yourself)

Preamble

Just under 11 years ago, on the third of February 1975, I arrived in Jakarta for a short pre-field work visit to Indonesia. I had commenced writing a detailed daily diary two weeks earlier while travelling around Malaysia and Singapore, a practice which I have continued whenever I am in Asia. This chapter examines a research project on the informal sector in Indonesia, and is largely based on the experiences recorded in those diaries. It concentrates on the period up until my departure from Indonesia, eyes yellow with hepatitis, in December 1976.

My experiences on fieldwork were not remarkable; I was not kidnapped by dissidents, nor did I directly experience any of the other exceptionable Indonesian events of the mid-1970s. However, fieldwork had a profound impact upon my character and person, and is therefore something I feel is worthy of exploration. More importantly, perhaps, my experiences were not atypical of others engaged in detailed field research in Asia. Yet we find these experiences, so often discussed with friends and colleagues late into the night, are rarely recorded for posterity, let alone as descriptive contributions to the debates about methodology in social and economic research.

Geographers have re-discovered biography in the past few years (Buttimer, 1983; Billinge et al, 1984; Eyles, 1985). This literature is both fascinating and highly stimulating, and a welcome move towards demystifying the methodologies of social science. I am not without criticism of the trend. Too often human recollection homogenizes our past experiences; at other times complexities are conflated and become absurdly short and superficial. Yet, on balance, the benefits of recapturing the essential complexity of making geography are worth the effort. It is only now, 11 years on, that I feel comfortable about going back to these diaries and looking critically at the experiences they reveal.

A Place and a Problem

Geographers, unlike many social scientists (and here I include economists), think in terms of places. Because problems and places are closely entwined it is rare for a geographer to conceptualize one without the other. It is one of the many subtle forms of conditioning which our training encourages: in fact these subtle messages are ultimately of greater significance to our view of the world than the more easily discarded theories and models by which the discipline is more formally defined. Geographers can, and often do, pass themselves off as specialists of another ilk – a transport planner, urban sociologist or regional scientist, for instance. The corollary is that it is rare, in Australia at least, for prominent scholars or senior bureaucrats to call themselves geographers. However it is much more difficult to restructure thought processes so as to hide such taken-for-granted connections as that between problem and place.

In my own case an interest in Indonesia marginally preceded an interest in urban geography. Ironically it was during my second year of university undergraduate work, while immersed in a course on the arid lands, that I developed a firm intention to specialize in the humid tropics, of which Indonesia was an excellent example. Alaric Maude, later a supervisor of my Honours dissertation, had a strong interest in Indonesia at the time and introduced me to the writing of Keith Buchanan (1967, 1968), and it was at this time that I decided to specialize in urban and development geography.

My first appointment to a tutorship at the University of Papua New Guinea in 1972 was as a specialist in urban geography. I developed a new course on urbanization in the Third World, and later taught in it jointly with Richard Jackson after his appointment in 1973. My research in Papua New Guinea ranged widely, from participation in urban fresh-food marketing by peri-urban villagers, to squatter settlement rehabilitation, the impact of dam construction on villagers, and growth-centre policy for the highlands. Research work in Kenya and Tanzania was a major influence at the time, and the equity issue in particular was beginning to assume a new importance, in conjunction with the development of 'basic needs' approaches to development planning.

Papua New Guinea was an early participant in the experiments with equity-oriented policies. The most pertinent to my interests was the aim which encouraged 'an emphasis on small-scale artisan, service and business activity, relying where possible on typically Papua New Guinean forms of business activity' (Papua New Guinea, Central Planning Office, 1974). My M.A. dissertation focussed on local business activity, the food marketing by Koiari villagers, particularly their participation in Port Moresby's markets. The terminology of the 'informal sector' was only in sporadic use in Papua New Guinea, but, as a set of concepts, it underpinned my interests (for an introductory review of this literature see Forbes, 1984, pp. 166–75). The programme rehabilitating squatter settlements in Port Moresby, which had been formalized with the publication in 1973 of a government White Paper, also incorporated a direct concern with the problems of the urban poor, and attempted to find realistic, low-key solutions to their plight (Papua New Guinea. Government White Paper, 1973).

With the completion of my contract at the University of Papua New Guinea at the end of 1974, I decided to pursue my growing interest in the informal sector further, but chose to focus on Indonesia. The chief drawcard of Asian work was the infinitely larger and more complex natures of urban development and the informal sector. Terry McGee's work on the informal sector was outstanding, and followed directly on from his well-known work on *The Southeast Asian City* (McGee, 1967). Of particular interest were his papers on 'anti-development' and a later review of the development of a 'proto-proletariat' (McGee, 1974, 1976). These incorporated explicit denunciations of Asian city planners' obsession with modernization, and put the case for allowing the informal sector to continue unhindered. As in Papua New Guinea, the argument that the urban poor had developed workable solutions to their housing and employment problems was gaining ground in the academic literature. It was increasingly argued that central and municipal government policies which sought the destruction of these survival mechanisms should be abandoned. Informal sector workers would be better off left alone, or better still, supported by new policies which would provide credit and other forms of assistance to small informal sector enterprises, and low-key assistance to inhabitants of squatter settlements.

An Interlude in Australia

Australian universities are generally recognized as having a comparative advantage in economic, political and social research on Indonesia. This was important to me, as I wanted to study something in the mainstream of contemporary Australian research. Admittedly, then as now, neither Asian studies nor development research are particularly important in Australia compared to research on western societies and economies. In the past few years most Australian politicians, and even the populace at large, have begun to pay lip-service to the 'new realism' of foreign policy.

That is, they recognize that Australia's strategic, political and economic future is bound up with its Asian–Pacific location. Nevertheless, the reality is that our primary interests are still, firstly, ourselves, and secondly North American and Western Europe. A sea-change in attitudes is required before Australians as a whole come to accept the geographic imperatives of our membership of the Asian region.

At the time of my return to Australia in 1975, as now, there were two main centres of research on South-East Asia which were also prominent in geography – Monash University and the Australian National University (ANU). I applied for a scholarship to both, and was accepted at Monash. As I regarded it as the best geography department in Australia at the time (although Terry McGee had joined the staff at the ANU), I decided not to wait for the outcome of the scholarship allocation process at the ANU. But this was not the only reason for my choice. The ANU was very strong in Indonesian studies, publishing in fact the *Bulletin of Indonesian Economic Studies*, the most authoritative journal within the field of Indonesian economics. The university also had an impressive array of talent in demography, anthropology and history. Though far from homogeneous, Indonesian research at the ANU was also known for propagating a conservative political message, particularly in economics. Many staff were strong supporters of the New Order, or post-1966 government of Indonesia. Monash, in contrast, was widely regarded as closer to the left, and was associated with critics of the New Order in Indonesia, notably Herb Feith and Rex Mortimer. The latter had shortly before my arrival edited a book on the political economy of Indonesia, which set forth a critique of 'Coca-cola capitalism' and included a bitter chapter attacking the chief pro-New Order figure in the ANU economics department, Heinz Arndt (Mortimer, 1973, pp. 101–30; see also Arndt, 1985, p. 65).

I was further attracted to Monash by the reputation the university had carried for most of its short life. The Faculty of Arts was housed in a huge barn-like building, nine storeys high and located in the midst of Melbourne's south-eastern suburban sprawl. The location could not have been worse; far from public transport or any sort of commercial centre or entertainment. Yet the students had a well-earned reputation for being in the vanguard of student protest in the 1960s, and the academic staff had forged a reputation for excellence that had catapulted the university into the handful of top academic institutions within the country. The geography department boasted two professors, Bob Smith and Mal Logan, a rare enough event in Australian universities, and had made a name for itself in the fields of urban and regional development.

My first task at Monash was to narrow down the choice of place of research, and develop the topic I wished to work on with greater precision. In practice, language development occupied a large part of my

time. Although a group of friends and I had been meeting regularly in
Port Moresby with an Indonesian exile to discuss events in Indonesia,
and develop our skills in Bahasa Indonesia, my understanding of the
language was very rudimentary. I was frequently assured by those with
a smattering of Indonesian that it was a simple language by Asian
standards. However, no language is simple – rather there are grades of
difficulty. Recent experience in China and Vietnam has convinced me
that there are more difficult languages to master, but for me Indonesian
was a handful.

My study of the language was not assisted by recurring bouts of
malaria. I vividly recall sitting in a sunny classroom in early spring,
reciting short passages of Indonesian, and gradually breaking out in a
cold sweat. Forty-eight hours later, after a series of fevers and chills, I
would be ready to start eating again. Eventually I sought treatment from
an initially sceptical doctor, and have not suffered from malaria since.
My initial reluctance to consult a doctor was the result of a mistaken
belief that the illness was incurable. I had learned to cope with malaria,
as my colleagues had done in Papua New Guinea, and that was all that
mattered. But the health risks of working among the poor in tropical
Third World cities are significant but tend to be ignored. In my case,
however, illness was a significant and intrinsic risk associated with the
research project.

Geographic field research was in my mind located somewhere between
anthropology and economics on a spectrum of intensity. Anthropologists
might expect to spend around two years deeply involved in a field site.
Economists, on the other hand, seemed, if at all, to stay in the field
under a year. For a geographer expecting to come to grips with the
working of a medium to large Asian city, around one year seemed a
minimum. In the end my field research lasted for almost 14 months,
which allowed me sufficient time to travel within South Sulawesi, the
Indonesian province within which the city that I chose for study, Ujung
Pandang, was located, and soak up the flavour of the city itself. Moreover,
I was well aware at the time that it was a once-in-a-lifetime opportunity
to examine an issue in depth. Like Farmer (1973, p. 11) and others I
firmly believe in the importance of 'dedicated specialization by area'.
Language skills and an appreciation of the intricate nature of the political,
cultural and physical environment are difficult and time-consuming to
acquire. Yet this information is absolutely vital to a contextual discipline
such as geography. Where I differ from the proponents of traditional
regional geography is in the choice of theoretical structures for collecting
and interpreting contextual data (Forbes, 1984, pp. 48–55).

It was in this initial preparation stage that I first began to experience
one of the perils of the contextual approach, namely information overload.
Once my fellow postgraduates and staff in both the Department of

Geography and Centre of Southeast Asian Studies, with which I was also affiliated, understood the nature of my research, advice flowed to me thick and fast. Names and contacts in Indonesia and elsewhere, references to new work on decolonization, dependency and development, seminar papers on Indonesian politics and history, debates on the Second Five Year Plan (1974–79) and the significance of regional planning within it, new material on the informal sector, and to top it off, a course in Bahasa Indonesia and some discussion of the possibility of learning Dutch, combined to send me scampering from one end of the campus to another. I found it hard to hang onto the thread of my project, and did a poor job of synthesizing the material fed to me.

The research design I sketched out reflected the dual research traditions common to geography in the mid-1970s. On the one hand, Third World research, particularly in the informal sector, placed great emphasis on qualitative data collection, language skills and participant observation. On the other hand, geography had experienced its quantitative revolution, and most research work sought to include at least some quantitative data in the search for respectability. I decided to pursue both qualitative and quantitative avenues of research, the former through techniques of participant observation and the latter through a survey of informal sector participants. I reasoned that the data I required could quite readily fit into either of the categories. Survey research would ensure the availability of statistically significant data on the structure of the enterprise, the migration and work history of the respondent, demographic information, and the household. Participant observation and long unstructured interviews of key workers would provide detailed material on financial aspects of the enterprise, richer material on individuals, and a sense of how the sector fitted together. Moreover, the research design meant I had some fall-back positions: if survey work proved impossible I could improve the participant observation component, and vice-versa.

The next question was where to work in Indonesia? Research in Indonesia is often criticized for being Java-centric. This was certainly the case with existing informal sector work, which had concentrated on Jakarta (Lea Jellinek) and one or two other towns on Java such as Bandung and Pare (Clifford Geertz). A city in the outer islands therefore seemed to be a good choice. I eliminated Kalimantan and part of eastern Indonesia because the cities were either too small, too rich, or simply too much like Papua New Guinea, i.e. without a particularly large informal sector. This left Sumatra (Medan) and Salawesi, where Ujung Pandang was a possible choice: both were large (over 500,000), and major regional centres. Ujung Pandang was my final choice because it was the more neglected of the two as far as socio-economic resarch was concerned. I have since often wondered what led me to choose one of the least well-understood cities in Indonesia. Was it a desire to simply break new ground, or did I want to avoid the scrutiny of my peers who were concentrated on Java? Like the anthropologist, once my territory was marked out it took on a deep significance.

In the end, my preparations for field research were cut short. I delivered the mandatory research proposals, received excellent advice from those knowledgeable in such things (including the economist Colin Clark and Benedict Anderson) and applied to LIPI (Lembaga Ilmu Pengetahuan Indonesia), the Indonesia Institute of Sciences, for permission to conduct research in Indonesia. Jamie Mackie, then Director of the Centre of Southeast Asian Studies, decided it would be better to bring forward my fieldwork, and agreed to pay for me to visit Indonesia in October and November 1975, to be followed by a longer visit starting in early 1976. My preparations for field research could have gone on for much longer – I had not finished the course in Bahasa Indonesia – but I seized the opportunity and packed my bags. Though somewhat unprepared, I was anxious to get back to Indonesia, and begin to find at first hand more about my subject. During presentations I had been conscious of an overwhelming ignorance of the Indonesian informal sector, and had frequently elaborated on Papua New Guinea examples to make my point. This did not satisfy the Asianists in my audience, who felt the two countries had nothing at all in common. Nor did it satisfy me. The only solution was to acquire some first-hand experience in Indonesia.

Lain Desa, Lain Adat (Another Place, Another Culture)

The informal sector may have been invisible to scholars, but it hit residents and visitors to Jakarta square in the jaw. After passing through customs at Halim Airport it was impossible to find a taxi, but I was inundated with offers to travel into the city in 'informal' taxis. These were privately owned vehicles being used or borrowed to earn an extra income. They were usually parked outside the airport perimeter to avoid the airport police. Along the road we passed numerous stalls selling cooked food, and small stalls specializing in tyre repairs. Particularly in the densely settled parts of inner Jakarta, almost every conceivable good or service could be purchased in the street. I was offered drugs by a gangly youth with flared trousers and platform-soled shoes covered in fur. An old man with a shoulder-pole carried jars filled with goldfish. A fellow Australian, a worker on an oil rig in the Java Sea, with whom I shared an airport taxi, earnestly lectured me on the market in prostitution in Jakarta.

Indonesian scholars and planners were, on the whole, not sympathetic to the people in the informal sector. National economic planning was growth-oriented, while municipal planners clung tenaciously to the concept of the city-beautiful (Clarke, 1985). Yet by the mid-1970s a number of groups had developed an interest in the informal sector in Indonesia. The Canadian International Development Research Centre (IDRC) had sponsored a study of the informal sector in Jakarta and Bandung by W. J. Waworoentoe and T. B. Mohamad Rais (see IDRC, 1975), the Institute of Rural and Regional Studies at Gadjah Mada University commenced in 1975 a study of low-cost transportation (Kartodirdjo, 1981), and the International Labour Organization (ILO) (Sethuraman, 1976) and the Indonesian Institute of Sciences (Moir, 1978) had both mounted studies of Jakarta. There were also a handful of individuals in the early stages of informal sector research. These included Lea Jellinek and labour market researchers Chris Manning and Gavin Jones.

Most of this work was sympathetic to the problems of the informal sector, and urged informal sector workers be given increased latitude to pursue their opportunities. My project fitted into this genre. It sought to investigate the structure and dynamics of the informal sector, and argued for an approach to development which explicitly recognized the contribution which the informal sector made to employment and the provision of services within the city. The project was not propositional: I had no explicit hypotheses to test, nor any explicit method of establishing or verifying truth. My task was to describe the informal sector, and evaluate it in terms of contemporary debates within the development literature. More explicit arguments, I reasoned, would emerge in the course of the field study.

Ujung Pandang, or Makassar as it had earlier been known, was described as 'like Jakarta 20 years before'. It had a population of 592,740, and similar to Jakarta was sited on a flat coastal plain surrounded by intensively farmed wet-rice (sawah) fields. It was the major centre of the province of South Sulawesi (population 5,189,000), but had in recent years gradually lost the role of chief city for eastern Indonesia to the Javanese port city of Surabaya. Ujung Pandang had a workforce of over 126,000 and low labour participation rates. Unemployment was estimated at 7.6 per cent, but overall 38.6 per cent of the workforce was under-utilized – i.e. were unemployed (7.6 per cent), worked short hours and would like more work (7.2 per cent), or earned a very low income (23.8 per cent). Unlike in the cities of Java, most (90.9 per cent) of the city's 'own-account workers' (a category that roughly approximates with the informal sector) earned less than Rp5000 ($ US10.00) per week. Finally, the city had an inflated tertiary sector, with only 8.0 per cent of the workforce in manufacturing, and a further 4.6 per cent in construction and utilities. The tertiary sector accounted for upwards of three-quarters of the urban workforce (Forbes, 1979, pp. 75–87).

My field research commenced immediately on arrival, and took two forms. First, as I had done in Jakarta and Surabaya en route to Ujung Pandang, I set about trying to describe what I could of the informal sector. This meant recording the different forms of activity, counting numbers involved where possible, and long detailed descriptions of individual enterprises. One such description of a foodstall took place over several hours and occupies pages and pages of my notebook, together with sketches of the site and the equipment used.

Second, I spoke at length with anyone willing to talk bout the city's society and economy. I stayed in very cheap tourist hotels and frequently struck up conversations with itinerant western travellers. Many were on a 'hippie' trail through mainland Asia, and were heading for Bali. Others, usually Australians, were heading in the other direction. Some complained incessantly about Indonesia. Less frequently I met young research students who spoke knowledgeably about life in a Yogyakarta kampung (urban village) or the hydrological cycle in a West Javan River Basin. Chance meetings of this sort, as on aeroplanes, have provided me with some excellent contacts in Indonesia. More importantly, perhaps, I talked with as many residents of Ujung Pandang as I could find. These included academics and officials from the city government, as well as trishaw riders, market stallholders, and itinerant pedlars; in fact anyone who could speak knowledgeably about the city. The reception was generally good. Often a discussion would lead to an invitation to meet someone else, and so I was handed along a chain of contacts. This multiplier effect can usually be relied upon to build up a long list of people to see, although it can also send the researcher off on a tangent.

The remainder of my first visit to Ujung Pandang was taken up with securing sponsorship for the project from the Faculty of Economics at Hasanuddin University, searching out municipal government officials such as the Mayor, M. Daeng Pattompo, and a short visit with a colleague from the university to his home area in Pinrang. I also made the first of several trips to the mountain province of Tanah Toraja, a very beautiful and interesting part of Indonesia that is inexplicably better-known to French tourists than English-speaking visitors. Back in Ujung Pandang I was prevailed upon to deliver a seminar to a collection of planners from regional planning offices who were attending a refresher course in the city. I was not sufficiently confident in Bahasa Indonesia to attempt a delivery in the local language, although it was clear early on that only a few of the audience understood my slow, deliberate English. Nevertheless I persisted, encouraged by my host who was adamant that the planners had to acquire English and therefore should be given no sympathy. Training and education in Indonesia are performed in a very hierarchical manner, not an approach I feel comfortable with. As a guest, however, I acceded to my host's request.

The Urban Informal Sector

I returned to Indonesia to begin the main part of my fieldwork in February 1976, accompanied by Janet Williams, a palaeo-ecologist and close friend whom I later married. Getting formal permission to stay in Ujung Pandang proved a protracted affair. While at Monash I had applied for permission to undertake field research in Indonesia. Apart from various forms which needed to be completed, and a research proposal, I was also required to get police clearance. When the main visa did not arrive, I decided to enter Indonesia for my reconnaissance trip on an easily obtainable tourist visa. In Jakarta I approached LIPI, only to discover my file had been misplaced. When I returned from Ujung Pandang it had been rediscovered, and I was given permission to undertake research. There was a condition. Elections were due in 1977, and I would have to depart by the end of 1976.

The visa stamps in my passport, which I duly presented to immigration officials in Jakarta in February 1976, were only the beginning. First, there were negotiations in Jakarta and multiple visits to LIPI, various immigration and security offices. Then in Ujung Pandang, much the same occurred, as I carried letters between the governor's office, the university, immigration offices and police department. Eventually I acquired the appropriate documentation, and was asked to report to police every time I left the city. This I did, and duly received a *surat jalan* or travelling letter, with photograph and stamps, at quite a reasonable cost. It was not quite the burden it seemed. Not everyone in the provinces cared about the documentation, and where they did, in Sinjai province, the policeman escorting us around went home at 1pm each day and did not return.

Janet was not so lucky with a visa. She never did receive a year-long visa, and instead returned to the immigration office every month to fill out forms, pay for stamps and 'administrative costs' and sit around for hours on end until her passport was ready for collection. While the bureaucracy angered us with its corruption and inefficiency, it was expected and accepted. The last thing I wanted was to be diverted from my main task in Ujung Pandang, and therfore I reasoned it was better not to fight against the system. It is one of the compromises we were forced to make when time and resources were scarce.

The backbone of the research work I undertook in Ujung Pandang consisted of observation/description and discussion with key informants. I mentioned earlier that on a number of occasions I sat and observed the setting up and operation of street stalls (*warung*). When I found accommodation with the Indonesian family of Dr and Mrs Rahardjo Adisasmita in the southern suburbs, I could extend observation to the mobile informal sector. The household was supplied by three regular pedlars; opposite was sited a small collection of trishaw riders, adjacent to a series of *warung*, and day and night would see a procession of sellers plying cooked food, medicines and cheap household goods. With help from Janet I also visited local markets and began to document the layout, flow and type of commodities, numbers of people involved and so on. Some of these, such as the large fish auctions on the coast, were scenes of intensive activity in the early morning, others were mid-morning, late afternoon or evening markets. I was impressed with the quality of service provided to the residents of Ujung Pandang, if they could afford to buy from the informal sector operatives.

As my confidence with the language grew, and I came to understand at least the rudiments of the informal sector system, I increasingly supplemented observation with long, loosely structured interviews with key participants in the sector. These were not always a success. Often information provided would be contradictory, or it would, of necessity, be based on guesswork. The main fish auctions, for instance, did not weight fish coming in or going out. All taxes were based on estimates of volume and value, and so aggregated data on fish transactions were merely rough estimations. At other times my language skills let me down. One interview I conducted early on was with the Kepala Sub-Direktorat Dinas Pelelangan Ikan – the head of the sub-directorate in charge of the fish auction. As he warmed to his theme I began to lose track of the argument, and after a while I could understand nothing of what he was saying. I was embarrassed, because the longer the monologue went on, the more hopeless my predicament became, yet I did not want to intervene for fear of embarrassing him. In the end I heard him out, made some perfunctory thank yous, and escaped home on my bicycle, completely rattled.

For my dissertation I used 40 major informants. Of course, my cut-off point was necessarily quite arbitrary, and could easily have doubled if I included everyone with whom I discussed the project. For instance, I did not include non-Indonesians in the list of key informants, yet discussions with fellow-researchers were important to my work. An American volunteer English teacher, Russ Dilts, spent many evenings in Ujung Pandang in the small drinking houses scattered around the city talking with trishaw riders as they sipped their palm wine (*bollu*). The city was convulsed during this period by a war between rival trishaw riders. Scuffles and occasional stabbings in the late night or early mornings would be the topic of conversation among the trishaw riders, yet many in the city remained relatively unaware of the details of the conflict. Russ awoke me to the undercurrents of life among the trishaw riders, and was a source of many anecdotes about the trishaw riders' view of the world. Being a very shy person I did not at first feel comfortable sitting around in drinking houses or striking up casual conversations, although now it is second nature to me in the field.

Just prior to my departure for Indonesia Herb Feith showed me a draft of an account of a Jakarta street trader by Lea Jellinek. The paper was subsequently published by the Centre for Southeast Asian Studies at Monash, and has appeared in one of the main readers on Third World urbanization (Jellinek, 1977). I was deeply moved by this portrait of 'Ibu Bud', a food seller and inhabitant of the inner city kampung called Kebun Kacang. Other publications had included single-paragraph sketches of informal sector participants, but none had given such a deep impression of life for an informal sector worker as Jellinek's account of 'Ibu Bud'. I resolved therefore to undertake a similar exercise in Ujung Pandang.

However, the circumstances were different. Jellinek had built up a friendship with 'Bud' over a number of years whilst mainly involved in other work in Jakarta. My sole role in Ujung Pandang was research. Therefore I felt that I would have to contrive to develop such a relationship and, besides, it would be unlikely to develop to the same depth as between Jellinek and 'Bud'. My strategy was therefore to choose a small group of informal sector workers for more detailed discussions. I wanted to visit their houses, meet their families, record their life histories, ask them to complete a household budget, and generally fill out a picture of their lives in all its complexity. Such oral records are now *de rigueur* for informal sector research, but like much of the description of the sector, I suspect, provide diminishing marginal returns. They do add what is known in the newspaper world as 'colour', but at a cost.

'Daeng Rappung', an itinerant fish seller, was the best interviewee. He invited me to his house, a small bamboo annexe to a larger timber and bamboo house in the suburb of Mamajang. Here he shared a room, two metres by five metres, with his wife, two small children, and a cousin, a trishaw rider. Furniture was limited to sleeping mats and a small bamboo lounge suite, and cooking was done outside. When I analysed Daeng Rappung's household budget I realized the precariousness of his existence. Total income for seven days amounted to Rp2750, and total expenditure Rp2735. During my visit to his house Daeng Rappung had provided tea, sugar and bananas. This very modest hospitality had cost the family around 10 per cent of net weekly income, and was more than twice the daily food budget. This posed a dilemma. Payment of Daeg Rappung was out of the question, as it would have caused him severe embarrassment. A packet of cigarettes were left opened on the table, as a token gesture of thanks, but beyond that it did nothing to help the family. Nor could I refuse an offer of food, for that also would have caused embarrassment. Furthermore, we were staying in an

Indonesian household where entertaining a pedlar was unthinkable. I therefore resolved to limit my visits to Daeng Rappung, and build up the data from the survey side of the research methodology.

Socio-economic surveys were the mainstay of the work being done on the informal sector at the time, due in large part to the inadequacy of official data sources when it came to the marginal groups in the informal sector. I found a number of interview schedules that had been used in Indonesia for *kampung* surveys, informal sector surveys and migration surveys, and drafted out a schedule of nearly 50 questions. My original intention was a total of around 400 completed schedules from the four main sectors to which I had narrowed down the study: fish sellers, fruit and vegetable sellers, trishaw riders and prepared food makers and sellers. My final sample was 320, with only 38 in the latter category.

In order to administer the survey, and to help out in the project in general, I resolved to employ a research assistant. Through contacts in the local teacher's college (IKIP) I was put on to two talented and enthusiastic students, Mohammed Amin Rasyid and Mohammed Nasiruddin. Both struck me as able and competent, and very sharp, so I was delighted when they agreed to work part-time on my survey. It was an excellent choice. We got on very well together, they performed the tasks that I set them diligently, and both have gone on to prestigious jobs in tertiary institutions in Ujung Pandang, and have travelled overseas on work. Like our host and friend Dr Rahardjo Adisasmita and his family, they provided me with a great deal more information about Bugis and Makassarese society than I had the wit to ask for. In the end it was the random discussions about Bugis history and culture, patterns of behaviour, custom, traditional law, food preferences and even traditional medicine, that provided me with notebooks full of valuable contextual material.

After preparing and pilot testing a survey schedule, I settled on a set of 45 questions. Informal sector workers, being largely an itinerant group who worked long hours, proved to be a hard group to sample. I rejected a *kampung* study in favour of a sectoral approach, but how do you draw a systematic sample from such a mobile population? I was warned by a visiting colleague that many a research student at ANU had come to grief on sampling technique. The solution was to stratify the sample into groups. First, trishaw riders and pedlars were ubiquitous, so I chose three suburbs, in the inner city (Gaddong), middle (Maricaya) and outer suburbs (Rappocini), and drew my respondents from informal sector workers in those areas. Second, I drew another sample from the concentrations of fresh food sellers in the city's markets, and for prepared food sellers I went to their houses where the food carts would line up each morning as their operators readied themselves for the day ahead.

It was not an elegantly drawn sample, but it avoided any serious bias in the selection of respondents.

The schedule was administered in either Bahasa Indonesia or, where necessary, in the *lingua franca* of the city, Makassarese. Between 8 and 10 per cent of respondents refused to be interviewed, and of those interviewed, 13.1 per cent were indifferent and 2.8 per cent uncooperative. In the circumstances the response to the survey was good, but it must be said that informal sector workers are, on the whole, not an easy group to deal with. The itinerant pedlars, in particular, were busy and always anxious to continue with their work. In contrast, trishaw riders work intermittently and were usually less troubled about answering questions.

Therefore I devised solutions to the sampling problem, and dismissed as inevitable refusals to be interviewed or indifference to the questions. I took less care over question structure, interviewer training, sample design and repetitive questions for checking accuracy, than more recent work to which I have been exposed, particularly by demographers. This does not mean my survey was poorly done; rather that in the field practical solutions took precedence over pure concepts. A complicating factor was the limited resources, particularly time, available for research, which again favoured practical solutions to problems. It is interesting that contemporary socio-economic researchers are facing up to this paradox. The push for greater specialization, more replicability in research methodology and a more precise division of academic labour is being opposed by a series of views which argue the importance of rapid socio-economic assessment techniques, the subjectivity of research and the diminishing marginal returns to particular types of research effort. It is clear to me that there is as yet no universally agreed-upon methodology within the socio-economic 'sciences', but what is not clear is whether such a thing is possible at all.

In Ujung Pandang I joined the local library and took the opportunity to read widely in background material on Indonesia. The local bookstores were poorly stocked, but occasionally had paperbacks worth buying. Apart from literature of direct relevance to the research I was particularly interested in travelogues and fiction with a strong Asian or developing country setting. I took it for granted that this sort of writing had a greater potential for evoking the significance of place and the importance of everyday life in poor countries than academic material or government reports. Graham Greene was undoubtedly my favourite author, and I consumed with relish his fragments of autobiography (*A Sort of Life*), his brilliant novels (*A Burnt-Out Case*) and his account of an expedition through Liberia (*Journey Without Maps*) (Greene, 1963, 1971, 1982). V. S. Naipaul's (1968) *An Area of Darkness* was another book that left a deep impression upon me, as did Somerset Maugham's (1963) collections of short stories. It would have been pointless to attempt to imitate these

writers, though frequently in my notebooks I recorded material that
could later form the basis of a personal view of Indonesia, but instead I
found inspiration in the grace with which they handled such complex
subject matter.

Not all my research was restricted to the city of Ujung Pandang. On
occasions we were invited to travel to rural villages, which I eagerly
accepted. It became clear early on during my period in Ujung Pandang
that a lot of informal sector workers were recent arrivals in the city, and
kept in close contact with the rural areas. They returned for festivals
and family celebrations, and the more mobile would return to help with
the planting of the rice crop and its harvesting.

Therefore it made sense to me to visit some of these villages to get
some understanding of this process. And as the city was hot and congested
it was a great relief to travel through the open countryside. During my
first short visit I was taken to the district of Pinrang in the north-west
of the province, and also managed a few days in the Toraja region in
the central north of the province. Later, during our extended stay in
South Sulawesi, Janet and I returned to Toraja on several occasions, as
well as visiting Sinjai and Wajo provinces on the east coast of the
peninsula. At times like this the geographers' ready acceptance of
fieldwork and the significance geographers place on contextual rationale
that is the envy of the practitioners of less flexible disciplines.

Getting by in Ujung Pandang

The urban poor in Asian cities 'get by' – they eke out an existence on
the margins of the formal economy, and survive rather than prosper.
The phrase is also appropriate for my field research. My aim was to
survive the experience and write a competent dissertation. By bringing
to the fore the functioning of the informal sector I also hoped to influence
the ideas of academics and urban administrators, but this, I realized,
was an ambitious goal and one that remained secondary to the completion
of a dissertation. At no stage of my field research did I feel in control
of my circumstances or the environment. My mood swung from the
depths of depression to wild elation, depending on the immediate
circumstances. I was not able to smooth out the ups-and-downs of
everyday existence as I was able to in Canberra or Melbourne. I always
felt an outsider, peripheral to the society and economy, with a poorly
defined task and no identifiable niche in which to fit. This was certainly
not the fault of the community in which I lived. Nor was it my own
fault. I think we need to recognize the essential artificiality of the
experience of the research student, trying to cope with a dramatic shift
in cultures, and set the task of inquiring into the way people's lives are
organized.

After my original choice of South Sulawesi as a site for field research it puzzled me that the literature on the region was fairly scant, at least by comparison with places like Java, Bali and Sumatra. I have since concluded that the region is difficult to work in, and this has inhibited researchers. There are two sources of problems.

First, Islam is strongly entrenched within the region, and the Bugis and Makassarese, like the Acehnese of northern Sumatra, are fiercely proud of this heritage. This leads inevitably to a difference in outlook, over such things as alcohol consumption and the treatment of women. I had no wish to adopt Islam, or any other religion.

Second, Bugis and Makassarese culture caused concern. People spoke openly about *panas hati*, literally the 'hot liver' of local people, and the fact that they are easily angered. Crowds of children often plagued us when we walked in the streets, would sometimes pinch Janet, and throw stones at us. It was a nightmare for the children of some anthropologists we met, who, being fair-headed, were always the focus of attention. Our Indonesian friends would frequently urge us to ignore the attention, arguing the children would soon go away. However, on one occasion we drove to the province of Gowa, south of the city, and stopped on the side of the road for a picnic. We were soon surrounded by people, pointing and giggling. Janet and I had become accustomed to this, and took no notice. Our Indonesian hosts, however, became angry and called for them to go away. They did not, and so we cut short the picnic and drove to a local town, there to buy fruit and vegetables in the market. As we wandered around the market our host was quoted exceptionally high prices, due mainly to our presence. This angered him further and we quickly returned home, arriving well before midday. We had become used to the constant attention but our friends had not. I must confess to not always being so calm when annoyed by people intruding upon my privacy. My notebooks record two instances when I responded very rudely, and many others when I reacted angrily in private. Such behaviour I now regard as unnecessary, but it was a clear response to the pressure of the situation.

Living in the city we did not experience the intense rivalry over status and hierarchy – *siri*, or self-esteem – that is apparently common in Bugis and Makassarese villages. One anthropologist friend visited every month or two in the city. It was clear she needed a break from the village, where there was a great deal of jostling for status. One mechanism was to *kurang* – put down – someone of slightly higher status. The outsider, though not really part of the system, was fair game in the battle. Throughout my stay in Ujung Pandang I was rarely aware of being manipulated for status, though our friend saw meaning in events that I did not.

A real danger fieldworkers face when they fell conditions are not optimal is that of sliding into the usually welcoming arms of the local expatriate community with its round of tennis, cocktails and dinner parties. I avoided this by living for half the period with an Indonesian family, and for the second half in the home of Peter Goethals, an anthropologist teaching in a local research centre. Peter was part of the first group of American anthropologists to work in Indonesia, in his case Sumbawa, and knew the country well. The advantage of living in a house with a fellow scholar was that the separation of classes which happens in Indonesian households was not at all important. I could socialize with my assistants, or invite in a pedlar or trishaw rider for a drink and a talk, something that was not possible elsewhere. Admittedly we developed a network of friends within the foreign community, but they were mainly researchers or volunteers, and without exception all had close ties with the local community either through their work, or residence, or both.

Of course, most of the time both Jan and I found the cultural and social life fascinating. Jan set herself the task of exploring the role of women in society. Each morning she would spend an hour or two sitting on the front verandah of our house talking with Mrs Rahardjo about local practices. Mrs Rahardjo was descended from the nobility of Sinjai, a kingdom situated on the south-east coast of the peninsula, and had trained as a lawyer, but never practised. She had a good understanding of Bugis culture, and explained the significance of the various ceremonies and celebrations we attended with her and her family, and had an even better grasp of the politics of large extended families. (Her mother was the fourth wife of the former Aru of Sinjai.) Jan concluded that interpersonal relationships were much the same everywhere, even though Bugis culture gave them an appearance of something different.

Local politics did not intrude upon my research project to any great extent. Of course I was aware of the political nature of the project I had undertaken, but I invariably projected it into a research and policy framework, rather than seeing it as a part of the process of political mobilization. Though political, I am not an activist, and I am especially cautious about getting too involved in Indonesia. While my career is closely linked to Indonesia, and I have a strong concern for the well-being of the urban poor, I have always realized the locus of my life was elsewhere. In the late 1970s and early 1980s my writing became more explicitly left-wing, before moderating again to a cautious radicalism. This has had repercussions for me in Indonesia, where the largely conservative academic community shuns work with a left-wing bias.

Of more importance during my fieldwork in Indonesia was the issue of international politics. The relationship between Australia and Indonesia has been variable. Australia's post-war Labor Government was the second to recognize the independence of Indonesia in 1949, creating a large store of good-will between the two countries. However the annexation of Irian Jaya, the Indonesian 'confrontation' of Malaysia, the bloody aftermath of the 1965 coup, and the invasion of East Timor all contributed to a deterioration in relations between the two countries. My fieldwork coincided with Indonesia's invasion of East Timor. While there is some suggestion the Labor Government gave tacit approval to this action, the majority in Australia, and particularly the media, opposed the action very strongly. To make matters worse five Australian journalists were killed in the fighting in East Timor, many believe deliberately by Indonesian armed forces.

I was largely unaware of the details of these events, being dependent for news solely on local newspapers and letters from Australia. However, I was asked by friends and acquaintances in Ujung Pandang about Australia's motivations, and at times made to feel uncomfortable. In Indonesian eyes their government's actions were necessary, and press reaction in Australia naive and unnecessarily hostile. I had to admit the existence in Australia of a xenophobic anti-Asian lobby, but I took great pains to point out that many in the press were critics of the Indonesian government, not the Indonesian people. In the end both my friends and I probably felt our respective cases had been inadequately appreciated, but at a personal level the differences were soon resolved. In Australia, however, the issue remains an important one and a source of friction between the two countries.

Finally, a further comment about health is appropriate. During our time in Ujung Pandang both Janet and I experienced the expected range of maladies and illnesses prevalent in a developing country city. Our most frequent symptoms were stomach cramps and diarrhoea, caused by contaminated food and drink. People in Ujung Pandang offered us a range of explanations for our illnesses, the most frequent of which was *masuk angin*, exposure to the wind. Remedies included stroking the upper arm with a coin, or rubbing the stomach with a eucalyptus ointment. None had any effect, of course, and although I am sympathetic to the value of traditional Asian medicines it was generally not the appropriate circumstances for trying new medicines.

Most crippling of all, though, some four weeks before I was due to leave Ujung Pandang I was diagnosed by a Chinese doctor as having severe chronic hepatitis. He wanted me hospitalized, but we managed to persuade him that I could be treated at home. I felt demoralized. My skin and the whites of my eyes began to glow yellow, I felt itchy all over, and I was prescribed total bed rest, and even discouraged from browsing through notes. Janet took over the research project, finishing the last few survey interviews, carrying out the last intensive interviews, and doing the rounds of thanking everybody we had been in contact with in the city. Then she had to get passport clearances, purchase tickets, and arrange inoculations. It was an awful way to leave the city, and I felt disappointed the fieldwork had to end that way. I was not given the all-clear by doctors in Melbourne until May the following year.

A Summing Up

As an undergraduate at Flinders University I was once asked to prepare an essay in economic geography on the problems of small businesses. Coming from a family of shopkeepers I blithely set about preparing an account based on my family's experiences, with minimal references to the academic literature. The essay was a spectacular failure. This autobiographical account has also been based on experience with little reference to academic literature. Yet I hope it makes more sense than my undergraduate essay. I have presented a simple narrative, devoid of excessive introspection and theoretical anchor points, owing more to the style of Galbraith (1983) than to the current literature of social theory.

Research projects, like development projects, go through a cycle of stages, and no matter how much we seek to stress our own individuality, researchers share much in common through their stages. I have concentrated on the preparation and fieldwork stages of the research project, not because these are more important, but because it is useful to document the experiences encountered during this period. Working in a foreign land can be traumatic, even when it does not require the courage and intense commitment of a Neil Davis or a Wilfred Burchett (1980). I was physically changed by the experience, and I think my outlook on life also changed. But how, precisely, I cannot tell. I had no scale by which to measure divergence, nor detailed before-and-after studies, as psychologists studying a group of my peers at Flinders have had (see Ellerman and Feather, 1976). Perhaps most importantly, fieldwork reaffirmed my belief in the essentially subjective nature of socio-economic research, and recalibrated the limitations to my own knowledge. Socio-economic research may be a putative science, if by science we mean an objective body of knowledge, but I am more inclined to the view put by Zelinsky (1975) that all science is, ultimately, social science.

References

Arndt, H. W. (1985) *A Course Through Life, Memoirs of an Australian Economist.* National Centre for Development Studies, Canberra.
Billinge, M., Gregory, D. and Martin, R. (eds) (1984) *Recollections of a Revolution: Geography as Spatial Science.* Macmillan, London.
Buchanan, K. (1967) *The Southeast Asian World.* Bell, London.

Buchanan, K. (1968) *Out of Asia. Asian Themes 1958–66*. Sydney University Press, Sydney.

Burchett, W. (1980) *At the Barricades: The Memoirs of a Rebel Journalist*. Quartet, London.

Buttimer, A. (1983) *The Practice of Geography*. Longman, London.

Clarke, G. T. (1985) Jakarta, Indonesia: planning to solve urban conflicts. In J. P. Lea and J. M. Courtney (eds), *Cities in Conflict: Studies in the Planning and Management of Asian Cities*. World Bank, Washington, pp. 35–58.

Ellerman, D. A. and N. T. Feather (1976) The values of Australian student activists, *Australian Journal of Education*, 20(3), 260–77.

Eyles, J. (1985) *Senses of Place*. Silverbrook Press, Warrington.

Farmer, B. H. (1973) Geography, area studies and the study of area, *Transactions of the Institute of British Geographers*, 60, 1–15.

Forbes, D. K. (1979) Development and the 'informal' sector: a study of pedlars and trishaw riders in Ujung Pandang, Indonesia. Unpublished Ph.D. dissertation, Department of Geography, Monash University, Melbourne.

Forbes, D. K. (1984) *The Geography of Underdevelopment: A Critical Survey*. Croom Helm, London.

Galbraith, J. K. (1983) *A Life in Our Times*. Corgi, London.

Greene, G. (1963) *A Burnt-Out Case*. Penguin, Middlesex.

Greene, G. (1971) *Journey Without Maps*. Penguin, Middlesex.

Greene, G. (1972) *A Sort of Life*. Penguin, Harmondsworth.

IDRC (International Development Research Centre) (1975) *Hawkers and Vendors in Asian Cities*. IDRC, Ottawa.

Jellinek, L. (1977) The life of a Jakarta street trader. In J. Abu-Lughod and R. Hay Jr (eds), *Third World Urbanization*. Methuen, New York, pp. 244–56.

Kartodirdjo, S. (1981) *The Pedicab in Yogyakarta*. Gadjah Mada University Press, Yogyakarta.

McGee, T. G. (1967) *The Southeast Asian City*. Bell, London.

McGee, T. G. (1974) In praise of tradition: towards a geography of anti-development, *Antipode*, 6(3), 30–50.

McGee, T. G. (1976) The persistence of the proto-proletariat, *Progress in Geography*, 9, 1–38.

Moir, H. (1978) *Jakarta Informal Sector*. LEKNAS/LIPI, Jakarta.

Mortimer, R. (1973) From Ball to Arndt: the liberal impasse in Australian scholarship on Southeast Asia. In R. Mortimer (ed.), *Showcase State: The Illusion of Indonesia's Accelerated Modernization*. Angus & Robertson, Sydney, pp. 101–58.

Naipaul, V. S. (1968) *An Area of Darkness*. Penguin, Harmondsworth.

Papua New Guinea: Central Planning Office (1974) *Strategies for Nationhood. Programmes and Performance*. Central Planning Office, Port Moresby.

Papua New Guinea: Government White Paper (1973) *Self Help Housing Settlements for Urban Areas*. Minister for the Interior, Port Moresby.

Sethuraman, S. V. (1976) *Jakarta: Urban Development and Employment*. ILO, Geneva.

Somerset Maugham, W. (1963) *Collected Short Stories* (four volumes). Penguin, Harmondsworth.

Zelinsky, W. (1975) The demigod's dilemma, *Annals of the Association of American Geographers*, 65(2), 123–43.

8

Interpretive Social Research in the Inner City

David Ley

In recent years human geography has increasingly shared in and contributed toward a broader interpretive turn in the social sciences (Rabinow and Sullivan, 1979; Ley, 1985). Interpretive research is concerned to make sense of the actions and intentions of people as knowledgeable agents; indeed, more properly it attempts to make sense of their making sense of the events and opportunities confronting them in everyday life. From this simple statement flow a number of consequences. First, for the geographer places, regions or landscapes are seen as the active construction of social groups, a human achievement, with all of the flux, dynamism, discontinuity and local nuances which this implies. Places are not the inevitable outcome of seemingly irreversible and impersonal forces. Rather people make over places in their own image as they confront the opportunities and limits of a local environment, an environment which is itself anything but stable, as, for example, economic contexts shift and political priorities evolve. In this manner places become, as the French regional geographers so aptly put it early in this century, a medal cast in the likeness of a people. In more contemporary jargon, every place is an object for a subject, an intersection of human objectives, physical possibilities and contextual contingencies, developing together through time.

But this statement highlights a second point concerning modern interpretation. Whereas the older regional geographies spoke of a collective human response, an undifferentiated regional 'man', this is far too much of a simplification. Any place is more properly an object for a plurality of subjects; there is a regional sociology, and the realities of social stratification introduce class, status, power, lifestyle and interest group cleavages to the intersection of people and place. For example, John Western (1981) in his penetrating social geography of the Coloured community in Cape Town could not provide an interpretation of their residential areas without also introducing race politics in South Africa, the politics of a dominant white minority classifying groups and assigning them areas through apartheid legislation, while at the same time endeavouring not to push the Cape Coloureds into political alliance with the black majority.

A third point we shall return to later is that interpretive research requires an interpretive methodology, a set of operating procedures in the field (techniques is often too formal a term) which are simultaneously able to pick up the nuances of social life in a place while not missing the broader contexts which structure the life chances of local people – sometimes in ways that may not be readily apparent to them. It follows that interpretive research is concerned with the case study, or less commonly, a comparative assessment of case studies. There is a limit to the number of cases which an individual researcher can manage and still gain sufficient local knowledge for the interpretation to be convincing. Beyond this threshold, interpretive method breaks down and is replaced by the collection of statistical data which provide a far more summary proxy of the nature of places. There is, however, no necessary limit to the geographic scale of a case study which can range from the village or neighbourhood to the city, the region, or the nation.

A fourth and final point is that the significance of intentions and actions guides the researcher to a philosophy of science where such qualitative dimensions as the sense of place, or the relations between landscape and identity, may be accommodated more successfully than is possible with the object-orientation of positivist philosophies of science. The so-called philosophies of meaning, including existentialism, pragmatism, and social phenomenology are centrally concerned with the character of human experience, including of course the experience of place (Ley, 1977; Ley and Samuels, 1978; Jackson and Smith, 1984). But while a philosophical underpinning provides logical coherence to a research programme, it should be held loosely, for too often the purity of philosophical discourse has run aground upon the rocks of geographic practice. Without a whole series of compromises and accommodations there is always the danger that the researcher will not be truly open to the problem at hand, and will force reality into a preconceived template of his or her own making.

There is now an extensive literature which discusses these issues. The first part of this chapter will briefly review several interpretive traditions in the humanities and social sciences. This section is mainly for reference purposes, for most of this literature was quite unknown to me when I began my inner city fieldwork in Philadelphia! These after-the-fact justifications do, however, provide a significant and helpful body of material to orient the reader towards the character and range of interpretive research. Following this section the major portion of the chapter will be devoted to an exposition of my inner city research in Philadelphia and, to a much lesser extent, in Vancouver.

Interpretive Traditions

A classic example of interpretive research is Max Weber's monograph *The Protestant Ethic and the Spirit of Capitalism* (Weber, 1958). In this copiously documented essay (the footnotes are almost as long as the text) Weber argues that the origins of capitalism are, at least in part, associated with the deeply held religious values of some of the more ascetic Protestant groups such as the Puritans, whose doctrine of a calling imbued the pursuit of business with a divine purpose and created such a fastidious (though not worldly) prosecution of commerce that capital accumulation and investment became an inevitable outcome. Weber's methodology is characteristic of hermeneutic enquiry of the past, as he minutely assembles a range of texts, including sermons, theological expositions, the declarations of businessmen, and where possible statistical tabulations, to describe the worlds of meaning enveloping the Protestant groups, to interpret their declared values in terms of less visible contexts, and to show the sometimes unintended consequences as values were translated into practice. Examples of recent and penetrating historical interpretations are two studies of the intersection of culture, politics, and creative expression in Vienna from 1870 to 1930, a place and time which helped define the shape of the modern movement in philosophy and the arts (Schorske, 1981; Janik and Toulmin, 1973; also Gibson, 1978).

The interpretation of contemporary rather than historical social groups may be illustrated from the ethnographic studies of urban sociologists based primarily at the University of Chicago. While the ecological, statistical research of the Chicago School has been an important influence upon urban geography, the more qualitative interpretation of urban neighbourhoods and social worlds has not (but see Jackson and Smith, 1984; Smith 1984). Yet this research tradition, stretching from the 1910s to the 1970s, and including such writers as Robert Park, Louis Wirth, Robert Redfield, Erving Goffman and Gerald Suttles, has been enormously influential in the development of not only urban sociology but also the discipline more broadly (Thomas, 1983; Suttles, 1984), while its methods continue to be discussed and elaborated (Burgess, 1984; Plummer, 1983). Though the subject-matter later included the study of a range of social worlds, including those of work, perhaps the typical study was of the inner city ethnic neighbourhood, for example Chicago's Jewish ghetto (Wirth, 1928), Boston's Italian district (Whyte, 1955), or a segment of Chicago's multiracial west side (Suttles, 1968). Before he arrived at Chicago's sociology department Robert Park had been a newspaper reporter, and the practical experience of tracing a story across the city streets inculcated a strong field tradition which was passed on to students and colleagues. The methods of these community ethnographies were essentially qualitative and unstructured, and included individual case histories (e.g. Thrasher, 1927), field observation (Cressey, 1971), the interpretation of letters and other documentary sources (Thomas and Znaniecki, 1918), unstructured interviews in almost all instances, and increasingly in the later years, participant observation (Whyte, 1955; Suttles, 1968) where the researcher became a resident of the community under study in an attempt to gain a more precise understanding of the values and practices of its everyday life. Though qualitative, these ethnographies had a rigour derived in part from a meticulous field programme; for Suttles, three years spent as a participant observer in Chicago's Addams area, for Thrasher, the study of over 1000 adolescent gangs in inner Chicago.

A third source of considerable current importance is the interpretive anthropology of Clifford Geertz, who sees the hermeneutic task as one of deciphering the webs of meaning which give coherence to the wide range of artifacts, rituals, statuses and practices which constitute a culture. The interpretive goal is to read the symbolic code which gives coherence to a diverse set of cultural forms: 'Arguments, melodies, formulas, maps, and pictures are not idealities to be stared at but texts to be read; so are rituals, palaces, technologies, and social formations' (Geertz, 1980, p. 135). Clearly the symbolic web which ties together such a variety of phenomena may not be at all self-evident to people in their everyday life, and conceptual development by the researcher is required to make sense and bring order to such apparent diversity. Such concepts as the Protestant ethic, or the four wishes (social psychological needs) employed by several of the Chicago sociologists, or the dramaturgical concept of Bali as a theatre state, employed by Geertz (1980), organize and integrate an interpretation, and mark the distinction between thick description (or interpretation) and thin description which simply repeats the unexamined accounts of informants. Concept formation is a creative (and often difficult) act of the researcher to bring a unitary interpretation to diverse forms: 'Small facts speak to large issues, winks to epistemology, or sheep raids to revolution, because they are made to' (Geertz, 1973). Concepts do not exhaust reality but, as Weber pointed out in *The Protestant Ethic*, present one viewpoint of it and do not for a moment preclude the existence of others. According to Geertz, the accumulation of knowledge is secured less by providing a single total account of people and place than by a continuous refining of one's concepts.

There are some affinities between certain geographical traditions and interpretive method, though it is a moot point as to whether regional geography in particular represented thin or thick description. Certainly the impoverished sociology, anthropology and psychology in older forms of regional, cultural and historical geography limited the possibilities of concept formation and invited the criticism of 'mere' description. These criticisms have been addressed to varying degrees by more recent work in these fields (Harris, 1978; Meinig, 1979; and especially Cosgrove, 1985). Perhaps a clearer sense of the pursuit of conceptual development in case studies was outlined by research on primitive societies, mainly in the South Pacific, where geographers (sometimes in collaboration with anthropologists) engaged in participant observation of local communities with the objective of making sense of agricultural practices and settlement forms as the outcome of the intersection of cultural prescriptions and ecological (and later, market) possibilities (Brookfield, 1962, 1968; Brookfield and Brown, 1963).

During the 1970s, as human geography undertook a closer dialogue with sociology and anthropology, more explicit interpretive research was conducted by social geographers in advanced societies, leading to a small literature on the use of qualitative methods, primarily participant observation and unstructured interviews, in case studies (Rowles, 1978; Jackson, 1983; Western, 1986). Empirically, fieldwork in the inner city was conducted among Puerto Ricans in New York (Jackson, 1980), the elderly in Massachusetts (Rowles, 1978), and an elite in Vancouver (Duncan and Duncan, 1984); other studies considered native Indians in Arizona (Winchell, 1982), the Cape Coloured community in South Africa (Western, 1981), and, in a particularly ambitious study, the intersecting social worlds of British Columbia Indians and the federal Department of Indian Affairs, where the researcher gained access to the institution through employment as a field worker and then a middle manager (Kariya, 1987).

Formulating a Research Area

Little of the preceding literature was available or familiar to me (aside from the Chicago ethnographies) when I began a participant observation study in a part of the North Philadelphia ghetto in January 1971. It is perhaps worth retracing the steps which led to the identification of the research field, for it was not at all part of the academic agenda I had anticipated on arrival at graduate school at the Pennsylvania State University in the autumn of 1968. Like many British citizens of the period my knowledge of race relations was minimal, as British racial minorities at that time were smaller and largely invisible to middle-class households. However, the United States had just passed through three years of inner city convulsions as the civil rights movement, continuous poverty and institutional discrimination, a growing black consciousness, and the murder of Martin Luther King together moulded the urban race riots of the late 1960s. The publication of the report of the US

Government's special advisory commission on the urban riots in 1968, which found America to be splitting into two nations, separate and unequal, raised race relations to the level of a critical public issue, while through its use of Disraeli's forceful phrase, the two nations, the report also evoked nineteenth-century British precedents. In addition to a student imbued, like others under Paul Paget's tutorship at Oxford, with the spectre of the plural society (cf. Clarke, Ley and Peach, 1984), there was the sense of an intellectual challenge already part engaged.

After some perseverance I was able to secure a summer position in 1969 as a tutor in a remedial education programme in the American South, inland from the industrial city of Tampa, Florida. This position was sought in order to familarize myself with both the intellectual and the moral challenge of American race relations. This encounter, like the longer field programme to follow in Philadelphia, was motivated by the belief that there should not be a separation between private values and public practices, and that personal commitment to a Christian view of justice should help define an appropriate academic research project. That summer, spent in a residential complex with mainly black, but also white and hispanic, high-school dropouts in their late teens served as an intensive apprenticeship in the realities of race relations in the American South.

The institutional nature of racism soon became apparent. The telephone of the apartment I shared wth three black counsellors was bugged, and a police cruiser drove slowly past several times each day; one of the students was a leader of the black student union at a nearby university, an association perceived with suspicion by the police. The lives of the teenagers showed powerfully the consequences of deprivation and degradation, and the circumscribing of personality which so readily accompanies poverty. At the same time their aspirations had not been quenched – they were after all a group who were aspiring to make good a lost opportunity to secure a high school diploma – though their creativity had been moulded into a capriciousness which could in most instances cope with, and in some instances make good in, the rough vagaries of street culture. The most surprising group were the mainly white, middle-class teachers, counsellors, and supervisors. Aside from the formal educational goals, an ostensible objective of the project was to inculcate the students with 'middle-class American values'. For a conspicuous minority of the overseeing group these values were professional incompetence and sexual predation. An important lesson to be learned (and re-learned later in Philadelphia) was that things are rarely as they appear. This lesson has, of course, an epistemological as well as a practical application. The geographer's charge to interpret the complex relations of people and place requires a methodology of engagement not detachment, of informal dialogue as well as formal documentation. There is both an ontological and epistemological requirement that place as a human construction be granted more respect and complexity than the profile it displays from the pages of the census (useful though this may be). In Philadelphia these considerations suggested participant observation as an appropriate method.

Making Contact

The participant observer's selection of a field area is invariably purposeful rather than random. An area is chosen either because it appears to fit a prescribed set of characteristics, or else because of pre-existing contacts with it. In *Street Corner Society*, William Whyte (1955) in his youthful exuberance selected an Italian district in Boston for study because it most closely approximated his preconception of a slum area! But unfamiliarity then presented the difficulty of making contact with the place and its people – an initial task for which Whyte showed enterprise if not always success, as he amusingly recounts in the methodological appendix to his book. More commonly researchers take advantage of existing contacts to launch their own projects: either using professional or outreach programmes already in place (as Suttles (1968) did in Chicago), or else working from the base of their own neighbourhoods of residence (see Bunge (1971) in Detroit, or Ley (1981) in inner Vancouver).

The selection of Philadelphia as a field area was determined by its ease of access, a half-day's journey from the rural campus I attended, and more importantly by an orientation and visit with Dr Julian Wolpert, at that time a faculty member at the University of Pennsylvania with numerous inner city contacts. The identification of a smaller and more manageable district (the County of Philadelphia included over 650,000 black residents in 1970) was aided by the knowledge of a community development programme initiated by a professor from my own university in a district of North Philadelphia. He agreed that I could move into a house he rented near his own, already occupied by several community development interns and a group of African students. Before agreeing to this arrangement I met with a local neighbourhood association and planning group, which I had determined would provide a major entry point to the community, to secure their cooperation with my research objectives in return for my full-time unpaid services as a community planner. With this informal contract in place, and together with Roman Cybriwsky, a fellow graduate student who later completed a participant observation thesis elsewhere in inner city Philadelphia (see Cybriwsky, 1978), I moved into the 'Monroe' neighbourhood on a cold day with snow on the ground, at the beginning of January 1971.

Settling In

It took some time before the house became a home. Indeed in some respects it never did, and after a few months I moved to a room in a more central location in the neighbourhood. The first residence had some limitations. It became the scene of casual drug-taking, and in the case of one of the interns a rather more serious problem. This raised several dangers for the research, including police detection and labelling of the house and its occupants by neighbourhood people which could raise barriers to their participation in the research (cf. Hannerz, 1969). In addition it prompted the ethical problem, not uncommon in participant observation, of peer pressures to conform in unwelcome activities. As pressing were the structural limitations of the housing. It was in considerable disrepair and important services, notably heating, operated only intermittently. During the cold winter on more than one occasion, following a heating failure, one of the African students was to be found sitting in the kitchen with his feet in the heated oven, the only source of warmth in the building.

While independent accommodation eventually proved more satisfactory, permitting quiet reflection of the day's activities as I wrote up my field notes each evening, in the first few weeks a multiracial group home proved a useful base for entry into the neighbourhood. For moving into an unfamiliar community, especially one with a reputation for hostility and danger, can be emotionally draining. In the early weeks there is a constant sense of being misplaced, a sensation I commented on during the research:

All are black, everywhere is an unrelieved tide of blackness, carrying on a life with no apparent reference to anything white. To travel by car through such a scene is an isolating experience; to walk down a block a white man feels as conspicuous as a Santa Claus, as naked as a Godiva. Anonymity is a closed option; whether present or not the curious and penetrating stare of a dozen eyes is felt (Ley, 1974, p. 58).

Indeed, during this initial period the capacity for misperception is considerable. As Gans (1962) noted in his work in inner Boston, there is a tendency to confuse signals and noise in the environment and fall victim to the 'bias of exotic data' (Naroll and Naroll, 1963).

From this beginning, place learning occurred. I attempted to maximize opportunities for encountering the district through the use of local shops and services, a role in two community organizations (to be discussed shortly), and by walking the streets, varying routes in order to cover every block in the neighbourhood. A new topography began to take shape. On the walk from the planning office to my house, for example,

I was accompanied several times by a neighbourhood teenager, though without explanation he always stopped at a particular corner and ran off quickly. On the next block I was challenged during my first week by a group of adolescents, but walked on, paying no attention to them. Only later, in part through reading the language of the walls (Ley and Cybriwsky, 1974), did it become clear that the teenager was stopping at a gang boundary, and that the group who challenged me were keepers of their own turf. Street danger was always a possibility in what was a high-crime area, especially for a solitary pedestrian. Certain blocks were negotiated with caution, and walking after dark was limited. While random violence occurred, it was present to a lesser extent than sensational media images led one to expect. As a (British) white in a district most of whose streets were 95–100 per cent black I was treated as a curiosity on blocks I was known, and as a nonentity elsewhere.

Relations were closer in the two neighbourhood organizations with which I had a continuous association during the seven months of residence and more intermittent contacts over a longer period. It is useful for a participant observer to have a separate community role besides that of researcher for several reasons. First it creates an identity which may appear more legitimate to other residents than the status of researcher alone. Second it provides entry points to the community where a research apologetic is not required. And, third, in setting a fair contract with the community one is studying, voluntary service in particular offers the community a return in kind. As mentioned earlier, an informal contract was established with an umbrella neighbourhood group prior to moving into the district. The research objectives were shared fully with the director of the association; in return for a free hand in pursuing research in the community I would offer my services as a volunteer on a daily basis. This was acceptable to him, and he recommended my presence to his board 'as an expert in demographics and proposal-writing' (a more salient local adaptation of the skills I had laid out), a status that was approved by the board aside from some misgivings from a Black Muslim. Writing funding proposals was indeed my unlikely mandate for a couple of months, to a range of public agencies and philanthropic foundations. One contract that had already been secured by the association was to prepare a neighbourhood plan as part of an experiment in decentralization of its planning function by the City of Philadelphia, and I spent some time researching and writing the social planning component of the document. The association, in the breadth of its local linkages, provided a critical network of contacts, as well as a fascinating laboratory in its own right (Ley, 1974, chapter 7).

A second encounter with the neighbourhood occurred through a local church. This had not been prearranged, and indeed was not without mishap when on the first Sunday I attended the closest facility, a Baptist congregation, and in the midst of a highly culture-specific order of worship, was asked politely but firmly to stand up and account for my presence as the only white in a packed building of some 400 people. I retreated to a safer, if more distant, spiritual haven the next week upon the invitation of a teenager I met at the office of the community association. This proved to be a more manageable challenge, and I was soon invited to lead the youth group of the church, an opportunity which also offered important insights to adolescent perceptions and experiences in the inner city. While interpretive method requires a continuous broadening and filling out of the text and context of the research question, an immersion in the multidimensionality of people and place, the community association and the church provided the foci of an expanding network of neighbourhood contacts.

Making Sense

With limited experience to fall back on, aside from the intuition gained from a British field tradition and knowledge derived from a number of ethnographies, devising a method was in part a matter of learning on the job. The principal method was participant observation. The period from January to July was set out as the length of continuous residence in the neighbourhood; while much shorter than some field studies, such as that of Whyte (1955) or Suttles (1968), it was compatible with the length of others, incorporated the variety of three seasons of the year, and fitted the constraints of my period of graduate funding. It is essential to establish a systematic procedure for recording field data in any ethnographic research, and my own practice was to write up field notes each evening, ranging in size from a paragraph to (occasionally) 1000 words. These notes were records of impressions, events and conversations, sometimes reconstructed from brief phrases or sentences scribbled down during the course of the day. In these unstructured, everyday encounters the use of a tape recorder would have been an intrusion, and it was only used on a few occasions at public meetings. Field observation was a second method. While conventionally used by urban geographers in land-use mapping, in the inner city work it was employed principally to map unobtrusive measures, such as graffiti, vandalized cars or abandoned properties, each of which provided a visible indicator of less visible attitudes and practices.

Agency data and documents from police, planning, and school board authorities were made surprisingly accessible upon serious request, and the wealth of material made available, for example the addresses of street gang members or of children absent from school, would have repaid far more detailed study than was possible (Ley, 1975). Interviewing is a major tool of the participant observer which was conducted throughout the research period in an informal and unstructured way. Towards the end of the field season I decided to bolster the essentially qualitative research material with a more formal round of questionnaire interviews. Funds and time permitted a cluster sample of 120 interviews to be sought. Four community members were employed as interviewers and the data provided not only research material but also documentation for the social component of the neighbourhood plan.

Consequently the range of research methods was more varied than is usual in participant observation studies. In part this was a product of my own (disciplinary) insecurity with qualitative methods, but a more mature judgement has suggested that a varied methodological arsenal is an asset. The qualitative material is indispensable and forms the basis of the interpretation, but it can be usefully supplemented and confirmed by more formal methods – though only after the structuring of these methods has been sensitized by field study. It does seem, however, as if the use of exclusively qualitative data introduces an unnecessarily purist limitation to interpretive research. The justifiable scepticism against the abuses of some positivist work should not rule out of hand the use of quantitative data which are contextually accountable. More recent work in Vancouver has continued to incorporate quantitative description and analysis in interpretive studies (Ley, 1980). The qualitative–quantitative dualism separates unnecessarily hermetic categories which, like others in human geography, should profitably be integrated together.

Participant observation is usually described as an inductive strategy, a matter of progressively making sense as the data accumulate, and such it is, though it would probably be more accurate to speak of an intellectual process of tacking back and forth between concept formation and data collection. Certainly I began my fieldwork with clear expectations of the principal configurations of place and identity in the black inner city. The nature of the black community seemed to be consistently defined by black middle-class writers, the media, and a progression of white social scientists over several decades, leading to a tenacious image defined tightly around a few dimensions – cultural separateness, a singular sense of collective identity and purpose, and hostility to white America, a hostility which had so recently erupted into widely distributed insurrection in the cities. This image could have been sustained by a perfunctory or detached contact with the black inner city, but as the weeks passed the validity of participant observation emerged as a method which is not, as critics sometimes claim, an exercise in rationalizing the initial biases of the researcher. In the face of field notes which consistently refused to support my *a priori* interpretation, my preconceptions were shattered and for some time no compensating *gestalt* took their place, a condition of conceptual nudity which was quite unwelcome. Then slowly a new interpretation began to be pieced together, culminating in a 'eureka experience' not unlike that mentioned by Whyte (1955), when the pieces of the puzzle fell suddenly into place. The occasion was shortly before I moved out of the group house. For a period the music of Isaac Hayes was very popular in the house, played at a high volume over and over again. One evening, when constant repetition of one album reaching every recess of the house had reduced one's mind to a near-hypnotic state, a lateral connection between two apparently dissimilar events occurred as I reviewed my field notes, and a new conceptualization took shape, a configuration around which the eventual interpretation was constructed.

Following the elation of this discovery there was a clearer focus and orientation to the research. What had previously seemed chaotic now appeared far more ordered. The images with which I had entered North Philadelphia were those of an arms-length outsider, and exposure to the relentless barrage of everyday pressures in the inner city revealed an experience where stress and uncertainty precluded the coherence, the fusion of unity and uniformity, I had anticipated. The enemy was perceived to be within rather than without; a fissiparous individualism characterized everyday life and showed the appearances of community organization to be shallow masks concealing a more persuasive reality of interpersonal distrust and competing agendas.

Ethics

Ethical issues are far more conspicuous in ethnographic research because of the close relationship between the researcher and the community. Indeed relationship is precisely the right word, for in engaging other people, sometimes closely, in field research, one can scarcely escape personal involvement in the place (Western, 1986; Rowles, 1978). At the same time the privileged information one has access to confers a certain sense of power, and requires considerable responsibility in the course of writing. There are various biases which may enter the interpretation, including the bias of going native and allowing sympathies for the community to transform one's account into an apologetic which presents people and place only in the terms that they would fondly reserve for themselves.

Ethnographic research represents an intrusion into the lives of others, and the intruder senses (and is sometimes obligated) to strike a fair contract with the community. In return for withdrawing information, what will be returned: the findings, professional skills, political influence, a cash settlement? Or will the research represent extraction without due return, a more sophisticated form of the shady dealings of the door-to-door salesman? There are no set pieces in answering those questions, and indeed answers will vary according to the circumstances of the community, with perhaps an example of contemporary research in Cape Town's Coloured neighbourhoods posing some of the most wrenching questions (Western, 1986). But the questions must be asked and answered in good faith. As mentioned earlier, my own unwritten contract involved offering professional skills to the principal community association and other skills to church youth work. In the questionnaire survey both interviewers and interviewees received modest cash stipends. The communication of findings was more problematic. The questionnaire results immediately became public information as they were incorporated into planning reports prepared by the association for implementation at City Hall. Conveying the qualitative interpretation to the community was more difficult as identifiable individuals were not necessarily presented in the best light, or at least not as they might choose to present themselves. Nonetheless copies of the book inevitably did find their way back to the neighbourhood, and seem to have generated interest rather than indignation. Whether these arrangements constituted a fair contract I cannot say, but they nonetheless represented my best efforts.

Intrusion necessarily invokes further questions of privacy and confidentiality. Thick description can scarcely avoid a discussion of personalities, and their privacy must be protected, especially as incidents and conversations recounted were rarely acted out or uttered for the record. The concealment of identity requires the casting of fictitious names, but for the geographer an additional problem is presented, for if locations cannot be specified, and maps cannot be included, a great deal of relevant material is likely to be discarded. After experiments with map rotations of the street pattern, my eventual solution was to use maps, but to rename all streets and take a few other cartographic liberties, which were inconsequential for the research but did confuse further the identity of the neighbourhood. I have yet to meet anyone, who did not already have insider information, who has accurately located 'Monroe'.

In Retrospect

The practice of thick description or interpretation remains a small, if growing, genre within human geography. In part this reflects the rather uncritical embrace between geography and self-styled scientific philosophies in the 1960s and 1970s which created a peculiarly insular view in the discipline about the definition of rigour and scholarship. To such a viewpoint interpretive methods seem irrevocably tainted with subjectivity, the intuitive skills of a single investigator.

There is, however, an important distinction to be drawn between subjectivity and rigour. All methods are, to a significant degree, subjective in the sense that they call for informed but personal judgement by the researcher, and one should not confuse the quantitative–qualitative dichotomy with a different dichotomy separating objectivity from subjectivity. For example, a quantitative procedure like factor analysis requires a series of personal judgements including the selection of variables, the choice of factor model, the form of rotation, the interpretation of factors, and the number of dimensions to be extracted. These decisions are all subjective, but they may be defended as rigorous against a canon of approved standards. So too interpretive research can be rigorous, whether historical (Harris, 1978) or ethnographic, when calibrated against its own standards. Is there enough evidence for the interpretation? Is it internally consistent? Was the methodology sound? How do the research results square with existing findings? How robust is the relationship between the evidence and the conceptualizations which give it coherence?

There is another question that is concerned less with rigour and more with the quality of an interpretation. To what extent does a piece of work present thick as opposed to thin description? Thin description has rightly been criticized as mere description, an inventory of facts that takes reality at face value, and presents it as a form of narrative photograph. But as I stated earlier, everyday life is rarely so transparent that things are precisely and no more than what they seem to be, and the conceptual task, the task of making sense, is the difficult and creative act which defines thick description. It requires that the researcher be simultaneously insider and outsider, closely familiar with the local knowledge of people and place, but not limited by it; able to interrogate its taken-for-granted categories, to introduce a scepticism which presses the interpretation a stage further and towards abstraction.

Concept formation also answers the criticism that interpretation is concerned with the contemplation of the unique, with individual community studies manifesting a precious singularity which precludes any cumulative growth of knowledge. In one respect places are unique and the importance of their contextuality should not be forgotten. Again, some places are of such significance that they are worth understanding for themselves. But more commonly we are searching for knowledge which goes beyond the specifics of a single time and place – how far beyond is a separate question to be resolved by the imagination and boldness of the investigator. Conceptual heuristics are a vehicle for making sense of a particular place, while at the same time projecting local circumstances into a broader discourse – as the concept of the Protestant ethic projected the writings and sermons of individual English Puritans into an argument about religious values and the rise of capitalism. Such conceptual heuristics are relational rather than phenomenal, invoking linkages which are not limited to a single case study, but which may be imaginatively extended to other comparable cases. They are heuristic because they are treated as fluid and evolving, rather than fixed and static, and as contingent as the investigator tacks back and forth between concept formation and the evidence. But they have enough form to give an interpretive study coherence and introduce lines of determination to the account, factors and relations which mould the character of a place. In the Philadelphia study the dominant concept was the model of the community as a frontier outpost, islands of knowledge and security in a sea of stress, distrust, and uncertainty, islands which were shown by the fieldwork to shrink frequently to the level of the individual household. Like a pioneer venturing into the wilderness, much of inner city life is concerned with engaging the unknown. Perhaps rather too boldly, I attempted to generalize the cognitive and behavioural processes involved in living with uncertainty to analogous circumstances outside the inner city. More recent research in urban Canada has been working with a new set of concepts, exploring associations between (amongst others) the new middle class, the culture of consumption, and the post-industrial city.

Thick description creates new knowledge as it fixes upon reality from a different perspective, as, in Alfred Schutz's phrase, it makes questionable the unquestioned. While thin description is content to reveal new data, thick description seeks to interrogate old or new data before the conceptual power of an idea, an idea which can be illuminating and might even be liberating. A major challenge then is communication to a broader audience, and here geographers have displayed a range of styles from the capricious (Olsson, 1980) to the literary (Meinig, 1983). Some would find it an abuse of the problem one has laboured with to over-intellectualize an interpretation, to reduce its audience to a specialized speech community. Such a privatization of knowledge seems particularly ironic for research which explores the contours of everyday life. Far better that the pedagogy be outward-looking, available and comprehensible even to the community under study, where its insights can perhaps be given the most compelling assessment of all (Hasson, 1983). For ultimately interpretive research should contain a catholic and non-hierarchical view both of community and learning, contributing an integral dimension to the spirit and purpose of a humane education.

References

Brookfield, H. C. (1962) Local study and comparative method, *Annals of the Association of American Geographers*, 52, 242–54.
Brookfield, H. C. (1968) The money that grows on trees, *Australian Geographical Studies*, 6, 97–119.

Brookfield, H. C. and Brown, P. (1963) *Struggle for Land: agriculture and group territories among the Chimbu of the New Guinea Highlands*. Oxford University Press, London.

Bunge, W. (1971) *Fitzgerald: geography of a revolution*. Schenkman, Cambridge, Mass.

Burgess, R. (1984) *In the Field: an introduction to field research*. Allen & Unwin, London.

Clarke, C., Ley, D. and Peach C. (eds) (1984) *Geography and Ethnic Pluralism*. Allen & Unwin, London.

Cosgrove, D. (1985) *Social Formation and Symbolic Landscape*. Croom Helm, London.

Cressey, P. G. (1971) The taxi-dancehall as a social world. In J. Short (ed.), *The Social Fabric of the Metropolis*. University of Chicago Press, Chicago, pp. 193–209.

Cybriwsky, R. A. (1978) Social aspects of neighbourhood change, *Annals of the Association of American Geographers*, 68, 17–33.

Duncan, J. S. and Duncan, N. (1984) A cultural analysis of urban residential landscapes. In J. Agnew, J. Mercer and D. Sopher (eds), *The City in Cultural Context*. Allen & Unwin, London.

Gans, H. J. (1962) *The Urban Villagers*. Free Press, New York.

Geertz, C. (1973) Thick description. In *The Interpretation of Cultures*. Basic Books, New York, pp. 3–30.

Geerz, C. (1980) *Negara: the theatre state in nineteenth century Bali*. Princeton, Princeton University Press.

Gibson, E. (1978) Understanding the subjective meaning of places. In D. Ley and M. Samuels (eds), *Humanistic Geography*. Croom Helm, London, pp. 138–54.

Hannerz, U. (1969) *Soulside: inquiries into ghetto culture and community*. Columbia University Press, New York.

Harris, C. (1978) The historical mind and the practice of geography. In D. Ley and M. Samuels (eds), *Humanistic Geography*. Croom Helm, London, pp. 123–37.

Hasson, S. (1983) *The Neighborhood Organization as a Pedagogic Project*. Institute of Urban and Regional Studies, Hebrew University of Jerusalem.

Jackson, P. (1980) A social geography of Puerto Ricans in New York. Unpublished dissertation, University of Oxford.

Jackson, P. (1983) Principles and problems of participant observation, *Geografiska Annaler*, 65B, 39–46.

Jackson, P. and Smith, S. (1984) *Exploring Social Geography*. Allen & Unwin, London.

Janik, A. and Toulmin, S. (1973) *Wittgenstein's Vienna*. Simon & Schuster, New York.

Kariya, P. (1987) Keepers and kept: British Columbia Indians and the Department of Indian Affairs. Unpublished dissertation, Clark University.

Ley, D. (1974) *The Black Inner City as Frontier Outpost: images and behavior of a Philadelphia neighborhood*. Association of American Geographers, Monograph Series No. 7, Washington, DC.

Ley, D. (1975) The street gang in its milieu. In G. Gappert and H. Rose (eds),

The Social Economy of Cities. Sage Publications, Beverly Hills, Calif., pp. 247–73.

Ley, D. (1977) Social geography and the taken-for-granted world, *Transactions of the Institute of British Geographers*, NS 2, 498–512.

Ley, D. (1980) Liberal ideology and the post-industrial city, *Annals of the Association of American Geographers*, 70, 238–58.

Ley, D. (1981) Inner city revitalization in Canada: a Vancouver case study, *Canadian Geographer*, 24, 124–48.

Ley, D. (1983) *A Social Geography of the City.* Harper & Row, New York.

Ley, D. (1985) Cultural–humanistic geography, *Progress in Human Geography*, 9, 415–23.

Ley, D. and Cybriwsky, R. (1974) Urban graffiti as territorial markers, *Annals of the Association of American Geographers*, 64, 491–505.

Ley, D. and Samuels, M. S. (1978) *Humanistic Geography: prospects and problems*, Croom Helm, London.

Meinig, D. (ed.) (1979) *The Interpretation of Ordinary Landscapes.* Oxford University Press, New York.

Meinig, D. (1983) Geography as an art, *Transactions of the Institute of British Geographers*, NS 8, 314–28.

Naroll, R. and Naroll, F. (1963) On bias of exotic data, *Man*, 25, 24–6.

Olsson, G. (1980) *Birds in Egg: eggs in bird.* Pion, London.

Plummer, K. (1983) *Documents of Life.* Allen & Unwin, London.

Rabinow, P. and Sullivan, W. (eds) (1979) *Interpretive Social Science.* University of California Press, Los Angeles, Calif.

Rowles, G. (1978) Reflections on experiential field work. In D. Ley and M. Samuels (eds), *Humanistic Geography.* Croom Helm, London, pp. 173–93.

Schorske, C. (1981) *Fin-de-siècle Vienna: politics and culture.* Cambridge University Press, Cambridge.

Smith, S. (1984) Practicing humanistic geography, *Annals of the Association of American Geographers*, 74, 353–74.

Suttles, G. (1968) *The Social Order of the Slum.* University of Chicago Press, Chicago, Ill.

Suttles, G. (1984) The cumulative texture of local urban culture, *American Journal of Sociology*, 90, 283–304.

Thomas, J. (ed.) (1983) The Chicago school: the tradition and the legacy, *Urban Life*, 11, whole issue.

Thomas, W. I. and Znaniecki, F. (1918) *The Polish Peasant in Europe and America.* Alfred A. Knopf, New York.

Thrasher, F. (1927) *The Gang*, University of Chicago Press, Chicago, Ill.

Weber, M. (1958) *The Protestant Ethic and the Spirit of Capitalism.* Scribner's, New York.

Western, J. (1981) *Outcast Cape Town.* University of Minnesota Press, Minneapolis.

Western, J. (1986) The authorship of places: reflections on fieldwork in South Africa, *The Syracuse Scholar*, 7, 4–17.

Whyte, W. F. (1955) *Street Corner Society.* University of Chicago Press, Chicago, Ill.

Winchell, R. (1982) Space and place of the Yavapai. Unpublished dissertation, Arizona State University.
Wirth, L. (1928) *The Ghetto*. University of Chicago Press, Chicago, Ill.

9

A Welfare Approach to Human Geography

David. M. Smith

The origin of an idea is not always easy to explain. It is seldom a case of the penny dropping, far less the apple – a moment of instant revelation with cries of 'eureka' and a rush to print. More likely, an intellectual innovation is the product of a lengthy gestation, with the final outcome involving subtle interaction between the individual scholar and the context within which he or she lives and works.

To trace the development of an idea for which one carries responsibility requires more self-awareness than many of us possess. It involves not only an ability to reconstruct elements of life experience which have a bearing on scholarly conduct, but also insight into aspects of personal motivation, creativity, ambition and so on (along with whatever element of arrogance or self-delusion is required to make claims on originality). To understand the intellectual context in which the work in question was undertaken may seem easier, but this itself is deceptive. Academic activity is a reflection of broader societal conditions, both material and cultural; we are simultaneously scholars and members of society, playing out these roles (if indeed we can distinguish between them) in our own unique way. And the element of chance must not be overlooked: chance encounters, fortuitous moves, crucial references found by accident and that element in the creative process which leads these paragraphs today to be different in detail and nuance from those composed in the mind earlier – just as the painter's precise brush-strokes and the composer's notes are a matter of mood rather than mechanics.

Early Influences

The development of a 'welfare approach' to human geography began, at least as a conscious project, in the latter part of the 1960s. When it came to the surface in print it represented a significant departure from the academic identity of an industrial geographer with a predilection for theory, expressed most substantially in an advanced-level text (Smith,

1971a). Some of the background has been set out in another autobiographical piece (Smith, 1984) so this contribution will be confined to what seem, in retrospect, to have been the crucial elements in the shift from location theory to spatial welfare analysis.

We begin with an individual – a British trained geographer (with 'subsidiary' economics) in an American mid-western university (Southern Illinois at Carbondale), working in a lively department, and married to someone teaching sociology. I was not particularly ambitious, except in the sense of wanting to be known and noticed, and found in writing an outlet for personal creative expression and, through the printed word, a means of establishing a public identity hitherto denied to someone diffident in personal encounters. Having come upon the quantitative revolution rather late (after a Ph.D., two years in planning, and an excursion into industrial archaeology), I was turned 30, eager to catch up, and determined not to be left behind again.

The writing of *Industrial Location: an economic geographical analysis*, along with conversion into quantifier, took place at a time of great intellectual excitement in American geography. This provided a stimulus lacking in Britain, with its stultifying hierarchical structure and geographical profession dominated by dull old men. But it was also an era of social turmoil, with the civil rights struggle and voter registration in the South fresh in many memories, the discovery of poverty in Michael Harrington's 'other America', and the Viet Nam war boiling up into an issue to split the nation and radicalize a generation of students. It was the time of the Beatles, 'All you need is love', invitations to 'turn on', long 'rap' sessions, and struggling with a hangover and the latest book chapter next morning on the kitchen table. Conventional culture and lifestyles, as well as the social order, were being challenged. So were the foundations of the so-called new geography of statistics and models, as some of the actual subjects of the factorial ecologies of American cities tried to burn them down.

Of the individuals who played a part in my reorientation, the most influential at Carbondale was Don Eggert. A cultural geographer working on the Ohio Valley, he introduced me not only to the local landscape and some of its meaning, but also to the radical stance which young faculty as well as students were just beginning to adopt. He saw Appalachian poverty and war in South-East Asia as proper topics for his teaching, and many students responded avidly. My own perception of both geography and academia had changed significantly by the time Don left in 1968 for the anti-war resistance movement in Palo Alto.

Another important influence was Margaret. Practising as a social worker when we married, Margaret was offered an instructorship in the Sociology Department on arrival at SIU, and one of her assignments was a course on social problems. This helped to bring the literature and contemporary debates home, in a literal as well as figurative sense, as the issues of poverty, hunger, discrimination and, eventually, the environment unfolded on the TV screen as expressions of growing popular and government concern. We were, together, enlarging our experience of America in all its aspects, throwing our cases, Michael and (from 1968) Tracey into the back of the station wagon and taking to the road every break between teaching.

Three others made more specific contributions to a framework for (academic) action that was beginning to take shape. The first was Eric Rawstron, who had initially inspired my interest in location theory at Nottingham and who, even before I left Manchester for SIU in 1966, had written suggesting investigations of geographical patterns of social conditions such as public service provision. This idea eventually bore fruit in a book on Britain (Coates and Rawstron, 1971); it took the American experience for me to grasp its full significance. The second was Denis Fair, colleague in geography at SIU, whose knowledge of contemporary development theory stimulated my own interest in that field, and whose return to South Africa was partly instrumental in my own later sojourn in that troubled but fascinating land. The third was Ron Beazley, an economist at SIU, who in a seminar for incoming graduate students offered me the first indication that the concept of social justice could be handled with analytical rigour; it was to him that I wrote, with such a helpful response, when I subsequently needed guidance into the tortuous literature of welfare economics.

By the time that the manuscript of *Industrial Location* had been completed, my changing interests were crystallizing around 'the geography of social problems'. The first step was to map a wide range of conditions that had thus far largely eluded geographical scrutiny. But it was not at SIU but in Florida that this probject came to fruition. The Geography Department at SIU degenerated into an arena of faction-fighting; it seemed to be time to move on, and the University of Florida offered a post in Geography with attachment to a new Urban Studies Bureau. The half-time research element in this job, along with a favourable impression of the then chairman Shannon McCune (who had an anti-war sticker on his car), and a substantial salary increase, brought us to Gainesville in September 1971.

Territorial Social Indicators

Florida. The heat, humidity, beaches, sunburn; Spanish moss draped on huge oaks reflected in swampland pools; the scent of orange blossom wafting across the interstate highway; the sound of crickets and bull-frogs in warm night air. So many senses assailed, against a backdrop of recently discovered Elgar. An environment which seemed to heighten awareness, encourage creativity. Things began to fall into place.

Shortly after arriving in Florida I discovered the 'social indicators movement'. For a few years a literature had been building up in American social science concerned with measures of social well-being or the quality of life, to augment the economic measures which tended to prevail in assessing whether a nation was making progress. This movement was a reflection of a growing unease, in times of unprecedented affluence, that the pursuit of still further economic growth was obscuring other less material sources of human satisfaction or happiness. The social indicators literature was focusing on the question of what conditions might be built into non-economic measures of the state of a society. There was also interest in the possibility of modelling social systems after the fashion of the economist, whereby some national goal or goals could be set and their attainment judged, and indeed planned for, in relation to resource allocation in an input–output or cost–benefit framework. The social indicators movement thus helped to provide some structure for what might otherwise have been an unsystematic search for social variables. However, the literature did reveal one serious deficiency – a neglect of the geographical dimension, with little concern for the territorial disaggregation of national data. There thus seemed something to contribute as well as to learn, and I adopted the term 'territorial social indicators' for measures developed at a sub-national scale.

The next step was to apply this concept in practice. While the primary aim was to work on the spatial disaggregation of the United States as a whole, two opportunities arose to operate at the intra-city level. The first involved collaboration with a colleague in the Geography Department – Joshua ('Dick') Dickinson. I had been warned about Dick even before I met him and had already noticed a poster for the only black candidate in the forthcoming elections on his office door. He was, by Florida standards, a rampant liberal, combining social concern with a background in ecology which led him to question some of the practices of agribusiness at home and US-backed development strategies in Central and South America. With a postgraduate student, Bob Gray, we did a social indicators study of Gainesville at the census tract level, combining census measures with other data collected locally (Dickinson, Gray and Smith, 1972).

The Gainsville study proved to be a useful dry run for a more ambitious project on the city of Tampa. As a contribution to the rather hesitant activities of the Urban Studies Bureau, I became involved with the City Demonstration Agency responsible for the successor to the Model Cities programme, as consultant in an exercise to assist the definition of a target area (i.e. the worst part of the city) to qualify for funds under a new federal scheme. Bob Gray was hired as research assistant. How much use was made of our work I am not sure, but inside access to data on crime, health, quality of local environment and so on, together with the assistance of Ray Jones in the University of Florida library in processing the first 1970 census tapes, enabled us to compile measurements on almost 50 variables at the tract level. The results were of academic as well as practical significance: when subjected to the inevitable factor analysis the data revealed a structure different in important respects from those of factorial ecology studies confined to census data which were then being replicated in various cities to reinforce what was in danger of becoming an accepted empirical generalization (Smith, 1973a, chapter 9).

The Tampa experience was helpful in another respect. It provided first-hand insight into urban planning in the American city. Whatever faith I had in this practice as a means of enhancing the lives of deprived populations was undermined by a growing recognition of the role of interest groups and powerful personalities within the broader political process. To be told at the outset that the primary job of one of the agency's senior staff was 'to keep the Mayor's ass clean' was hardly encouraging. Further insight was provided by Margaret's activities. Having turned down a post in Sociology she became involved in various voluntary organizations, including the active bi-racial Gainsville Women for Equal Rights. As well as broadening our contacts among the socially concerned and politically active members of the community, this brought more direct experience of the continuing exploitation of blacks, especially among the domestic workers who Margaret and her colleagues were helping to unionize. Again, local government seemed unable to do much to change a dramatically unequal city, run largely by, and for, the real-estate developers. Even the white middle-class community groups mobilizing to protect their own local environments seemed virtually impotent.

All this added to a broader disillusionment with America – its values, institutions, economic system and government (the Nixon era). We had to make a commitment to the country, and engage what would be an increasingly political struggle, or get out. We chose to go. In addition to general discontent we had the education of two children to consider, and experiences with the local school system gave us no grounds for confidence. My concerns now also included the academic setting in which I worked. Some of my colleagues were unhappy about my scholarship as well as my politics, in a department where the prevailing ethos was boots-on fieldwork with a Latin American focus embedded in what I described rather generously in an intemperate memo to my colleagues as cautious conservatism. It was not just the social activism of my work but also its theoretical and quantitative orientation that raised eyebrows. And I had failed to recognize the significance of some Southern cultural attitudes, including white and male supremacy and an expectation of deference, from which the Department of Geography was not itself entirely immune. To cap it all, Dickinson was refused tenure, having failed to respect the prevailing conventions of conformist and mediocre scholarship. The Department seemed destined for descent into richly deserved obscurity, though I hasten to add that the tables have since been turned and that Geography now flourishes at the University of Florida. I still greatly regret that the events of 1972 cut short what could have been a most fruitful academic collaboration between Dick and myself; I had so much to learn from his ecological perspective that could have enriched the emerging welfare approach.

The decision to leave precipitated the rounding off of the national-scale work which had been building up. Some of the first results were presented at the Boston AAG conference in 1971 (Smith, 1972) at a special session organized by Dick Peet when what I christened 'radical geography' made its first major public impact (Smith, 1971b). I was much impressed by the careful rigour of David Harvey's paper on social justice in spatial systems (Harvey, 1973, chapter 3). I also liked the increasingly activist stance of the *Antipode* group, although I did not at that stage grasp the full significance of their emerging interest in Marx.

What had been tentatively planned as a major alternative and 'socially relevant' text on the USA became two separate books, completed with the urgency of both scholarly conviction and the deadline of departure. One was an application of the concept of territorial social indicators to the geography of social well-being in the United States (Smith, 1973a), which comprised a draft initially produced internally for the Urban Studies Bureau and speedily accepted by McGraw-Hill thanks to the good offices of their local representative Terry Gets. Out of print for some years now, I still consider this book to be the most useful descriptive account of spatial variations in the human condition in the USA, and greatly superior to the standard texts with their tedious repetition of the same antiquated format of physical basis, masses of economic facts, and an assiduous avoidance of so many crucial if politically sensitive issues. The second book was a more popular treatment of life in the United States which Margaret and I wrote jointly (Smith, D. M. and Smith, M. R., 1973). The honesty of some of our account caused discomfort to the publisher's editor, steeped in the usual platitudes about America, but the book faithfully captured a country and people which we had come to know well – and in a strange sense love – at a particularly interesting time. It was a pity that David & Charles did not make more of it. Both these books would be worth revising, if only I had the time (and energy) now that I seemed to find then . . .

Spatial Welfare Theory

In June 1972 we left Florida for South Africa. A strange choice, perhaps, for an increasingly public radical who had been repelled by the racism of the American South and its nauseating religious hypocrisy, but the land of apartheid, Afrikanerdom and the Dutch Reformed Church seemed to offer new excitement as well as escape. In Florida our world-view had broadened, with glimpses of underdeveloped lands and their urban problems provided by visits to Mexico, Guatemala, Jamaica, Haiti and the Dominican Republic, and to extend this experience further seemed attractive. In addition, a serious interest in race as an element in spatial inequality was beginning to form as I came to terms with the emotional reaction. Furthermore, a strange experience at Leicester, and an even stranger one at Newcastle (in connection with applications for chairs), had yielded appointments to none of those concerned, and the opportunity to return to academic life in Britain seemed not to be an immediate prospect. So, four months at the University of Natal in Durban was followed by eight at the University of the Witwatersrand in Johannesburg.

The Durban days were dominated by teaching, tuning in to the new scene, and the personal indulgences associated with a nice flat overlooking the beach and a fascinating land to begin to explore. Within a couple of months we had crossed the country, from Kruger Park to the Cape. The first real academic encounter was, oddly enough, with Brian Berry at the quadrennial conference of the South African Geographical Society: he described social indicators as 'a bum steer', but I thought that they made more sense than his factorial ecology, and said so forcibly. The reaction to the fact that I had engaged this special invited speaker in vigorous public debate, American-style, brought home the fact that deference to status and seniority was the convention and expected courtesy in South Africa. This was linked to a more general attitude of respect for authority: I had already been told by the manager of our flats and by a traffic policeman that here you did as you were told.

In such an environment I could soon have encountered difficulties more serious than any in Florida. As it happened, I experienced a partial form of transformation back from political activist to more conventional scholar – as if some unconscious defence mechanism was at work. The role of activist was not fully abandoned: I was once pelted with eggs by Afrikaner students in a demonstration at Wits about some now unrecalled government assault on academic freedom. But in Johannesburg much of my time was spent reading welfare economics, which may seem a strange form of escapism from apartheid society but was a natural development of existing strands in my intellectual make-up. Additional stimulus was provided by the requirement that, as part of my role in the Department of Geography and Environmental Science, I should contribute to their *Occasional Papers*. This seemed to be a good opportunity to crystallize some thoughts on a conceptual foundation for the largely empirical work on territorial social indicators done in Florida. I had already made a contribution to location theory based on my knowledge of economics (neo-classical, of course, learned in two years of the Honours course at Nottingham taken along with geography). It therefore seemed sensible to seek guidance in welfare economics for a theoretical framework to handle issues of spatial distribution, and I read all I could find. Access to such abstract literature on inequality was no problem; had I turned to Marx and Lenin, which would probably have been the case in America, I would have found them as elusive as *Playboy* in puritanical anti-communist South Africa – where the authorities have a sensitive understanding of the frailties of both mind and flesh.

The outcome of this work (Smith, 1973b) turned out to be far longer than expected. It was in fact the first draft of the later book (Smith, 1977) in which the welfare approach was set out. What at Wits I saw as the new systematic specialization of 'welfare geography' involved the spatial extension of the formal framework of neo-classical welfare economics. I found a way of structuring problems of distribution among territories, in a manner which clarified not only the questions of choice of variables and their weighting but also what it means to judge one distribution pattern as better than another (i.e. a welfare improvement). Applying such a framework to practical problems helped the further development of empirical work. This included an attempt at a spatial welfare analysis of South Africa, which made some points about apartheid in an oblique form not unknown in lands where acceptable presentation and informal codes enable scholars sometimes to avoid censorship. I did insist on quoting Richard Turner, 'banned' author of a sensitive and incisive critique (Turner, 1972) which stood out in the literature on South Africa. To his great credit, Keith Beavon as head of department agreed to print this, at risk of publication being prevented. It was not banned; Turner remained so, and was later murdered.

The other product of six hectic months was a text on numerical methods (Smith, 1975), completed at Wits as part of a saga explained elsewhere (Smith, 1984). The relevance of this project to the present story is that aspects of territorial social indicator construction and a discussion of the identification of 'problem areas' still seem helpful as treatments of matters of practical interest neglected in other quantitative texts. But the broader purpose was to continue to demonstrate the relevance of the descriptive side of 'welfare geography', in the old pattern-identification tradition revitalized, as I saw it, by social concern.

The Welfare Approach

The foregoing provides the background which led to the planning and execution of *Human Geography: a welfare approach* (Smith, 1977). The year in South Africa was followed by six months in Australia, but soon after arriving at the University of New England an interview in London led to the appointment to a chair at Queen Mary College. The Australian visit was a hiatus from the point of view of creative scholarship, though it did provide familiarity with some new cities, a little case material, and opportunities on the lecture circuit to sharpen up the emerging theoretical framework (Monash, in particular, could provide a demanding seminar audience) – along with the occasional indulgence in sea, sun, Flag, Fosters and pottering around the early goldfields. After South Africa, Australia seemed a bland version of America, with only Fay Gale's students at Adelaide challenged and challenging over social issues such as the state of the aboriginal population.

Settling into QMC and London suburbia during the 1973–74 'winter of discontent' involved almost as much cultural shock as the first exposure to apartheid. We no longer felt or thought of ourselves as 'British'. However, we needed a stable environment for Michael and Tracey, and my new head of department – Eric Rawstron – was someone whose innovative mind I greatly admired. He ran the department (or let it run) in a way which gave me almost as much time for research and writing as I had enjoyed as an itinerant scholar not staying anywhere long enough to qualify for major administrative chores.

The Wits *Occasional Paper* (Smith, 1973b) was published soon after my arrival at QMC, and it was not long before I began to understand some of the weakness of the theoretical perspective. Roger Lee was immersed in the critique of neo-classical economics and he helped to expose the implications of my undue reliance on conventional welfare theory with its abstraction from social relations. Encounters with others showed me how far I had drifted, in almost two years, from the radical geography that was taking shape when I left the USA and which had, now, a growing affiliation in Britain. I recall the incisive response of Doreen Massey to my abstractions on social justice with particular pain, tempered by acknowledgement that she had a point. I began serious reading again, and soon found in Marxian economics a powerful counterpoint to the neo-classical view on which I had relied so heavily in the past.

To attempt a major text at this particular time was, in retrospect, misguided. I had five years of research and thinking to weld into a synthesis which, I was convinced, could advance human geography as an analytical and socially relevant field of enquiry. But the field was in a state of flux, and so was my own mind. As had happened before, the creative urge expressed in the exhilaration of writing, along with a contract deadline to meet, overcame what, academically speaking, might have been my better judgement had I tried to think the project through dispassionately. But is there a right time to write, paint or make music, other than when the urge is there? So I wrote.

The aim of the book was to redirect human geography from its traditional preoccupation with areal differentation to a concern for spatial inequality. The concept of welfare, as elaborated in welfare economics, was offered as a means of structuring not only description but also evaluation and planning for change in spatial patterns of social well-being. To me at least, these arguments still carry much conviction; the weakness of the work was its approach to explanation. The theoretical perspective had been broadened considerably from that in the Wits paper, but it lacked a coherent and persuasive sense of social process. Neo-classical economics has very little to say about the way in which real economic events occur, to generate inequality in geographical space (indeed, it can be used to demonstrate their elimination, given a number of absurd assumptions), and my reading in Marxism has not yet been broad enough to find an alternative theory of uneven development with the capacity convincingly to inform case studies. Although the essence of two different economics was conveyed clearly and accurately, for the most part, some attempts to bring them together (e.g. in dealing with the concept of value) did not bear rigorous scrutiny.

On the more positive side, the introduction of the concept of welfare to social indicators research did help to clarify some important issues. I still consider that the treatment of social justice in a spatial context (chapter 6) is as good as anything in print, and that the material on planning facility location so as to achieve redistributional objectives has stood the test of time. In fact, I had always regarded the practical application of the welfare approach to be more important than its explanatory capacity; just as in my work on industrial location, I had adopted Lösch's axiom that 'The real duty . . . is not to explain our sorry reality, but to improve it.' There is still something to be learned from *Human Geography: a welfare approach* in this respect, and despite its flaws I am satisfied that it does students more good than harm to read it, especially under the guidance of someone who actually understands its strengths and weaknesses.

Reactions to the book were predictably varied. It was greeted with enthusiasm by those seeking a reformation of human geography which gave inequality and social problems a central role, without fully embracing Marxism, though some 'liberals' did find too much Marx for their comfort. To many radicals it was not Marxist enough – especially at a time when grasp of Marxism in geography was itself primitive, with explanations for inequality extending little beyond the evocation of the 'logic of accumulation' or the 'law of value'. I recall discussions with Dick Peet in Australia in 1980, and the difficulty of finding common ground with those who seemed to inhabit a self-constructed cocoon: knowledge arrived at from different 'philosophical positions' could not possibly be reconciled, they maintained, so there was no scope for serious debate. Similarly, many who found helpful guidance in the welfare approach were, like me, unable to step far enough back to see some of its faults. My greatest regret about the timing of the book is that the field was too volatile and fast-moving fully to absorb the welfare approach, to give it mature and informed consideration, and to build on (or reconstruct) it in a manner consistent with other important developments in geographical thinking. Even now, it may not be too late: the grand synthesis of the various strands of argument in human geography since the eclipse of the quantitative movement has yet to come.

Subsequent Developments

The welfare approach has provided a frame of reference or point of departure for most of my subsequent work. This may be regarded as comprising specific applications or lines of further exploration, rather than a deliberate attempt to put flesh on a particular skeleton – as I described the structure in 1977. In fact, I have an open mind on the nature of the beast that may evolve, through my own efforts and the work of others, and I have as yet no clear view as to its capacity to engage in friendly and possibly fruitful intercourse with other creatures abroad in contemporary geography and social science. Some sense of an emerging synthesis is beginning to form; all I care to do here is to round off my own story, the significance of which others may judge.

Coming to terms with middle age can be a traumatic personal experience, which must have some bearing on scholarly practice. I approached the age of 40 with some trepidation, and it was more than usually satisfying to leave the following day for my first visit to the USSR. Perhaps I was ready for a new challenge; perhaps I wanted to prove (to whom I know not) that I was not too old, but this turned out to be the beginning of fresh experiences which have greatly influenced the direction taken since publication of *Human Geography: a welfare approach*. The academic justification for my emerging interest in the USSR was straightforward: I was increasingly dissatisfied with a radical geography exclusively concerned with inequality under capitalism, and which seemed to accept an unspecified form of socialism as a panacea without reference to actual experience. I had personally espoused 'socialism' since the early 1960s; living in the USA had convinced me of the evils of capitalism, and my reading was reinforcing an understanding that such a system was inconsistent with my own conception of a just society. It was therefore time to see socialism in practice.

I returned from the 1976 IGU conference full of enthusiasm for research on the USSR. I was known there for my work on industrial location, and my 'radical' reputation may have encouraged the feeling that I was sympathetic towards the country or at least not anti-Soviet. I found people more approachable and open than I had expected, from the first conversation with an interpreter in Novosibirsk who gave what seemed to be a frank answer to the question of what were the most serious problems in the USSR. A year learning some Russian was a practical as well as symbolic commitment to a new research field, and proved helpful on subsequent visits. These experiences, together with trips to Poland, opened up an important additional dimension to the study of inequality, as well as shattering some illusions about socialism as actually practised.

The first fruits of the Eastern European experience found a place in my next book, a more 'popular' account of inequality in living standards at different spatial scales written for Penguin (1979). I juxtaposed advanced capitalism with socialism along with the case of Peru to illustrate the underdeveloped world. (A consulting assignment with Dick Dickinson in Peru in 1976 had provided the necessary background here.) The interpretations offered were less rigorous than in the 1977 book, but more in tune with the enlarging realm of my first-hand experience: the intention was to show how different economic–social–political systems generate different patterns of inequality. The concept of welfare was subdued, in the interests of ease of comprehension, as I had in mind a general readership as well as students. I still build my first-year course 'Geography and Human Welfare' around *Where the Grass is Greener*. The only disappointment has been difficulty attracting an American readership – partly because of the distinctive style of American textbooks and their need to be 'politically neutral' (i.e. not anti-capitalist) and partly because Croom Helm, who published the hardback, disposed of the American rights to Barnes Noble, who priced their edition out of the market. How some of these publishers stay in business is beyond me, but their role in the dissemination or (in my case) otherwise of knowledge is important. The Johns Hopkins University Press now have a paperback for the American market; David Harvey wrote an introduction which seemed more generous than mere courtesy would demand.

Other developments running parallel with the Soviet experience included the revision of *Industrial Location* (Smith, 1971a), published in 1981. The welfare approach was reflected here, in particular in the conceptualization of industrial impact. The fact that I was content with only slight revision of the 'neo-Weberian' core of this work made me wonder how seriously my broader perspective had really changed over the decade since the first edition. I am still prepared to defend the approach (Smith, 1986), but am increasingly inclined to leave further exercises in location theory to younger and perhaps more agile minds.

Thus the past five years have seen a preoccupation with more empirical and social projects. Not that this implies a loss of interest in theory – far from it. What I firmly believe now is that what passes for theory in geography has consistently been advanced without adequate empirical reference – and those pursuing a Marxist approach may be even more guilty than the model-builders and quantifiers in this respect. Furthermore, I am increasingly of the view that the academic standing which geographers still so fervently seek, and that they thought at one time to be associated with the positivist scientific method, is most likely to be earned by convincing place-specific studies. Some think of this as a return to regional geography, others talk of theory-informed case studies. The essence of the approach is an ongoing interaction between observation and theory, rather than seeking somehow to fit reality into a preconceived theoretical structure in which non-conforming observations are dismissed as random errors or aberrant cases. The focus remains on inequality in human life chances, or uneven development, but recognizing the mutual interdependence of spatial form and social structure in its broadest sense, rather than taking spatial pattern as that which is to be explained. In this way spatial form can be incorporated into a holistic social-science perspective. The nearest thing to a convincing articulation of this view which I have read recently is in Doreen Massey's *Spatial Divisions of Labour* (Massey, 1984, chapters 2 and 3).

The case studies that I am attempting to build up are deliberately varied. One concerns Moscow, looking at inequalities in living standards as a reflection of, and with feedback to, the structure of contemporary Soviet society, with field observation and anecdotal evidence to supplement the scarce numerical data. The second is a study of trends in spatial inequality in Atlanta, examining some simple social indicators at successive census dates since 1960 against the background of racial segregation and residential change, as well as with reference to the local political process (Smith, 1985). Plans to extend this work to three Florida cities for comparative purposes reflect a continuing belief in territorial social indicators as helpful descriptive and diagnostic devices. The third case examines the relationship between urbanization and social change in South Africa (Smith, 1982). A second visit in 1979 enabled me to pick up on some important trends in the urbanization process, and it is in this context that I am continuing to develop some ideas concerning the distinctive spatial forms which arise from the organization of labour exploitation in South Africa, and which feed back into the ongoing process of social change.

One final aspect of my current work is worth mentioning, as I have found in this both opportunities for further applications of social indicator research and also elements in the broader perspective towards which I am working. An active Health Research Group has been built up in the Department of Geography and Earth Science at QMC, with a number of externally funded projects which seek to elucidate the concept of local need for health care in a manner helpful to the more efficient and equitable allocation of NHS resources. While most of this work has been the responsibility of others (Sarah Curtis, John Eyles and Kevin Woods), I find it a particularly satisfying application of welfare geographical research in an applied context, East London being one of the unhealthiest parts of any British city. If this is working for change 'within the system', I am happy to defend it. The research work does have a broader significance, of course, not only in refining survey methodology but also at a more theoretical level. We have been increasingly attracted by qualitative methods and approaches in the tradition of ethnography and interpretive sociology, led by some talented postgraduate students. The work of one of these (Cornwell, 1984) exemplifies the kind of place-specific theory-informed case study to which reference was made earlier. The direct reference to individual experience in such work evokes the humanism which on occasions seeped through the more dispassionate analysis in *Human Geography: a welfare approach*.

So, geography remains about place, and the people therein. We are now ready for a return of the local, even regional, monograph as a demonstration that, collectively, we have made intellectual progress since the days of the French school. The result may be far from the welfare approach as originally conceived, but I am convinced that this will not be entirely absent.

Epilogue

In an earlier autobiographical piece, somewhat flippantly entitled 'Recollections of a random variable' (Smith, 1984), I concluded with a crescendo of contrived cynicism about the field of geography and its strange introspection. (I have yet to find economists, far less physicists, baring their souls as they reconstruct the making of their disciplines.) Perhaps this is one of our strengths – that we are (increasingly) conscious of the role of individual creative scholarship, with the capricious element intrinsic to being human. As I see my fellow geographers striving for new structures of knowledge in an environment of growing self-awareness, my own faith is renewed. We still publish far too much trivia and pretentious theoretical posturing, but that long-revered capacity to synthesize and not to be unduly constrained by disciplinary boundaries has not been totally stunted by our years of number-crunching and law-seeking.

The problems facing geography today seem more external than disciplinary. I refer, of course, to the madness presently being perpetrated by the British government, via the UGC, in the guise of academic planning. Writing in the summer of 1985 I have recently completed my profile or plan, as what I now take to be manager of a 'cost centre' rather than head of an academic department: three pages of A4! Who knows who will do what with these reams of paper. All that can be sure is that the exercise represents a further stage in the tightening of central, state control over our universities. The irony is that the only other places where I have encountered state-imposed research plans are Warsaw, Moscow and Siberia; such precedents are hardly encouraging. I am struggling to avoid frozen staff positions, while as I write this piece in Gainesville the University of Florida is creating dozens of new posts (geography is doing well) in a conservative state in Reagan's America.

I decided to write this in Florida, partly because it is here that the welfare approach took shape, but largely because creative activity is increasingly hard at home. Four years as head of department, beginning with one financial crisis and ending with another, is taking its toll. And now three years as Dean, fighting for social 'studies' that the Education Secretary will not see as science. What I fear, as a cost of all this, is the demise of the creative spirit, not only my now but also that collective creativity which stems from the interaction of independent-minded scholars free to follow their own inclination without regard to state pressure or what ESRC are likely to support. While I have some respect for the innovative capacity of American academia, its seriousness of purpose heightened by self-seeking and aggressive competition, it is the more maturely reflective if less immediately invigorating environment in Britain which seems most conducive to real intellectual progress in geography. And central to this is the autonomy of the individual, able and willing to transcend current fashion and pressures to conform. We destroy such an environment, or allow its erosion, at our peril, for in place of the new and exciting synthesis that I sense forthcoming in human geography will be the consolidation of a dull orthodoxy, encouraged by the UGC and the ESRC as we revert to the technological gymnastics of digital mapping, remote sensing and the like. I shudder to think what the rest of the 1980s will bring.

Whither is fled the visionary gleam?
Where is it now, the glory and the dream?
(Wordsworth, 'Intimations of immortality')

References

Coates, B. E. and Rawstron, E. M. (1971) *Regional Variations in Britain: studies in economic and social geography*. Batsford, London.

Cornwell, J. (1984) *Hard-earned Lives: accounts of health and illness from East London*. Tavistock, London.

Dickinson, J. C., Gray, R. and Smith, D. M. (1972) The 'quality of life' in Gainesville, Florida: an application of territorial social indicators. *Southeastern Geographer*, 12, 121–32.

Harvey, D. (1973) *Social Justice and the City*. Edward Arnold, London; Johns Hopkins University Press, New York.

Massey, D. (1984) *Spatial Divisions of Labour*. Macmillan, London.

Smith, D. M. (1971a) *Industrial Location: an economic geographical analysis*. John Wiley, New York.

Smith, D. M. (1971b) Radical geography: the next revolution? *Area*, 3, 153–7.

Smith, D. M. (1972) Towards a geography of social well-being: interstate variations in the United States. In R. Peet (ed.), *Geographical Perspectives on American Poverty*. Antipode Monographs in Social Geography, Worcester, Mass., pp. 17–46.

Smith, D. M. (1973a) *The Geography of Social Well-being in the United States: an introduction to territorial social indicators*. McGraw-Hill, New York.

Smith, D. M. (1973b) *An Introduction to Welfare Geography*, Occasional Paper 11, Dept of Geography and Environmental Studies, University of the Witwatersrand.

Smith, D. M. (1975) *Patterns in Human Geography: an introduction to numerical methods*. David & Charles, Newton Abbot.

Smith, D. M. (1977) *Human Geography: a welfare approach*. Edward Arnold, London.

Smith, D. M. (1979) *Where the Grass is Greener: living in an unequal world*. Penguin, Harmondsworth.

Smith, D. M. (ed.) (1982) *Living Under Apartheid: aspects of urbanization and social change in South Africa*. London Research Series in Geography, 2. Allen & Unwin, London.

Smith, D. M. (1984) Recollections of a random variable. In M. Billinge, D. Gregory and R. Martin (eds), *Recollection of a Revolution: geography as spatial science*. Macmillan, London.

Smith, D. M. (1985) *Inequality in Atlanta, Georgia 1960–1980*. Occasional Paper No. 25, Department of Geography and Earth Science, Queen Mary College.

Smith, D. M. (1986) Neoclassical location theory. In W. Lever (ed.), *Industrial Change in the United Kingdom*. Longman, London.

Smith, D. M. and Smith, M. R. (1973) *The United States: how they live and work*. David & Charles, Newton Abbot.

Turner, R. (1972) *The Eye and the Needle: an essay on participatory democracy*. Spro-cas, Johannesburg.

10

Coming in from the Dark: Feminist Research in Geography

Linda McDowell

One does not see those who are in the dark (Bertolt Brecht)

In the past few years feminism has become part of geography. It may be, as yet, a relatively small part of the discipline, and one whose significance varies between subareas and departments; nevertheless feminism is on the agenda in geography in a way that cannot be ignored. Feminist theory has begun to influence how geographers conceptualize their subject-matter, how it is divided into subareas for teaching and research, how definitions and concepts – such as social class categories, work, skills, and the categories woman and man themselves – are operationalized. Feminist practice has started to influence social relations between geographers, how we treat our colleagues and students; how we prepare, undertake and disseminate research results, what and where we publish. Books, journals, articles and papers are now appearing that raise issues hitherto unknown in geography. Women geographers themselves are organizing for change within and outside conventional academic boundaries, and we are beginning to have an impact, to become visible, in ways that have not been true in the past.

For me and many others the past few years have been exciting, with memories of the 'relevance' debates in the 1960s, of challenging conventional geographic practice, but this time for ourselves. Our theoretical interests in feminist theory, in forms of women's oppression in a class-divided and patriarchal society and our own political involvement in a range of issues and campaigns around and within the women's movement, are coinciding in ways which are tremendously stimulating and challenging. For me as a feminist, feminism has an impact not only on what to choose to research and how I undertake particular investigations, but also on my daily life as a woman in a Social Science faculty within a university department. Uniting the different areas of my life and developing a feminist approach both to research and to everyday practice is, in a sense, the project in which I have been engaged lately. For this reason I have written a chapter that raises broad issues about feminism in geography rather than looking in detail at a particular research project.

The project in which feminists in geography are engaged is to change the very nature of the discipline. I want to argue that the philosophical and methodological bases of geography have been, and to a large extent still are, androcentric, concerned with maleness or masculinity, with men's experiences. The bias, which is common to all the social science disciplines to a greater or lesser extent, has meant that, in Brecht's terms, women have not been 'seen' by geographers. But it is not easy to develop new ways of seeing: as John Berger (1972) has shown in his critical analysis of cultural images, there are powerful hegemonic forces at work that ensure we see the world through the eyes of the establishment. Women tend to be perceived as objects, to be exploited or protected by men. They are defined in opposition to men, seen as 'the other', as fundamentally different from the rational behaviour and good sense of (most) men.

In academe the establishment is overwhelmingly male (see McDowell, 1979). Geography is defined and taught by men: what are and are not perceived as acceptable questions for research, and the ways in which we approach these questions, are also defined by men. What we have had, and perhaps still have, in geography is theory that is grounded in, based on and reinforces the perceptions, experiences and beliefs of men, although it must be emphasized that it is theory that purports to speak of human beings, of all people. Even when women have been the object of geographical study, it may be argued that the perspective and mode of analysis have remained masculine, derived as they inevitably are from the dominant culture, replete with a set of assumptions about what femaleness is, what it means to be a woman, or rather what it is assumed it should mean. Du Bois has argued that the result of this androcentric bias 'has rendered women not only unknown, but virtually *unknowable* (her emphasis)' (Du Bois, 1983, p. 106). Thus because, in geography, women have been defined through the eyes of men, there has, until recently, been little questioning in the literature about a set of commonplace assumptions about women's 'place' – as workers, in the home, in the private sphere and as consumers. Women are relegated to particular places, engaging in particular roles that are seen as secondary, both in the economy and also in other spheres, particularly the private place of the home. Because women's activities have been regarded as of secondary importance, the changing experience of women in contemporary society has tended to have been ignored as a valid area for research by geographers working in both developing and developed societies, despite the key significance of women's labour in these different types of societies.

Things are changing, though, in the world at large, in the social sciences and within geography. There are new developments in feminist research and theory that are influencing geographical research. In Western Europe and in the USA, centres for women's studies have been set up in many universities and other higher education establishments, and in a number of disciplines, geography included, women have formed specialist groups and associations, to further their own status and the academic analysis of gender relations and women's subordination. New research areas are beginning to attract funding and the number of postgraduate students working on different aspects of gender is increasing. In recent years, also, there has been a growth in feminist literature published. Feminist publishing houses, presses and bookshops have been set up, for example Virago, the Women's Press, Pandora and others. Generalist publishing houses and bookshops, too, have discovered women as a new market and have reserved a growing number of shelves for the developing feminist literature. However, these developments have thrown up a series of questions about the origin and nature of women's oppression to which there are no ready-made answers, and it is to these that feminist researchers increasingly are giving their attention, within geography and in other disciplines.

In the following sections I shall outline the implications of feminism for geographical research: in the choice of topic, in the development of new concepts and theories, in the methodology adopted and in the practice and personal relations involved between researcher and researched. The examples to illustrate my arguments will be drawn from within geography and from other social science disciplines. Such feminist research is raising questions about women's position in the labour market, their experience of waged and unwaged work, about the patriarchal basis of land-use and planning policies, about women's access to education, health and other social services, about their involvement in community politics and other areas that conventionally have been defined as part of the subject-matter of our discipline. Feminist geographers have published in all these areas; for example, in special issues of journals such as *Built Environment* in 1984 and *Antipode* in 1984, in the collective book *Geography and Gender*, also published in 1984. Feminism, however, is not a unitary phenomenon and there are many disagreements among feminists about theory and method. I shall attempt to give some indication of the range of approaches as I proceed.

The chapter is divided into several sections, including ones on research methods and on theory development. However, this is not to imply that the two are analytically separable activities. Theory, methods, and practice and policy are, I believe, integral parts of the same process. I have separated them here solely in order to be able to discuss a number of specific implications of feminism for the different aspects of the research process.

What does it mean to do Feminist Research?

What exactly is feminist research? What does it mean for geography? In a way it is easier to say what feminist research is not, rather than what it is. Feminist research is *not* research solely about women, where women are the object of study. In the past decade or so a new literature has developed in urban, economic and social geography in particular, that has women as its focus. (Good summaries of much of this work are to be found in McDowell (1983), Monk and Hanson (1982) and Zelinsky, Monk and Hanson (1982).) In this literature, researchers have documented in detail the discrepancies between women's and men's experiences, describing gender differences in access to a range of goods and services in the urban environment and in women's and men's experiences in the labour market and in the housing market. Despite being an essential starting point, it is perhaps not unfair to criticize this research on the grounds that it has tended to duplicate traditional research in its methods and perspectives. Knowledge about women has been added to existing knowledge about men. And although women's attitudes, behaviour, access to goods and resources or participation in waged labour differ from those of men, the point is that these traits exhibited by women in most cases were evaluated against a male norm. They are presented as different from *men's* attitudes, behaviour, access and work patterns. The methods used in such studies have tended to be the conventional methods of positivist research practice. The researcher was not seen as part of the research process but rather as an objective, or at least uninvolved, observer. The results typically have been disseminated in academic geography journals.

More significantly, it is now clear that this research did not challenge, or even analyse in any systematic way, the social bases of gender relations and the unequal distribution of power between women and men which is the basis of women's oppression. Geographers interested in 'women', and in what were defined as 'women's issues', tended to look only at the *consequences* of women's subordination, not at its origins. It is now argued by feminist geographers that we must shift attention to the social basis of unequal gender relations rather than continue to describe variations in women's roles and behaviour over space. We even need to challenge the very categorization of 'female' and 'male'. It is unsatisfactory to regard the qualities or attributes of femaleness and femininity, and maleness and masculinity, as somehow 'natural' and unchanging. The categories 'women' and 'men' are socially constructed. Over the years women and men internalize and reproduce feminine and masculine moulds in which 'she' is 'the other', evaluated against 'he' the norm. However, this dichotomy itself is historically and spatially specific. There have been significant changes, over time and through space and between cultures, in what are regarded as the particular attributes of femininity and masculinity. Feminist geographers are arguing that these changes must be examined and become part of the subject-matter of our discipline. What is regarded as typical of women in Britain today is different from the assumed attributes of femaleness at other periods or in other contemporary societies.

So, feminist research must recognize and take into account the social construction of gender. Indeed it must be centrally concerned with gender relations, with the inequalities in the structure of social relations between women and men and the nature of male powers, rather than focusing on women *per se*. This should be the focus of the research.

However, I would argue that there are two further prerequisites for defining what is feminist research. The first is that women's experiences, ideas and needs become accepted as valid in their own right, that the view of society through the eyes of the oppressed starts to have as great a validity as that of the oppressors: and not only in society at large but also within the academy. These experiences, views and ideas, of course, will not be uniform. Feminism has developed beyond the phase in which the communality of women's experience was emphasized at the expense of the variety. It is now recognized that women's experiences vary depending on their race, class, age, sexual preference and cultural identification just as those of men do. The second attribute that distinguishes feminist research is that it is research *for* women. It should be useful, instrumental research, research that aims to make a contribution to improving women's lives in one way or another, research that contributes to liberation. This is not to argue that all research must have immediately practical results. Ideas as well as actions are a potent force in altering repressive social structures. The power of the printed word and logical argument may have as much impact in the long term as political protest and more practical forms of organization for social change. However, feminist geographers are raising questions about where to publish, how to write in ways which are accessible to a range of audiences, questions about where and how to teach and about how to develop links between the academic world and women working in other areas, such as with community groups, in housing and health cooperatives, with minority group women, with the trade unions and with other organizations.

The implications of these questions, however, tend to be seen as threatening by many academics. Feminists are demanding a new way of doing things, a different approach to research and, perhaps above all, a share in the power that currently, in society as a whole and within education in particular, is held mainly by men. But this will not be easy to achieve. Research which admits to working for change, and thus to being 'political', is often regarded as 'biased', unscholarly, unacademic, evaluated as it commonly is against accepted canons that perpetuate the myths of value-free and objective scientific research. Further, work that acknowledges emotions, feelings, personal involvement, empathy and intuition may also be seen as unsound, even as journalistic or as, that ultimate academic insult, 'popular'. Feminists, in common with other researchers working from committed, radical or unpopular perspectives, have to challenge these misconceptions. But feminists teaching and researching within geography departments also have to face a further challenge that their male colleagues do not: that of being a woman in a male-oriented profession and discipline. Feminists are not usually in positions of power and influence within geography, and in some departments feminist research is not highly regarded. Individual researchers may be isolated, often working alone in a department and, more often than not, in a junior capacity. Articles about gender issues are still uncommon in the mainstream journals, and feminist research tends to fall into the cracks between the main divisions in the discipline. Although this is one of the main strengths of a feminist analysis, it makes it more difficult to gather support for teaching a feminist course. In the face of small numbers and male opposition, one of the key questions currently facing feminists in academia is how to influence the generation and distribution of knowledge, how to develop strategies to gain power. One way is through the development and dissemination of feminist research.

Choosing the Topic

The aim here, and in the succeeding sections, is not to offer a blueprint of how to go about feminist research, nor to report on existing work that measures up to what I have set up as the crucial requirements of feminism, but rather to argue for the importance of variety in approach and method, and for research that deals with what appears to be the commonplace, with everyday experience, as well as with the grander social structures and the links between the two. Existing systems of thought have tended to treat women's everyday experiences and understanding of social reality as peripheral or unimportant. Further they seldom question the existence of the sets of power relationships that result in women's confinement to these very areas that are seen as peripheral. Hence in geography, power relations within the 'private' sphere of the home are seldom seen as part of the subject, as an area appropriate for research investigation. Women's responsibility for domestic labour, for example, does not often enter into explanations of the changing spatial distribution of waged employment; nor does women's reluctance to travel about the city in the evening and at night enter into planning decisions about the location of employment or public sector facilities. Because it is too often assumed that women should be in the home, research conclusions and the planning decisions based on them tend to reinforce and strengthen conventional attitudes about what it means to be female today. Feminist research is centrally concerned with challenging these attitudes, and with demonstrating the centrality of an analysis of gender relations to an understanding of the structure of contemporary societies.

The construction of femininity and masculinity and women's subordination occur in many areas of personal life – in the family, in marriage, in work, in the education system, and the ways in which these processes occur and vary over time and between places can and should become accepted areas for geographic research. For all women do not share the same experiences – women in different class positions and from different ethnic backgrounds experience patriarchal domination in different ways. But the material forms of oppression also differ between places. Consequently, we need to know not only *how* but also *where* women's oppression occurs. One of the great steps forward that has been taken in recent feminist work is an acceptance of this variety, and it is a step in which geographers, among others, have been influential. During the past two decades or so, the ways in which the basic institutions and organization of particular forms of society oppress women have been delineated by feminist writers from different backgrounds. In 1963 Betty Frieden, in the *Feminine Mystique*, wrote about 'the problem that has no name' – individual women's experience of isolation and powerlessness. Since that time feminists have shown how the organization of contemporary society is based on the exploitation of women's domestic labour, which is done 'for love' in privacy, how contemporary cities are planned and laid out on the assumption that this domestic labour is undertaken by countless women in private at home, how women's skills are undervalued and underpaid in the labour market, how their positions in the labour market are connected to supposed attributes of femininity such as docility, dexterity, and caring, as well as to assumptions about their economic dependence on a male breadwinner and the oppressive nature of the patriarchal family. Feminists have shown how what many individual women regard as their own personal problems are the common experience of women today. 'Personal' issues of domestic violence, women's sexuality, the experience of childbirth and mothering have been put on the political agenda through the growth of the women's movement and other forms of feminist politics. In all these ways, through research, writing and political action, our knowledge of the structure of women's subordinate position, in Britain and elsewhere, has been altered over the past 20 years.

The key task now for feminists working in the social sciences is to deepen our knowledge of the *variety* of women's experience. There is a need to move beyond generalizations about women's oppression to understand its specificity at particular times in different places. One of the ways to do this is through empirical research. In a discussion of feminist research methods, Stanley and Wise (1983) recently suggested the types of questions that feminist social scientists should now be asking themselves. They included the following list: Are the particular experiences under consideration oppressive for all women? In all their aspects or only some? At all times or only intermittently? Does the concrete experience of oppression vary? If so, in what ways? If it varies why? There are thus many complexities and ambiguities to be explored. The experiences of women who are black, for example, clearly are different from those who are not. Women from different class backgrounds have different life chances. Women born or living in the north of Britain do not necessarily experience the same structures of oppression as those in the south. Geographers with their intrinsic interest in differentiation and their own varied experience are well placed to contribute to this new research agenda within feminist social science. Some feminists have argued that one of the ways to start this agenda is by research on women's own experiences, with the observed empirical variations in women's and men's opportunities and behaviour, and with women's own views on what it means to be a woman in a particular society. This is Stanley and Wise's (1983, p. 53) conclusion: 'feminism argues that systems and social structures, whether concerned with the economy, the family or the oppression of women more generally, can best be experienced and understood through an exploration of relationships and experience within everyday life.' However, there is a danger with such a sole focus on the individual, and other feminists would not agree with this argument.

As suggested earlier, feminist scholars are not interested solely in women's experiences and behaviour, but in gender relations – by which I mean the ideology, institutions, structures and practices that create and reproduce unequal material conditions and oppressive power relationships between women and men. By focusing exclusively on women's experiences there is the danger, already recognized in other studies of 'minorities', of *blaming the victim* for their own oppression and of searching for solutions in women's behaviour itself rather than focusing on and attacking institutionalized sexism.

There is, of course, a parallel here with the Marxist critique of behavioural and Weberian geography. Geographers working within a Marxist perspective have been influential in refocusing analysis in many areas of the discipline, showing how spatial differentiation is a key element in the structure of capitalist societies. However, this work may be criticized both for its over-emphasis, at least in certain versions, on structural factors, denying the validity of individual experience, and also for its neglect of the specific nature of women's oppression in class societies. As Carol Smart (1984, p. 151), a feminist lawyer, aptly put it 'the overdetermined concept of *man* [her emphasis] . . . in Marxism . . . has tended to absolve social actors of the responsibility, or even the consequences, of their actions'. In recent geographical work from a critical perspective, both Marxist and feminist, a new focus is emerging. This is the attempt to develop a simultaneous focus on institutions and agents, in, for example, work based on Giddens' idea of structuration (see for example Gregory, 1984; Storper, 1985) and Massey's and other arguments about the significance of local social processes and the uniqueness of localities (see Massey, 1985; Gregory and Urry, 1985). In feminist analysis the same aim, to put together the patriarchal structure of the key institutions of society and women's own experiences of oppression by and struggle against these forces, is evident. For feminist geographers the specific ways in which these structural forces and national changes in the economy, the nature of the state and its interventions in such areas as the family and welfare provision, in the ideology of the family and women's position interconnect, are influenced by and influence, the particular structure of gender relations in local areas should be the focus of research. At different times in different places, class, gender and racial differences are combined and re-created in particular ways to reproduce women's subordination. This may be exemplified by research on the Lancaster region and its changing employment structure by Linda Murgatroyd, and on spatial variations in women's paid work and unemployment by Sylvia Walby (Murgatroyd, *et al.*, 1986).

It is increasingly recognized by economic geographers that changes in the spatial division of labour in Britain cannot be understood without taking into account changing gender divisions. Ideas from feminist theory about the ways in which patriarchical power relations are used and manipulated by employers, and also by labour organizations, are providing a fresh input to more conventional geographical explanations of the restructuring of British industry. Other geographers are building on these ideas and, by uncovering the links between women's position in the home and in the labour market, are challenging the current divisions within geography between the social and the economic (see Lewis, 1984; McDowell and Massey, 1984).

One of the most interesting recent attempts by a geographer to use feminist ideas about how the patriarchical structure of contemporary US society structures female labour reserves is a study by Kristin Nelson (1986). Her aim was to explain the suburbanization of office employment in the San Francisco–Oakland Metropolitan area in California. This movement was highly specific, and factors such as land availability and low rental levels, access to highways, pro-business lobbies, even labour availability, were inadequate to explain the choice of a particular part of the region. She found that the relocating offices were looking for a very specific type of woman worker – white, middle-aged, not achievement-oriented and preferably with company ties through their husbands: 'biographical ties with entrepreneurial elements', as one interviewed manager put it (Nelson, 1986, p. 157). Thus Nelson's study combined ideas from feminism about the construction of particular types of female labour with a geographical analysis of their locational specificity to explain changing employment patterns in the metropolitan area.

Doing the Research

As well as raising questions about what topics to research, feminism is influencing geographical methods. Questions about how to do research, whether there is a particular method that is feminist, and whether this is even an appropriate question to ask, are being raised by feminist geographers.

There has been a long debate within the social sciences about methodology, showing how particular research aims and techniques embody a view of society and reflect the social conditions of the production of knowledge. For example, within industrial geography there has been a fierce debate about the relationships between theory, method and policy conclusions (see for example Massey and Meegan, 1985). Within feminism there has been a similar debate about theory and method (see Oakley, 1981; Roberts, 1981; Bowles and Duelli-Klein, 1983; Stanley and Wise, 1983). One element in this debate has been the rejection of the traditional values of the positivist, 'scientific' approach to research. In common with other critical perspectives, feminism has been critical of 'hard' empirical research based on taken-for-granted concepts and statistical analysis of representative samples. Stanley and Wise's (1983, p. 56) pithy summary of this rejection is hard to improve on: 'The western industrial scientific approach values the orderly, the rational, quantifiable, predictable, abstract and theoretical: feminism spat in its eye.' The type of approach that is being rejected here is that which tends to be taught in many undergraduate courses on geographical methods and research techniques. The research design is set up to establish regularities or common patterns in a representative sample of objects. Formal questionnaires and other survey techniques are the usual methods of data collection, and statistical analysis is commonly employed. The researcher is recommended to be as objective as possible and to remain uninvolved with her or his subjects.

Certain feminists, among them Reinharz (1983) in the USA and Stanley and Wise (1983) in the UK, not only reject the quantitative, 'scientific' approach to research, but argue that it is specifically a patriarchal model as it denies the significance of women's experience of oppression, classifies their concerns as private rather than shared, and embodies the values of traditional views of women's and men's expected positions in society. They have argued that feminist research should recognize and challenge the everyday experiences of women. In order to excavate women's experiences, feminist methods should value subjectivity, personal involvement, the qualitative and unquantifiable, complexity and uniqueness and an awareness of the context within which the specific area under investigation takes place. This has led some researchers towards a range of alternative approaches, especially from certain areas of psychology and sociology. Experiential analysis in which the research procedure is not a linear process but is grounded in the researcher's own experiences and perceptions, and which is as concerned with the unique and particular as establishing empirical regularities, has been adopted as one model. Recent work by geographers (see Allen, 1983; Sayer, 1984; and Sayer and Morgan, 1985) based on the ideas of realism, have something in common with this feminist critique. They have argued that 'extensive' research methods, by which they mean the search for regularities among representative samples, using formal techniques such as questionnaire surveys and statistical analysis, are unsatisfactory ways of revealing causal processes, and that 'intensive' methods such as case studies, interactive interviews, ethnography and qualitative types of analysis may be more appropriate in attempts to produce causal explanations.

These ideas and arguments about personal involvement, intersubjectivity and the practical usefulness of research have not, however, been completely absent from the geographic literature. Among more 'progressive' geographers it has been usual for many years to state one's 'bias' in the introduction to one's research and to acknowledge the truism that the questions asked determine the answers received. Politically relevant research, too, has an honourable tradition in geography. Developing from the geographic expeditions led by Bungé in Chicago in the late 1960s, there has been a strand of action research that has responded to social inequalities, though the focus has been on class or racial inequalities rather than gender differences. Other workers have acknowledged the validity of subjective data. Researchers in the behavioural and humanistic traditions – for example, Ley and Samuels (1978) and Tuan (1977) – have emphasized the need to take into account the feelings and perceptions of the researched subjects and, less commonly, of the researcher.

However, feminist geographers looking for examples of research that involves *women* as part and parcel of the research process, rather than as the 'objects' of analysis, have so far had to look mainly to other social science disciplines for ideas. A classic example of feminist research that recognized the importance of a personal relationship and involvement between the researcher and the researched is the work of Ann Oakley on attitudes towards, and the experience of, childbirth (Oakley, 1979,

1980). She argues that as a committed feminist as well as a researcher she could not fail to become involved with the pregnant women she interviewed. She always attempted to answer her respondents' questions in a way that made them part of the research process. In the passage below she illustrates the difference between her approach and that recommended in classic texts in interviewing techniques (Oakley, 1981, p. 48):

> The dilemma of a feminist interviewer interviewing women could be summarised by considering the practical application of some of the strategies recommended in the textbooks for meeting interviewee's questions. For example, these advise that such questions as 'Which hole does the baby come out of?' 'Does an epidural ever paralyse women?' and 'Why is it dangerous to leave a small baby alone in the house? should be met with such responses from the interviewer as 'I guess I haven't thought enough about it to give a good answer now', or 'a head-shaking gesture which suggests "that's a hard one" ' (Goode and Hatt, 1952). Also recommended is laughing off the request with the remark that 'my job at the moment is to get opinions, not to have them' (Selltiz *et al.*, 1965).

Although less explicit about the personal involvement with the women whom she interviewed about child care, Jackie Tivers' (1985) study, of the spatial constraints on the choices of women with small children, is a good example of similar feminist research in geography.

Great care needs to be taken, however, to ensure that a particular methodology is not accepted as the only appropriate way to engage in feminist research. An intersubjective approach, or even action-based research, is not necessarily appropriate in every situation. In some cases the circumstances in the lives of those involved in a research project will make it impossible, or inappropriate, for them to work closely together. A good example is contained in the work of Carol Smart. As a feminist committed to social change, she carried out a research project into the law and marriage to reveal the patriarchal basis of many decisions made in, for example, custody and divorce cases (Smart, 1984). Part of her study involved interviewing solicitors. In her own words, she describes the dilemma presented to her as a woman interviewing men who seldom, if ever, shared her political beliefs.

> The scope for employing feminist practice when interviewing lawyers and magistrates is more limited. I could open doors for myself or decline assistance with my coat but such practices are hardly revolutionary. In fact in my experience interviewing the legal profession and the magistracy gives very few opportunities for feminist practice to emerge. One important reason for this was the presumption in almost all the interviews that the interviewer and interviewee shared the same values and probably politics. This meant that in order to express a dissenting view the interviewer not only had to find an opportunity but would have, in the

process, shattered the inferential structure within which the interview was carried out. In other words the interview would have become impossible.

This dilemma is obviously not peculiar to this research and many researchers must have had to endure listening to sexist, racist and other views without responding. However a lack of response based on the desire to finish an interview can become complicity. In other words silence is consent and the views of the interviewee may have been reinforced by the experience of the interview in which the interviewer necessarily shows an interest in his or her views and does not express shock or outrage. I wish to argue that this problem is particularly acute where the interviewer is a woman and the interviewee a man. Dale Spender (1980), in her book on language, has argued that in conversations between men and women, women frequently operate as facilitators to male speech. That is to say that women tend not to interrupt but rather to encourage and help the flow of men's talk. Moreover women are expected to do this so that if they decline to do so or if they interrupt men in the way in which men usually interrupt women they are defined as aggressive and pushy. On this basis I wish to argue that the job of interviewing is intrinsically *feminine* because the interviewer's job is to facilitate speech and not to interrupt it. Hence when the interviewer actually is a woman and the interviewee a man the interview situation becomes especially loaded. It is extremely difficult for the interviewer to break the mould because not only does she jeopardise the interview but she has to challenge the conventions of 'polite' conversation. The feminist interviewer can therefore experience the interview as doubly oppressive. Firstly she is unable to express alternative views and secondly she reconfirms the typical model of male/female verbal exchange. This can be an extremely frustrating experience. (Smart, 1984, pp. 155–6).

Indeed, it is often so frustrating that many women researchers have begun to question whether the results from interviewing men who persist in refusing to take women researchers seriously actually justifies the effort required. Feminist geographers (including myself) have experienced just such problems when involved in research on a number of topics, including housing and employment policies, studies of new town planning and of retail policy and planning. However, in certain circumstances femininity can be used to advantage as a weapon to disarm these particular types of respondents. It is difficult obviously to know whether respondents would have answered differently if the interviewer had been a man. But in my own work interviewing union officials, housing managers, employers and so on it seemed likely that, because I was perceived as unthreatening or not 'official', confidential documents were often made accessible, or difficult issues broached relatively freely. A colleague working on the politics of environmental issues has had similar experiences.

It is important to recognize, however, that certain assumptions that seem to inform an 'alternative' feminist method, as argued for by feminists such as Reinharz (1983) and Stanley and Wise (1983), do not always hold. In many dicussions it seems to be taken for granted that feminist researchers mainly, or even solely, interview women, and that the power relationships involved in feminist research are basically in favour of the researcher. But this is not inevitably so. To uncover institutionalized sexism in modern society also involves researching the powerful. The power relationships in such cases are often stacked against the researcher and attempts to be open, vulnerable, to reveal feelings about the process of research will not necessarily be productive and may even, in some cases, positively hinder the conduct of the research. Feminists need to be flexible, to adapt their methods to the needs of each individual research situation and not become trapped in a set or rules or ideal method. As Smart (1984, p. 158) concluded from her research: 'Ultimately I suspect that the idea that there is an ideal type of feminist research is spurious and that although we may produce principles and ethics for doing research, we may have to recognise that there are as many types of feminist research as there are feminisms.' In some research situations, quantitative research methods, large-scale questionnaire surveys or the interviewing of representative samples may be appropriate techniques. It is important not to reject such 'hard' methods as inevitably empiricist or patriarchal. I believe that there is, in fact, no inevitable bias in traditional methods; it is rather the set of assumptions behind them that needs careful thought. Large-scale research based on the unthinking acceptance of, for example, official statistics, on conventional definitions of what is or is not 'work', of skill definitions, of who is head of a household, of how women are allocated to social class categories (see chapter 8 in *Geography and Gender* – Women and Geography Study Group, 1984) will disguise the structure of women's oppression and obscure the nature of oppressive social relations between men and women. But this is not necessarily an *inherent* bias in methods, rather it reflects a lack of clear thinking about the concepts that tend to be embodied in their use. Reconceptualization is one of the most important aims of feminism. It is a key element in the development of new theories about women's oppression and its construction in space.

Developing Theory

One of the key aims of feminist research is to develop, replace or substantiate sets of ideas about how and why women are oppressed: in grand terms, theory development. For feminist geographers the question of spatial variations in the form of oppression is also significant. Within feminism itself there is no one overarching theory, but rather sets of diverse types of explanation. The conventional split has been one between radical feminists and socialist feminists (see Bowlby, Foord and Mackenzie's short summary in *Area*, 1980) who disagree about the origins of women's oppression and the extent to which patriarchal relations are related to or are functional for a particular mode of production or are a completely separate set of relations. There is now less difference between these approaches than formerly, as socialist-feminists increasingly have argued that moral, social, familial, sexual and cultural issues, all stressed as important by radical feminists, must be part of socialism, and that unequal social relations between men and women are found at a number of levels: the biological, the unconscious and the ideological as well as the economic. But there is still disagreement between them about the relationship between wider social change and women's liberation and the strategies for achieving this.

Within feminist theory in general, there remains a clear emphasis on, and understanding that, theory must be relevant to and derived from women's experiences. Women's own responses to their oppression, their attitudes and beliefs are an integral part of theory development. However, and despite my earlier emphasis on the variety within women's experience, it is important to go beyond the documentation of women's hidden history and to develop theoretical concepts to explain the reasons for particular forms of oppression. As Sheila Rowbotham (1979) has argued, there comes a time when it is important to stop 'telling it like a story', otherwise we are continually refighting the same old battles, documenting the same pattern of inequalities. She has argued that theory is a key weapon in women's liberation, as it enables critics to be presented with a worked-out, coherent set of alternative arguments. However, she emphasizes that theory is not a fixed body of truth with universal applicability but rather, in an analogy particularly appropriate to geographers, a series of 'maps' that provide paths and footholds for challenging women's oppression.

Within the feminist geographical literature there is now a need to take the step forward into the realm of theory. We need to go beyond documenting spatial patterns of inequality between women and men, and to try and develop concepts that explain why these inequalities take the form they do. As I have already argued, the initial geographical work influenced by feminism was primarily descriptive and relied on the concept of gender roles to explain differences between women's and men's behaviour. A second strand of research developed that was based in the tradition of socialist-feminism and its development of Marxist theory. In this the concepts of production and reproduction were broadened to take account of the structures of male domination and female subordination that were missing from the Marxist concept of production. The ideas of patriarchal gender relations within the labour process and the links between the gender division in the home, women's domestic constraints and their labour market participation rates were included in work on women's subordination. Feminist geographers have used these ideas in combination with ideas from geographers about the spatial division of labour, rounds of accumulation and local specificity to argue for analyses of geographical variations in patriarchal gender relations. Foord, McDowell and Bowlby (1986), for example, have argued for research that has as its aim the understanding of how spatially specific gender identities are constructed in the home, workplace and community to produce local differences between places. In their paper they argue that only by focusing on the ways in which male power over women is constructed and reinforced in all areas of life will we be able to understand spatial variations. In a recent paper on feminist theory in geography, Foord and Gregson (1986) have suggested that a re-examination of the concept of patriarchy might be a way forward in developing a theoretical framework for a feminist geography. They suggest that although patriarchy has been a problematic term in the feminist literature, a realist approach to its conceptualization, isolating the necessary relations or basic characteristics of women's domination by men, might be helpful.

These developments within feminist geography are part of the more general development within social, human and economic geography as a whole towards types of theoretically satisfying empirical research that can reveal the ways in which national and local changes interact to create particular geographical patterns. Theory development and the critical use of methods, are, of course, inseparable, and these arguments are part and parcel of the earlier discussion under the heading 'doing research' about investigating the institutional structures of society as well as the 'victims' of sexism. Theoretical developments do not occur in isolation, but are part of the whole process of doing research.

Working Together for Change

In this final section I want to look at some of the implications for research practice of adopting an avowedly feminist view of the world. For undertaking feminist research is not only challenging and exciting but also very difficult. It involves rethinking your perspective on the world, being open and honest about feelings and fears, and integrating your own life into the research process, which at times can leave you feeling very vulnerable. It also means challenging existing ways of seeing the world and long-established codes of research practice and conduct: challenging in effect the structures of male power in the academy and in research institutions. This is not easy for feminist scholars who are often in junior positions, dependent on the support and patronage of male superiors. How many research projects finally see the light of day as books published under the name of the, usually male, head of department or leader of the research team with assistance from a, usually female, research assistant, acknowledged in the preface, along with a similar gesture to his wife for domestic support and his secretary for typing?

Within geography in particular, but also within other social science disciplines, feminism is a challenge to the very construction of knowledge and the way in which it is subdivided for teaching and research purposes. Feminists stress that the conventional separations between the public and the private, between waged work and work at home, between employment and domestic privacy, and so between urban and economic geography, are false separations. They operate as ideological devices that hide the interconnections between different parts of daily life, conceal women's domestic work, and the contribution this makes to the economy, negate women's experiences and deny their relevance to the discipline of geography. One aim of feminist research within the discipline is to alter the conventional understanding of these divisions.

One of the most exciting parts of feminist research is the challenge that it presents to develop new ways of working: to find ways of working together with other women – women in the research profession and women in the community. The challenge to bridge the gap between academia and 'real life' is enormously stimulating, as is working on research that has as its ultimate aim, social change. Within the profession, too, it is extremely rewarding to be able to challenge existing ways of seeing, to develop critical dialogues with feminists working in other areas and in other disciplines in efforts to bridge the gaps and to discover similarities. Being a feminist within geography at present has brought me some of the greatest rewards and most difficult moments in my academic career so far. The challenge and the rewards of working at a frontier that affects how I conduct my own everyday life are heady. It is difficult not to be too ambitious, to want changes to occur overnight. But we must be careful not to expect too much. I want to end by echoing some points made by Renate Duelli-Klein in a paper on feminist methodology published in 1983. She has argued that, first, we must take care not to create a supermethodology, by which she means piling on top of one another different approaches from a variety of disciplines. We must also be careful to write in plain, accessible language and avoid excesses of esoteric feminist jargon – always a danger when a new approach is attempting to establish its academic credibility.

Secondly, she argues that we must be patient. Working together, instead of competitively, is not easy. We need to be strong enough to accept failures as a constructive learning experience. We must not, although it is very difficult, expect too much of each other: we must never underestimate the barriers between women approaching problems from very different perspectives.

Thirdly, we should be very clear that it is going to be hard to shed the years of 'indoctrination' about what is 'good' research, how to approach geographical research, and accepted philosophical and methodological points of view. Experimenting with new approaches, with innovative methods, is risky.

Fourthly, as feminists we have to make ourselves visible. Women with academic jobs are in an extremely privileged position. At a time of financial cuts and threats to feminists, and other radical scholars, both within and outside academia, we need to develop networks of solidarity and to encourage other women to join us. There is no doubt that feminist scholars will continue to be charged with bias, advocacy, subjectivity – of being 'non-academic' – but this must be expected. Feminism poses an enormous threat to conventional ways of seeing and doing, and the powerful seldom give up their privileges without a struggle. Indeed, if feminist research is *not* seen as a challenge within geography, then we are on the wrong track with the wrong set of maps.

References

Allen, J. (1983) Property relations and landlordism: a realist approach, *Society and Space*, 1, 191–204.

Antipode (1984) Special issue on *Women and the Environment*, vol. 16, no. 3.

Berger, J. (1972) *Ways of Seeing*. Penguin, Harmondsworth.

Bowlby, S., Foord, J. and Mackenzie, S. (1980) Feminism and geography, *Area*, 14, 19–25.

Bowles, G. and Duelli-Klein, R. (1983) *Theories of Women's Studies*. Routledge & Kegan Paul, London.

Built Environment (1984) Special issue on *Women and the Environment*, vol. 10, no. 1.

Du Bois, B. (1983) Passionate scholarship: notes on values, knowing and method in feminist social science. In Bowles and Duelli-Klein (1983), pp. 105–16.

Duelli-Klein, R. (1983) How to do what we want to do: thoughts about feminist methodology. In Bowles and Duelli-Klein (1983), pp. 88–104.

Foord, J. and Gregson, N. (1986) Patriarchy: towards a reconceptualization, *Antipode*, 8, 186–211.

Foord, J., McDowell, L. and Bowlby, S. (1986) For 'love' not money: gender relations in local areas. Discussion paper 76, Centre for Urban, Regional and Development Studies, University of Newcastle.

Frieden, B. (1963) *The Feminine Mystique*. Victor Gollancz, London.

Goode, W. J. and Hatt, P. K. (1952) *Methods and Social Research*. McGraw-Hill, New York.

Gregory, D. (1984) Space, time and politics in social theory: an interview with Anthony Giddens, *Society and Space*, 2, 123–32.

Gregory, D. and Urry, J. (eds) (1985) *Social Relations and Spatial Structures*. Macmillan, London.

Ley, D. and Samuels, M. S. (eds) (1978) *Humanistic Geography*. Croom Helm, London.

McDowell, L. (1979) Women in British geography, *Area*, 11, 151–4.

McDowell, L. (1983) Towards an understanding of the gender division of urban space, *Society and Space*, 1, 59–72.

McDowell, L. and Massey, D. (1984) A woman's place. In D. Massey and J. Allen (eds), *Geography Matters!* Cambridge University Press, Cambridge, pp. 128–47.

Massey, D. (1985) *Spatial Divisions of Labour*. Macmillan, London.

Massey, D. and Meegan, R. (1985) *Politics and Method*. Methuen, London.

Monk, J. and Hanson, S. (1982) On not excluding half and the human in human geography, *Professional Geographer*, 34, 11–23.

Murgatroyd, L., Savage, M., Shapiro, D., Urry, J., Walby, S., Warde, A. with Mark-Lawson, J. (1985) *Localities, Class and Gender*. Pion, London.

Nelson, K. (1986) Labour demand, labour supply and the suburbanisation of low-wage office work. In A. Scott and M. Storper (eds), *Production, Work and Territory*. Allen and Unwin, London.

Oakley, A. (1979) *Becoming a Mother*. Martin Robertson, London.

Oakley, A. (1980) *Women Confined: towards a sociology of childbirth*. Martin Robertson, London.

Oakley, A. (1981) Interviewing women: a contradiction in terms. In H. Roberts (ed.), *Doing Feminist Research*. Routledge & Kegan Paul, London.

Reinharz, S. (1983) Experiential analysis: a contribution to feminist research. In Bowles and Duelli Klein (1983), pp. 162–91.

Roberts, W. (1981) *Doing Feminist Research*. Routledge & Kegan Paul, London.

Rowbotham, S. (1979) The women's movement and organizing for socialism. In S. Rowbotham, L. Segal, and H. Wainwright (eds), *Beyond the Fragments*. Newcastle Socialist Centre and Islington Community Press, London, pp. 9–87.

Sayer, A. (1984) *Method in Social Science*. Hutchinson, London.

Sayer, A. and Morgan, K. (1985) A modern industry in a declining region: links between method, theory and policy. In Massey and Meegan (1985), pp. 144–68.

Selltiz, C., Jahoda, M., Deutsch, M. and Cook, S. W. (1965) *Research Methods in Social Relations*. Methuen, London.

Smart, C. (1984) *The Ties that Bind*. Routledge & Kegan Paul, London.

Spender, D. (1980) *Man Made Language*. Routledge & Kegan Paul, London.

Stanley, L. and Wise, A. (1983) *Breaking Out*. Routledge & Kegan Paul, London.

Storper, M. (1985) The spatial and temporal constitution of social action: a critical reading of Giddens. *Society and Space*, 3, 407–24.

Tivers, J. (1985) *Women Attached*. Croom Helm, London.

Tuan, J. F. (1977) *Space and Place*. Edward Arnold, London.

Women and Geography Study Group (1984) *Geography and Gender*. Hutchinson, London.

Zelinksy, W., Monk, J. and Hanson, S. (1982) Women and geography: a review and prospectus, *Progress in Human Geography*, 6, 317–66.

11

Writing Geographically

R. J. Johnston

> Unpublished research isn't research . . .
> Publish or perish . . .

These clichés are widely used in academic circles, and encapsulate two of the major features of academic writing. They are positive statements, indicating how academic society operates. Without an appreciation of the norms that they express it is difficult to appreciate in full the nature of any academic writing.

The first of the statements identifies a major role of the staff members of universities, polytechnics and colleges. They are expected – in many cases required[1] – to undertake research, not simply as a way of indulging themselves and filling in their time, but to contribute to the advancement of knowledge. They are, in the widest sense of that term, scientists, working within communities that share five values, according to Mulkay (1975, p. 510):

1 *originality* – science is concerned to advance knowledge through original research (i.e. work that is not simply a full replication of previous research, except in certain conditions that fall under the fifth value);
2 *disinterestedness* – science is concerned to advance knowledge and is pursued by scientists for that reason alone, with personal rewards having no influence on the conduct of research;
3 *universalism* – scientific judgements are based on criteria which are applied impartially to the research and not at all to the researchers;
4 *communality* – all information is shared, and its provenance recognized;[2]
5 *organized scepticism* – all research results are subjected to constructive criticism, in order to evaluate their contributions to the advancement of knowledge.

Research findings must be reported, therefore, in order that they can be evaluated and added to the store of knowledge; researchers who do not report their findings are failing to contribute to scientific goals.

The need to report must be met by a reporting mechanism. Research results can be transmitted by word of mouth, in formal and informal situations; academic conferences provide major arenas for such communication among peers, as do smaller seminars, colloquia and other gatherings; teaching contexts allow researchers to report their findings to students, potential researchers and others. But such transmission is ephemeral, and the message is potentially distorted by the selective memories of the audience (including their note-taking) and the mode of presentation. It is also very partial, since it is extremely unlikely that all those who would like to hear the report can be present; repetition at different times and places is possible but inefficient, and still faces the ephemerality problem. And so publication, the permanent recording of the results, is the acknowledged way of contributing, literally, to the store of knowledge. Research that isn't deposited in that store, therefore, is widely regarded as unpublished research.[3]

Before turning to the nature of the store, and how material can be deposited in it, it is necessary to take account of the second statement with which I opened this essay. The scientific values set out above suggested an operation organized around very high ideals. As I expressed it elsewhere (Johnston, 1983a, p. 18), it appears that: 'academic work is carried out in a neutral fashion; there is a complete lack of partiality, self-seeking, secrecy and intellectual prejudice. The existence of objective criteria for assessment is assumed, as are high levels of ability and humility on the part of members of the academic community'. But academic communities rarely, if ever, achieve those high ideals, for they are peopled by individuals who, whatever their commitment to science, are pursuing careers: their quality of life, their status, and their power are closely linked to their success as scientists (see Dixon, 1976). This may not present a problem if both universal criteria of quality are recognized and applied, and all people of similar quality receive similar rewards. But neither is the case. Certainly the second is not, for successful scientists compete for a relatively small number of 'top jobs'. One must not only be good, therefore, but must prove that one is better. (Not all academics necessarily aspire to the 'top jobs'. Using the analogy of 'optimizing' and 'satisficing' behaviour – see Pred, 1967, for example – many are satisfied with a certain level of achievement below the top level.)

How, then, does one prove this quality? As already indicated, a major index of completed research is the publication of its findings; thus the nature of a scientist's published work is used to indicate the quality of work done. And, in a general sense, the more that is published, the greater the scientific contribution. (This creates a major problem for those evaluating scientists, since quantity is not necessarily to be equated with quality. One scientist may publish relatively little, for example, yet contribute more to the development of a field of study than another who publishes a great deal. A major contribution to the history of geography has been made by Clarence Glacken, for example, but he produced little (Glacken, 1983) apart from his magisterial (1967) *Traces on the Rhodian Shore.*) An academic's publication record, then, is used as the major index of the research record – within the context of the publishing norms of that individual's field of study, as set out below. It is used to assess both the individual's claims to occupy the various levels of the academic job hierarchy – hence 'publish or perish' – and applications for support to undertake further research.

Writing, then, is a fundamental characteristic of academic life: it provides a record of completed research and a portfolio of material that can be used to assess an individual as an academic. Within academia as a whole, the conventions relating to writing vary somewhat, but in terms of applying the guidelines set out above geography is clearly middle-of-the-road, though not without its pecularities. Illustrating the nature of that road is the purpose of the remainder of this essay.

Research in Geography: the Norm

There is a stereotype view of the nature of research in geography – frequently equated with *the* scientific method (as in Abler, Adams and Gould, 1971) – which presents it as a clear sequence of stages. A research area is identified, and a general *model* of the subject-matter is constructed, comprising a simplified representation of some aspect of the complex 'real world' – the pattern of land-use in a rural area, perhaps, or the changing shape of a river cross-section as one moves from source to sea. The purpose of that model is to guide empirical investigations, to structure questions that can be answered in an experimental or field situation. Such questions are usually termed *hypotheses*, which are hunches or controlled speculations, statements of what the researcher expects to find – that the intensity of land-use decreases with increasing distance from a market, for example, and that the cross-section becomes flatter and broader with increasing distance from the source. A piece of empirical research is then devised to *test* the hypothesis.

A report on a piece of research therefore should involve a discussion of the model that guided it, a presentation of the hypothesis and how it was derived, a clear statement of the methodology employed in the test, and an evaluation of the hypothesis in the context of that test. This is a general model of 'the scientific paper' – it is a statement of 'the question I asked, why I asked it, how I addressed it, and the answers I got'. In some disciplines (e.g. psychology: see Spencer and Blades, 1986) the papers are very terse and matter-of-fact; in others (including much geography) they are more discursive, and there is some general discussion of both the model and the implications of the test.

According to this model of the practice of science, each experiment can be equated with a research report, with a paper published in a scientific journal. As a consequence, one could infer that the design and implementation of a research project should include within it a report-writing stage, and that the whole procedure follows a very stereotyped pattern. Thus, for example, I became interested in the possible impact of campaign spending on British election results. A general model was devised which incorporated a series of relationships between a party's votes at a previous election, how much it spent at the next, how much its opponents spent, and how many votes it won. Specific hypotheses were derived, tests formulated and conducted, and reports of the various tests were published (e.g. Johnston, 1985a, b). To a considerable extent this work followed the model set.

A major question is raised, however. I stated in the previous paragraph that 'I became interested in . . .'. Why did I develop that interest and, more importantly, why did I translate that general interest into a piece of research? There are, after all, many other topics that I became interested in without these becoming the focus of any research endeavour. The things we choose to do research on are not random topics (or they shouldn't be!). They are part of a larger endeavour, of a concerted effort to understand a certain topic or body of subject-matter.

As researchers we are constrained, if not blinkered, by the academic environment into which we are socialized. Our education and training become progressively more specialized – in considerable part because the store of knowledge is now so great that we can only contribute to it by specializing in some small portion. Many of the questions that we might pose in our everyday life (why is it wetter on the west coast? why do many people choose to patronize the nearest pub to their home?) have been answered by others. There is no point in us replicating their work, since that would not contribute to scientific advancement. We need to know all that has been already achieved, so that we can focus on as-yet-unanswered questions. So much has been achieved that we can only master a small proportion of it, and so our education and training focuses us on particular subjects.

During that education and training we discover, for our chosen field: what is already known (i.e. the results of previous research); what questions (further hypotheses) this knowledge raises; and how those questions can be answered. We are educationally socialized into what Thomas Kuhn (1962) termed a *research paradigm*. Our own research is then not a random series of events. Rather it is a sequence of speculating and testing (and reporting) guided by a framework. The particular questions that we ask may be the consequence of our observations of the world we live in – of candidates spending money trying to convince us to vote for them, perhaps – but those observations themselves are influenced by the frame of reference provided by our research paradigms, as is our incorporation of them into our models.

Although each scientific paper can be equated with a particular piece of research, therefore, it should not be deduced from this that each paper is independent of all others. In the vast majority of cases exactly the opposite is true, and the research reported in a single paper is but one contribution that the researcher involved is making to that subject area. (An excellent index of this is self-citation, the referencing by researchers to other papers that they have written on the same topic. Such self-citation is characteristic of a majority of scientific papers, and indicates the research is perceived, by the researchers, as a cumulative process.)

Research, then, is cumulative, which suggests the need for forms of writing other than the *research report*. In particular there is a need for the *research synthesis and evaluation*. The findings of the individual pieces of research need to be brought together, in syntheses (sometimes known as *theories*) which integrate the various separate pieces. Without these, each individual researcher must maintain a continuing synthesis, reading and evaluating every separate research report. The syntheses allowed some of this work to be avoided, by identifying the key contributions to the area (those that should be read and evaluated and not cited – rather than sighted! – at second hand only) and pointing the way forward for future research, perhaps by proposing models that are improvements on those currently employed. As the volume of research work has increased, so the need for such syntheses has grown. Geographers now have two specialist journals – *Progress in Human Geography* and *Progress in Physical Geography* – oriented entirely to that task, and other specialized, non-serial publications provide periodic reviews. (As in the, now defunct, series that I edited with David Herbert – *Geography and the Urban Environment: progress in research and applications*. Specialist journals – such as *Urban Geography* – now provide reviews of subfields of subdisciplines, indicative of the explosion of research reporting: more is being done, and more people are faced with the 'publish or perish' syndrome.)

A further need is for writing on *research methods*. Many questions have to remain unanswered because we lack the ability – usually either technical or technological, but not necessarily so – to tackle them. Thus some research effort must focus on these methodological issues. The development of procedures should, of course, be set in the context of a particular research problem, and reported accordingly. But many procedures have wider applicability than the particular question to which they were initially addressed, and their separate presentation can more readily bring them to the attention of other researchers. (In some cases one can identify a 'have method, will travel' syndrome, of people with methods seeking valid applications: this was a charge levelled at some geographers during the 'quantitative revolution', for example. In others the general potential of a procedure is identified, and much effort is then expended realizing this potential: this is the case at present with remote sensing.)

As research proceeds, so more material is provided for the syntheses, and more methods are developed that may be relevant to other applications. The store of knowledge is being built up. New researchers are socialized into that store, into the contents of a particular research paradigm. For their education and training a particular form of synthesis is needed, not one which summarizes and evaluates recent research reports but one which encapsulates an entire field, which is a comprehensive state-of-the-art statement of what is known, of how knowledge is obtained, and of where we should go next. This is the *textbook*, the point of entry for the new, would-be researchers in a field. These could be very stereotyped. Some, especially in the area of research methods, are – as in statistical methods texts. But most are idiosyncratic, reflecting the authors' selection of material and framework for presenting it (compare, for example, Morrill's (1970) *The Spatial Organisation of Society*, Abler, Adams and Gould's (1971) *Spatial Organisation, the geographer's view of the world* and Haggett's (1965) *Locational Analysis in Human Geography*, all of which are syntheses of the same research paradigm. Note that Haggett's book was in two parts, one – 'Locational models' – providing the synthesis, and the other – 'Locational methods' – the procedures.)

Getting it Published

According to what we might call the standard model of scientific research there are several types of publication, therefore, each written in a particular way for a defined audience. How, then, is the process of writing organized? The discussion here is divided into two. In the first part the focus is on the writing of scientific papers – research reports and syntheses and presentations of technical developments. The second is concerned with books.

Scientific Papers and Academic Journals

Most researchers, when they set out on a piece of work, have it in mind that they will produce one or more papers to report their findings. (Not all do. Many are simply attracted by the research activity itself and find writing it up the hardest task. Indeed much research work lies incomplete because the researcher didn't publish a report – because of a 'writing blockage', perhaps, a lack of time, the attractions of new research, or whatever. The published record of completed research should not be equated with the 'unpublished incomplete research' record.) These papers will be sent to relevant academic journals. But which – for there are very many? And will they necessarily be published? Very few journals commission papers – they react to what is submitted to them rather than actively encourage (though an editor may solicit a piece). And extremely few accept all that is submitted to them; they evaluate the pieces very carefully, and many reject 50 per cent or more of what they receive, on a variety of grounds.

The choice of which journal to send a paper to would seem to be a straightforward one. The research is geographical, so it should be sent to a geographical journal. But there are many such journals – even in the English language and published in England. Basically, they are of two types. The first are the *general geographical journals* which cover the entire discipline (such as *Transactions of the Institute of British Geographers*, and *The Geographical Journal* in the UK and *The Geographical Review* and *Annals of the Association of American Geographers* in the USA). Most of these are published by *learned societies*, established to promote the subject as a whole, though some (the Royal Geographical Society and the American Geographical Society, publishers of the *Journal* and the *Review* respectively) serve a much wider, general audience than the more narrowly academic. Authors writing for readers of the latters' journals (i.e. *Transactions* and *Annals*) are thus addressing their academic peers, whereas those writing for the former's are presenting their findings to a wider audience, whose interests may not be the advancement of the frontiers of knowledge *per se*. Some general journals simply publish a wide range of research papers. Others focus on research reports and syntheses written for a certain purpose, such as contributing to materials that can be used in geographical teaching, as in the journal *Geography*.

The second type is the *specialist journal*. Most of these focus on a particular aspect of geography – such as *Economic Geography*, *Urban Geography*, *Journal of Biogeography*, and *Earth Surface Processes and Landforms*. Writing for them clearly involves the presentation of research reports, syntheses and methods to one's immediate academic peers. Most of them are produced by commercial publishers, and are aimed in particular at academic libraries. Few are very narrow, since overspecialization would probably mean a small potential market and relatively few sales. To achieve the needed market size, yet without generalizing the coverage too far (as with the first type) and thereby orienting towards a different type of writing, many such journals are explicitly multidisciplinary, focusing on a variety of approaches to particular subject-matter – as in *Environment and Planning A*, *Society and Space*, *Government·and Policy*, and *International Journal of Urban and Regional Research*, all of which serve geographers, among others.

Most of these journals operate very similar procedures. Authors submit papers to the editor, who sends them to referees, asking for comments and recommendations regarding the suitability of the paper for publication in that journal. *Environment and Planning A*, for example, asks the referee to rate each paper on the following scale:

1   The paper should be published in its present form.
2   The paper should be accepted for publication, subject to suggested amendments being made.
3   The paper should be returned for revision (along the suggested lines) and then resubmitted (with the possibility of being sent to referees again).
4   The paper should be withdrawn and a much shorter version submitted.
5   The author should seek publication elsewhere.
6   The paper should be rejected without qualification.

In addition, it asks the following questions:

1   Is there sufficient original material (results, theories) to warrant publication?
2   Are there any obvious faults in empirical basis and/or theoretical reasoning?
3   Are there demonstrable errors in mathematics, calculations, units?
4   Are the terminology, nomenclature and units correct?
5   Is the order of presentation logical (allowing reasonable latitude for individual preferences)?
6   Could some parts be condensed and/or others expanded?
7   Does the paper read well?
8   Are the title and abstract adequate?
9   Are the figures and tables satisfactorily and correctly labelled, or are some redundant?
10   Are the references appropriate and free from obvious omissions?

Editors and referees are important *academic gatekeepers*, therefore, with substantial power over both the development of the discipline(s) they serve and the careers of the individual researchers (if they can't publish, they perish). This power can be exercised partially. An editor may select sympathetic or unsympathetic referees deliberately; referees may be destructive or constructive. (Some editors send papers to referees with no indication of the author(s), although the practice of self-citation frequently destroys the anonymity that this seeks to create. In any case, most referees – supposedly expert in their field – should (and almost certainly do) recognize the work of a large proportion of 'anonymous' authors.) Even where no partiality is intended by the editor, the choice of referees can have an important influence on whether the paper is accepted. (A good test of this is the fate of rejected papers. The practice of many authors whose work is rejected is to submit it immediately to another journal, perhaps after some revision in the light of the referees' comments. The proportion accepted at the second – or subsequent – submission is not known; I have very few that have not found a home eventually! Of course, occasionally the same referees are used by the second journal. Problems sometimes arise when revisions are requested; authors have been known to resubmit the same paper, to the same journal, in the hope that either it will not be read in detail against the previous version or that a different referee will be used!)

One could deduce from this that there is a status continuum of journals – some have higher standards than others. This is probably a belief held by many writers, and correctly so in the case of some disciplines. But there is little evidence that it is so in geography. Some people do feel that greater prestige is achieved by publishing in some journals (the *Annals*, perhaps) than others, and I have been told by some that they would consider submitting something to such journals 'above them'. But there is nothing in the requests from editors to referees which suggest differentials in standards, and analyses of the 'value' of papers – such as citation counts – provide little evidence to suggest that the 'best' work appears in certain journals.

The differentials between journals are much more likely to reflect their varying markets, identified particularly by their titles. Thus, for example, the journal *Geographical Analysis* (founded in 1969 as a 'journal of theoretical geography': see Golledge, 1979) is aimed specifically at work with mathematical and statistical strengths (its theory is positivist), and not surprisingly it is a preferred journal for writers of such work. In part such specialized journals are favoured for their 'externality effects'. A paper in *Geographical Analysis* will be published among others of similar orientation, and is more likely to be identified by the casual reader (perhaps an economist looking for such work) than if it were in a general journal, only looked at by such readers when specifically referred to. (As already noted, many general journals are published by learned societies and distributed to all of their members. It is sometimes claimed that many members merely read the contents pages of such journals, find that there is nothing in their specialist field of interest, and put them straight back on the shelves unopened: Clayton and O'Riordan, 1977).

An important influence on the market definition for a journal is the editorial role, particularly with the commercially produced specialist journals. The editors of journals produced by learned societies have less freedom of action, because they are answerable to the governing bodies of those societies for the conduct of the journals, and members – who may be sore at the treatment of papers submitted – have a channel through which grievances can be expressed. Editors of commercially produced journals are answerable only to the publishers. These will no doubt be concerned that high academic standards are maintained, since a poor reputation is likely to affect sales. And the editors will not be expected to narrow the appeal of the journal and similarly reduce its saleability. But within those commercial constraints it is left to the editors to create an image for the journals, and to decide what sort of work will and will not be accepted. (They usually have unlimited terms in which to do this. Editors of learned society journals are almost all appointed – or 'elected' – for fixed terms.)

The differences between the two types of journal identified here are generalizations, of course, and no rigid classification can be imposed. Many writers can quote their experiences of what they identify as partial treatment by editors and referees, in both types of journal (see, for example, the comments by Brian Berry on the problems of getting the early quantitative work published, in Halvorson and Stave, 1978). Peter Gould (1979, p. 139) summarized such treatment in his analysis of the Augean period, when there were

new paths opening up, new connections being made, and real challenges being met. There was a sense of discovery and forging, of breaking out of the banal, factual boxes erected by the 'old men'.

But those 'old men' controlled the geographical communication system:

These were also the gate-keeping days, when the journals of the field closed ranks and stopped up the chinks to prevent the winds of new ideas from getting through. Some of the letters of rejection were extraordinary for their arrogance, sarcasm, and sheer venom, and we used to circulate the prize examples among ourselves as paper witnesses to the reaction of the current order. Eventually the reactions . . . became so predictable that few bothered to submit their writing thereafter, and in general this pattern has continued, so that even when a less conservative editor takes over, the traditional reputation of a journal lingers on. . . . One editor . . . has been forced to return papers containing mathematical notation to the authors without even sending them out for review (Gould, 1979, p. 142).

Some, at least, of the editors have been prepared to defend their positions. Wilma Fairchild (1979, p. 35) was editor of *The Geographical Review*. On her appointment she found that most of the Fellows of the American Geographical Society were not professional geographers, and so concluded that balance in content was essential, that each issue must contain articles of general as well as of professional interest – a circumstance that became more difficult to implement with the thrusting wave of the 'quantitative' surge in the 1960s.

But she also realized that the surge could not be denied, and that continued professional support required publication of such work:

Clearly, quantification was a force whose time had come. . . . In accepting manuscripts of this genre, I insisted only that the methodology illuminate a subject that had originality and meaning; too often . . . an author seemed merely to be carried away by his enthusiasm for the techniques (Fairchild, 1979, p. 38).

The editor of the specialist journal *Economic Geography* was less catholic. Raymond Murphy (1979, p. 39) noted that the journal was founded for geographers and others 'who wished to have a part in the intelligent utilization of the world's resources'. As editor (1949–69) he had sole control of the content:

Most journals use referees or an advisory board to help make editorial decisions, but I did not do this. It was too time-consuming. Besides, I believed that authors accepted the decisions of the editor more readily than those of anonymous referees or board members (Murphy, 1979, pp. 41–2).

Thus he fostered a journal which he identified as 'widely used in college and university courses in economic geography and urban geography' (p. 42). The quantitative revolution posed a dilemma, for 'the new statistically oriented papers could mean little to those users of the magazine who were not trained in modern statistical techniques' (p. 42). Should there be a shift, to a new clientele? The decision was taken by Murphy's successor, but his own position is clear:

the new editor . . . felt that the future of economic and urban geography lay in more, rather than less, use of modern statistical techniques. To some, the change was long overdue; to others the magazine lost much of its interest and usefulness (p. 42).

Editors, working alone or in concert with publishers/sponsors, can determine a journal's style, and thus the pattern of geographical writing that it represents. Most, if not all, display some idosyncracies. In 1969, a short paper was published in *The Professional Geographer* (a 'forum and journal of the Association of American Geographers'; the Institute of British Geographers publishes a similar quarterly – *Area*) on 'The bicycle as a field aid' (Salter, 1969, p. 369), which concluded that 'For reasons . . . of economy, mobility, independence and rapport with the field country population a bicycle is suggested as an important purchase after arrival in the field.' This intrigued me and some of my colleagues, and over lunch one day we wrote to the editor (tongue-in-cheek; we presumed that the piece on the bicycle was similarly written and was published as 'light relief') proposing a series of such articles on: boots and their use; the surfboard and coastal research; the value of a dog in fieldwork; the tape recorder; the biro vs the pencil; and the benefits of automatic transmission in field surveys. (Incidentally, we had a departmental bicycle, available for local field work!). The reply we got told us that

The article which you found so objectionable reached us from a thoroughly reputable source – the chairman of one of the largest American geography departments – and we published it deliberately to call attention to the inadequacies of the desk-bound computerized geographer. I judge that you missed the point.

We were duly chastened! But the statement on the provenance of the paper interested us even more, and I responded that

It suggests that it is not what you know but who you know that matters. Over the last few years you have rejected two contributions from me. I was disappointed, but believed this to be on academic grounds, and so did not complain. Am I now to understand that if I had not sent these items to you myself . . . but had forwarded them via a 'big name' in American geography, then they would have been published?

The correspondence closed with me being told that my papers were probably rejected because the journal had a long backlog, and that

My remark that a reputable source recommended the bicycle article came about because I was aware that the article was prepared by a student and not by a faculty member, but the chairman of his department (and it is one of our largest and best), felt that what the boy had written was well done and of value. I concurred . . .

This is not to imply that the short paper should not have been published, nor that this is normal editorial practice; far from it. But it does illustrate the power of the gatekeeper – and of other senior members of the academic community – in the control of geographical writing.

We know very little of the process of writing in detail, and so do not know whether people have a clear end in view (a paper in a particular journal) when they set off on a piece of research. Clearly at some stage they must decide if they are going to write the paper, in what form, and for what journal (the latter is necessary at a pragmatic level because of differences in formating conventions and because a paper can only be submitted to one journal at a time; some ask for a signed statement that this requirement has been honoured). Choice of journal is influenced by a variety of factors such as the intended audience (local, national, international; specialist, general; etc.). This may be important because, for example, of what can either be left unsaid or briefly alluded to in references and footnotes: referees and editors for specialist journals are more likely to assume readers know the academic pedigree (the theoretical framework) of a piece of work than are those working for general journals.

One decision faced by many geographers is whether to seek publication in a geographical journal (specialist or general), a multidisciplinary journal, or a journal of another discipline (or indeed whether to publish in more than one of these, using the same material in different ways for the separate audiences). Although geographers draw heavily on the work of researchers in other disciplines, this interdependence is only rarely reciprocated: there are, for example, many more references to the works of political scientists by political geographers than vice-versa (see Laponce, 1980). Some geographers try to place papers in the specialist journals of other disciplines in order to 'display their wares', and some are rebuffed through, it seems, the territorial politics of the other discipline (see Gudgin and Taylor, 1979, Preface). Some see it as more prestigious to publish in that way: a physical geographer may feel that his or her scientific reputation is enhanced further by publishing in, say, *The Journal of Glaciology, The Journal of Soil Science,* and *The Journal of Hydrology* than in a geography journal.

There are strong pressures within academic geography to publish. Further, those pressures point in particular towards the publication of papers in reputable journals (i.e. those which use the refereeing system, sometimes grandly known as peer review). Lists of such papers are the key parts of the CV of an application for an academic post, including promotion, and for a research grant, because they indicate a commitment to the completion of research projects at acceptable standards. (In some universities, lists of 'acceptable' and 'unacceptable' journals exist – although these are rarely made public!) Because of the importance of publication, researchers as writers must accept the dictats of the gatekeepers, the editors and referees in particular, and most orient the reporting of their research to the acceptable ways (they must even, some claim, orient their research as a whole in order to meet the publication criteria).

How About a Book?

As already indicated, textbooks play a central role in a research paradigm, although their production is not necessarily considered to be research.[4] They are, however, only one type of book produced by academic writers. The following classification suggests six types.

1   *The instructional text,* which teaches methodological topics –

statistical applications, computer programming, etc. These can vary in how the material is presented, but little more; they are evaluated on their success in getting the material across (assuming the absence of factual errors).

2   *The synthesis text*, which summarizes the substantive material in a discipline or, more probably, some segment of it. These are more likely to vary (as noted above) because of differences in the selection and organization of material; they are evaluated for their structure and coherence, as well as their presentation.

3   *The essay*, which is similar to the synthesis text except that the presentation is oriented more to the argument for a particular approach to the subject than to a summary of previous achievements; it is evaluated on the strength of the argument.

4   *The research monograph*, which is the report of a major piece of research that cannot be summarized in a single paper or split into several papers; it is evaluated in the same way as a paper.

5   *The collection*, either of previously published essays or of specially commissioned pieces, around a particular theme. Such multi-author texts usually reflect the inability/unwillingness of any individual to cover the entire field under consideration, so a group of experts is brought together to do that. Evaluation then is based on the overall coherence of the pieces as well as their individual qualities; coherence is usually harder to obtain if the pieces are reprints, frequently though not invariably of research papers.

6   *The reference work*, which in many cases is a particular form of synthesis text, such as a dictionary or encyclopaedia. Geographical reference works of course include atlases.

Four of these types (1, 2, 5 and 6) are clearly aimed at the usual textbook market – i.e. students. Those in the third type are more likely to be aimed at the writer's peers; those in the fourth certainly are.

Leaving aside type 5 for the moment, the size of the potential market for a book will decline from types 1 and 2 and 3 to 4; type 6 should have the largest market of all. Instructional texts are likely to attract most purchasers, and research monographs least. Thus it is not surprising that commercial publishers favour types 1 and 2, and that unsubsidized publishers (many university presses receive hidden, if not direct, subsidies, for example) are very chary of research monographs, especially in a discipline such as geography that has no market outside the academic (i.e. either the 'interested layman' or a profession of graduates).

Publishing a text is the result of negotiations between potential authors and publishers, negotiations which either may commence: an individual may wish to write a text, and will sound out publishers; a publisher may identify a lacuna in the supply of texts and seek an author to fill it. A contract is then signed, either before anything is written or, if the publisher is uncertain, after sample chapters have been produced and opinions received (much like referees' opinions on papers, except that saleability is under consideration, as well as quality; most publishers seek expert opinions on book proposals, which are only a few pages long). The author is writing for a specified audience. The publisher will want this to be as large as possible, hence the frequent advertising of British geography books that they are suitable for both introductory undergraduate courses and school sixth-form syllabuses.

Publishers vary in their market orientation. Most British publishers are content to ensure that there is a market for a proposed book and then, unless the delivered manuscript fails to meet the agreed criteria (too long perhaps, or badly written), will go ahead, publish and sell. They would like large sales, and the use of the book in many courses, but rarely undertake any major marketing 'hype'. Of course, outright flops have to be avoided. Some publishers take great care over offering contracts, therefore, whereas others are more liberal – but price their books higher to cover their gambles. The most successful are those able to judge potential authors as likely producers of good books. Many American publishers, on the other hand, are seeking to tap very big markets, especially in the large introductory undergraduate courses. To do this they will spend a lot of money and energy in ensuring that the book is 'right' for the market. The manuscript will be read by several referees, and much rewriting may be asked for. Copyediting will be substantial and, if necessary, a lot of effort will be put into the design of illustrations. They are making a major investment, and the writer may feel little more than a puppet (writing for an established market – perhaps even producing something very similar to another publisher's popular book on that subject rather than branching out into something new and risky, which may or may not create its own market). This can be irksome: as Gunnar Olsson (1975, p. vii) expressed it in the preface to *Bird in Egg*: 'It was then that Philistines offered to publish a book'.

Essays and research monographs are harder to publish than texts, especially in geography which has only a small number of academics plus students as its potential market. (Geographers often bewail their inability to attract an audience among the general reading public in the same way as, say, historians. Few have really tried, however.) Learned societies may publish them, as part of their subsidy to research publication, but few can be produced in that way.

The situation with collections is ambiguous. Some publishers are keen on them, but reviews are rarely favourable. Many collections have little coherence – especially those based on the papers offered at a conference

– and many teachers find them of little use as teaching texts. (This is especially so with collections of reprinted research papers, which assume that readers are already socialized into the relevant paradigm.) For this reason other publishers, especially those aiming at big markets, are reluctant to contract for them. Pioneering, purpose-written collections are more favourably viewed, however.

There are three major differences between writing research papers and writing books, therefore. First, the paper is usually written without any prior agreement to publish it, while the reverse is the case with books. Secondly, the audiences differ: most books are written for students; most papers for one's peer group of researchers. And thirdly, the rewards from publishing papers are charisma, status and, perhaps, promotion whereas those from books are additionally financial. Such differences mean that the production processes involved are very separate; a good writer of research papers is not necessarily a good textbook writer, or vice-versa.

But is it all Like That?

All of the discussion in the previous section has presented a particular view of scientific activity, one in which progress is linear as new research builds upon the findings of that which went before. According to this view, geographical writing involves one of: synthesizing what we already know; suggesting the next set of questions to be asked; proposing means of answering those questions; and reporting the results of posing one or more questions. Work of the last type is the most frequent, providing empirical research reports that add to the store of knowledge within a clearly defined framework.

But is all science like that? Is all geographical writing set in that framework? In physical geography the answers are almost certainly yes, but in human geography they are not. In the last two decades there has been considerable reaction to the framework! A full review of the debates and their foundations is not called for here (summaries can be found in Johnston, 1983a, b), but a brief overview is needed for an evaluation of other forms of geographical writing.

Varieties of Science

Definitions of science abound. Most focus on it as a frame of mind, as a means of carefully scrutinizing evidence in order to account for some phenomenon or event. It is, as Dixon (1976, p. 36) tells us, 'no more than scrupulously applied common sense'. But is there only one form of scrupulous application, the hypothesis-testing procedure outlined above?

The answer to this question is a focus of much debate. Among human geographers in recent years, three separate types of science have been identified and promoted.

1 *The empiricist/positivist*, in which the scientist is portrayed as a neutral observer recording and analysing empirical phenomena (the pattern of land-use; choices of shopping centres, etc.) according to the tenets of natural science. The outcome of such work is the explanation of individual phenomena/events as exemplars of general laws, whose applicability is spatially and temporally invariant (e.g. the laws embedded in central place theory).

2 *The humanistic*, in which the scientist is an insider rather than an outsider, seeking to understand how events have occurred not as exemplars of general laws but as the outcomes of individual decisions. The scientific goal is appreciation not explanation.

3 *The realist/structuralist*, in which the scientist argues that the proximate causes of an event (the appreciations provided by humanistic studies) provide insufficient explanations, since they do not also account for the mechanisms that underpin those causes. (That I let go of my pen provides the proximate cause of why it falls to the ground, but does not tell me why my pen must fall if I do not hold it. The answer to that is provided by the law of gravity – which I have a theory of, but which I cannot apprehend; I know it by its consistent outcomes, not its existence. Similarly, industrialists introduce new machinery in order to increase productivity and profits, and we can appreciate their actions. But we can only understand why they do that through our theory of capitalism, which demonstrates the necessity of increasing productivity. The theory of gravity does not predict why I let go of my pen, and the theory of capitalism does not predict the introduction of new machinery – there are other way of increasing productivity; the theories provide the context for studying the proximate causes.)

All three of these are scientific approaches, since all are concerned to provide rigorous accounts. (Some argue that humanistic accounts are not scientific since they deal with the subjective. This is a misrepresentation. Humanistic studies are concerned with the study of the subjective, but are themselves no more subjective than are studies in the other approaches.) The nature of those accounts varies, however. Empiricist/ positivist approaches explain individual events as cases of general laws; humanistic approaches appreciate the reasons for actions, as expressed by the actors; and realist approaches explain individual events as the outcomes of particular cause–effect sequences – which may be unique (though not singular: Johnston, 1984, 1985a) and in no sense replicable.

The Uses of Science

Science is usually portrayed not just as scrupulous analysis but also as the production of 'useful knowledge'. But if there are three approaches to science, are there also three types of 'useful knowledge'?

1 *Science, engineering and control.* The empiricist/positivist approach to science is geared to produce tools that can be used to manipulate – whether matter or society. Physical laws are used to ensure that buildings can withstand certain stresses, for example, and (assumed) economic laws are used to promote the economic health of a society (as in the manipulation of the money supply to influence the rate of inflation). This type of science is linked to environmental and social control, therefore, with the laws suggesting what needs to be manipulated to achieve certain ends and avoid others.

2 *Science and awareness.* The goal of humanistic approaches is not to provide laws of behaviour that can be used to predict and/or modify action, for such approaches deny the existence of any laws and their implications that people lack self-control. Instead the goal is to promote awareness, both self-awareness (increased appreciation of oneself, as in psychoanalysis) and mutual awareness (increased appreciation of others). The outcome of such increased awareness is a greater ability to exercise self-control and to accommodate the variety of others.

3 *Science and emancipation.* Both empiricist/positivist and humanistic approaches deal with events but ignore the mechanisms underlying those events: people appreciate why actions are taken to increase productivity but not why such actions are necessary in a capitalist social formation. Only a theoretical understanding of capitalism can provide the latter appreciation, thereby emancipating people from their ignorance of the forces driving society and hence identifying the possibility of altering those forces.

These brief paragraphs provide only the barest outline of the differences between the various approaches to science (for a fuller discussion, see Johnston, 1986). They are sufficient, however, to indicate that each approach must be associated with a separate style of geographical writing. As already demonstrated, empirical/positivist science is a cumulative process, and each new piece builds on previous ones. This allows for the development of the textbook–research paper writing framework.

Realist science is also cumulative, in that its goal is to build a coherent theory of the mechanisms underlying action. Individual pieces can be written either as extensions to the existing theory – as illustrated in journals such as *Society and Space* and the *International Journal of Urban and Regional Research* – or as uses of the theory to illustrate the mechanisms underlying particular empirical events. But since the theory is intended to be coherent, it is often necessary to reconstruct the whole as one tackles a part (as in Harvey, 1982). And individual pieces cannot be made to conform to a set framework.

Humanistic science is not cumulative, however. It is concerned with the individuality of events, people, and places, and with conveying that (though there are difficulties in expressing individuality through the use of language the words of which imply generality). Presentation of such interpretations does not fit the mould of the 'classic' scientific paper, since there are no hypotheses to be tested, no conclusions to be drawn; instead, a method is being applied to assist in the appreciation of a topic. That method involves the scientist addressing the texts (verbal, written, symbolic – including landscape etc.), and putting the material together in a coherent interpretation. Presentation of that interpretation is usually in essay form – which may be of book-length – and evaluation of it involves other scholars asking 'does that interpretation square with mine?', etc. The interpretation is itself personal, and there are no 'objective' criteria to say whether or not it is 'right'. For this reason, editors of journals find it difficult to assess essays sent to them according to their usual criteria: 'Is it telling a good story, which helps me appreciate the time/place described?' is rather different from 'Are there any demonstrable errors in mathematics, calculations, units etc.?'

Because humanistic essays are personal interpretations, they are both difficult to evaluate 'objectively' and yet easy to attack. This is well demonstrated in historical research, in which critical evaluation – in book reviews, for example – is frequently much harsher than is the case with reviewing in geography (and frequently much more personal too). This suggests that either the reviewer or the scholar whose work is being reviewed has been unscientific. But this need not be so. If I were to write an essay about, say, Swindon as a place it may be very different from that which somebody else would write, because we have experienced Swindon in different ways (see Eyles, 1985). Neither of us is wrong, for we are both describing the place as we experienced it. In historical research, including historical geography, we don't experience places directly, but through the materials left by others – and if, as is almost certainly the case, two or more people have provided materials then the interpretations we have access to are likely to be different. We must assemble and reinterpret those materials. We cannot approach them in a position of theoretical agnosticism, for to do so would be no more than random empiricism. We have a structure into which we think the material fits, and as we fill out that structure so we test its continued coherence in the face of new material; if it fails, we must restructure. In this, of course, we are acting very much as people do in their daily lives. They have a coherent structure – a model, if you wish – that provides the framework for living, for interpreting new material; at times the framework cannot accommodate new material, and so it must be altered. As humanistic scientists, therefore, we operate as people do daily, assimilating new material into our interpretative framework. The difference is that we then seek to transmit that framework to others – so that they can better appreciate the worlds that they and others inhabit.

There are many similarities between humanistic and realist writing, since both are aiming to increase awareness. There are two major differences, however. The first is that humanistic work remains at the empirical level of events and actors; realist work is interested in these too, but in people acting within the context of mechanisms. The second relates to the purpose of the writing. Humanistic work is aimed only to increase awareness of those events and actors, and is linked to no larger goal – it is typical of what is often termed 'liberal education', broadening the mind. Realist work, on the other hand, is linked to emancipatory goals, aimed at enabling people to appreciate the mechanisms that constrain their lives, so that they might then seek ways of removing them. The latter is clearly a political goal, linked by many to Marxism as a programme for action as well as a theoretical structure for the social sciences. As such, realist writing is viewed with distaste, if not outright disapproval, by many of the gatekeepers, since it promotes change – it doesn't square with either the claimed objectivity of empiricist/positivist science or the studied non-involvement of humanistic science. The latter is seen as harmless, the former as subversive (of the established order within geography, as well as beyond it).

In Summary

This treatment of 'writing geographically' has been very largely concerned with 'publishing geographically'. The two words – writing and publishing – are not synonyms, but since unpublished geographical writings are inaccessible the only sort that can be discussed are those which are published. And getting work published involves conforming to the norms of the publishers. (There are exceptions, of course. Most learned societies elect presidents, who deliver addresses to plenary sessions of their annual conferences. Those addresses are then published, unrefereed and unedited; the 'refereeing' took place at election time.)

In geography at the present time there is no one set of norms to which all conform. There are several different conceptions (or philosophies) of geography, with separate goals that lead to different forms of writing. Conflict between those various conceptions has led to the establishment of separate publishing outlets, journals specifically launched for a particular type of writing (as, for example, with *Geographical Analysis* and *Antipode*). To the extent that the discipline is divided within itself, so these would seem to be 'natural splits'. But the discipline also seeks to be united (see Johnston, 1985d, 1986), and its learned societies (which act somewhat like trade unions) in particular seek to promote a coherent geography. Their general geographical journals must reflect this, and so accept – reluctantly, and probably slowly – the various types of writing. It sounds like schizophrenia!

One of the problems of the different styles of writing, especially when they are new, is that they use language differently – and maybe invent some, known often (and pejoratively) as jargon. Thus Spate (1960, p. 388), reacting to the presentation of the 'new quantitative geography' wrote of the 'smoke screen of formulae. The *cognoscenti* have their own radar to see through it: the uninitiate may be completely bluffed'. And 23 years later, focusing on humanistic writing, Billinge (1983, p. 400) wrote of 'the Mandarin dialect':

nothing corrupts the geographical literature of our time more than fadishness, verbal trickery and the uncritical employment of unnecessary literary conceit. . . . The sonorous phrase is in, clear expression is out. Ostentatious, nonsensical and artificial by turns, the new form is increasingly *de rigueur*. It has balance and elan, passion and commitment, it has imagery, metaphor, simile and hyperbole, flamboyance and energy – in fact everything save honesty of intention and meaning.

People write in the way they believe that their audience wants them to, and assume that if they pass the gatekeepers then they have got it right. Some write more than others, perhaps because they have a greater dread of perishing: or perhaps they publish more because they simply enjoy it, have some deep need for public recognition, or just know how to please the gatekeepers. To understand fully the contents of the geographical literature we would have to appreciate the writers as well as their writings. As yet, neither autobiographies nor biographies have given us much insight into geographers, and our concern is only with their geography.

It is becoming commonplace these days for writers (not least me) to paraphrase Marx's comment about people making their own history but not in conditions of their own choosing. But it is a very insightful statement, which certainly applies to geographical writing. Academic geographers are socialized into a way of life which sees the conduct of research and the publication of its findings as the main performance indicator. Within that general way of life they are socialized into disciplinary and subdisciplinary frameworks that identify both 'good' research and 'good' writing. In order to succeed within those frameworks they must accept their norms. Over time the norms may change, and they may have some part to play in bringing about the change. But for most geographers, most of the time, the process of writing is a necessary activity which must be undertaken within the generally accepted rules. As Dixon (1976, p. 39) expressed it (in part quoting Cottrell)

The scientific genius may have his [sic] flashes of inspiration while in solitude, but if he is to be an effective scientist he must be very much part of the community of science. . . . 'He has to take the ideas and problems as they exist among his fellows, transmute them in his own personal way, and then bring them back as offerings to his community. He both takes and gives, in the scientific currency of his time.'

Notes

1. My contract as a Professor of Geography at the University of Sheffield makes me 'responsible for the prosecution and encouragement of original studies in the subject of . . . [my] Chair'.
2. Hence the copious provision of references and footnotes.
3. There is a problem if researchers cannot get their work published in the recognized outlets of their discipline, for reasons discussed in detail below. They may initiate new outlets that will accept their work. Initially, however, they are likely to circulate reports to interested persons in mimeographed form (often known as 'fugitive' or 'underground' publications), so that 'publication' is restricted to those who are members of a network, or linked to it. In addition some authors circulate early drafts of their research reports in similar formats, and many institutions have formalized this through the publication of Departmental Discussion/Seminar Paper series. Some reports circulated in this way never enter the 'formal' literature!
4. Promotions committees in the University of Sheffield, especially that of the Faculty of Pure Science, have been very reluctant to consider the publication of textbooks as an index of research activity.

References

Abler, R., Adams, J. S. and Gould, P. R. (1971) *Spatial Organisation: the geographer's view of the world.* Prentice-Hall, Englewood Cliffs.

Clayton, K. M. and O'Riordan, T. (1977) The readership of *Transactions* and the role of the IBG, *Area*, 9, 96–8.

Billinge, M. (1983) The Mandarin dialect: an essay on style in contemporary geographical writing. *Transactions, Institute of British Geographers*, NS8, 400–20.

Dixon, B. (1976) *What is Science For?* Penguin Books, London.

Eyles, J. (1985) *Senses of Place*. Silverbrook Press, Warrington.

Fairchild, W. B. (1979) The *Geographical Review* and the American Geographical Society, *Annals of the Association of American Geographers*, 69, 33–9.

Glacken, C. J. (1967) *Traces on the Rhodian Shore: nature and culture in Western thought from ancient times to the end of the eighteenth century*. University of California Press, Berkeley.

Glacken, C. J. (1983) A late arrival in academia. In A. Buttimer (ed.), *The Practice of Geography*. Longman, London, pp. 20–34.

Golledge, R. G. (1979) The development of *Geographical Analysis*, *Annals of the Association of American Geographers*, 69, 151–5.

Gould, P. R. (1979) Geography 1957–1977: the Augean period, *Annals of the Association of American Geographers*, 69, 139–51.

Gudgin, G. and Taylor, P. J. (1979) *Seats, Votes and the Spatial Organisation of Elections*. Pion, London.

Haggett, P. (1965) *Locational Analysis in Human Geography*. Edward Arnold, London.

Halvorson, P. and Stave, B. M. (1978) A conversation with Brian J. L. Berry, *Journal of Urban History*, 4, 209–38.

Harvey, D. (1982) *The Limits of Capital*. Basil Blackwell, Oxford.

Herbert, D. T. and Johnston, R. J. (eds) (1978–84) *Geography and the Urban Environment: Progress in Research and Applications* (six volumes). John Wiley, Chichester.

Johnston, R. J. (1983a) *Geography and Geographers: Anglo-American Human Geography since 1945* (2nd edn.). Edward Arnold, London.

Johnston, R. J. (1983b) *Philosophy and Human Geography: An Introduction to Contemporary Approaches*. Edward Arnold, London.

Johnston, R. J. (1984) The world is our oyster, *Transactions of the Institute of British Geographers*, NS9, 443–59.

Johnston, R. J. (1985a) Political advertising and the geography of voting in England at the 1983 general election, *International Journal of Advertising*, 4, 4–10.

Johnston, R. J. (1985b) A note on local spending in the 1983 general election: differences between the Liberal and SDP parties in England, *Environment and Planning, A*, 17, 1393–1400.

Johnston, R. J. (1985c) To the ends of the earth. In R. J. Johnston (ed.), *The Future of Geography*. Methuen, London, pp. 326–48.

Johnston, R. J. (1985d) Introduction: exploring the future of geography. In R. J. Johnston (ed.), *The Future of Geography*. Methuen, London, pp. 3–27.

Johnston, R. J. (1986) *On Human Geography*. Basil Blackwell, Oxford.

Kuhn, T. S. (1962) *The Structure of Scientific Revolutions*. University of Chicago Press, Chicago.

Laponce, J. A. (1980) Political science: an import–export analysis of journals and footnotes, *Political Studies*, 28, 401–19.

Morrill, R. L. (1970) *The Spatial Organization of Society*. Wadsworth, Belmont.

Mulkay, M. J. (1975) Three models of scientific development, *Sociological Review*, 23, 509–26.

Murphy, R. E. (1979) *Economic Geography* and Clark University. *Annals of the*

Association of American Geographers, 69, 39–42.

Olsson, G. (1975) *Bird in Egg*. University of Michigan, Ann Arbor.

Pred, A. R. (1967) *Behavior and Location, Part I*. C. W. K. Gleerup, Lund.

Salter, C. L. (1969) The bicycle as a field aid, *The Professional Geographer*, 21, 360–2.

Spate, O. H. K. (1960) Quantity and quality in geography, *Annals of the Association of American Geographers*, 50, 377–94.

Spencer, C. P. and Blades, M. (1986) Pattern and process: a review essay on the relationship between behavioural geography and environmental psychology. *Progress in Human Geography*, 10, 230–48.

12

Thinking Geographically: the Editor as Tailgunner

John Eyles

After I had succeeded in planning this collection, and convincing both contributors and publisher that it was worthwhile, I rather thought that I had coming a coherent set of essays, each and every one of which would illustrate in broadly similar ways (although in different arenas of human geographical analysis) all or most of the themes which I have already set out in the introduction. As most editors know, it never quite works out that way, and it is perhaps a good thing that it doesn't, as such a collection may well be a rather tedious object to behold. It would have been an object rather like Peter Gould's 'great research proposal' in that we know how something is going to turn out before we do it. So instead my contributors provide us with their stories in the light of their great variety of experience, career development and stage, and interpretation of my guidelines for contributions. Some, therefore, emphasize research practice (e.g. John Goddard, Phil O'Keefe and Dick Peet), others research orientation (e.g. Linda McDowell, David Smith). There is stress on the contexts of research, societal (e.g. Chris Rogerson and Keith Beavon), practical (e.g. Barry Garner, John Goddard, Ron Johnston), personal (e.g. Dean Forbes, David Smith) and theoretical (e.g. David Ley). Further, ethical questions (e.g. David Ley), the mode of discovery (e.g. Peter Gould, Barry Garner) and the importance of contacts (e.g. John Goddard) are also highlighted. It is of course churlish to exemplify in this way because all the contributions inform in a variety of ways on the process of research in human geography. The different natures of their projects mean that their stories will have different emphases. And I hope that readers take on board what the authors have said and interrogate the other pieces in the volume in the light of these statements.

Not only did I, as a 'formalist' editor, think that I had similar contributions in different topic areas, but I also was sure that I had a ready-made running order with an essay on thinking geographically to open the volume and one on writing geographically to end it. The papers in between would run from the more quantitative through policy to the more interpretive. Again things did not work out quite as planned. I failed to get the people I wanted to write the opening chapter, and after reading all the essays I thought that they could be linked together in what for me was a far more interesting way than the one planned. It is the order in which they appear. I hope that the reader agrees. If the order could be settled, the problem of the opening chapter on thinking geographically remained. I resolved to do it myself.

I therefore drafted an outline and got to work. The outline took the following form: the essay would emphasize the 'naturalness' of geographical thinking in terms of something we take for granted. With this status, it is something that we have to consciously think about. Thus

1   This status of geographical thinking will be examined in terms of: (a) spatial coordinates and order; (b) geography and intersubjectivity; and (c) geography and culture. Spatial coordinates and order can, for the purpose of analysis, be looked at at different levels, namely the micro, with its focus of the body and personal space; the macro, in terms of the need for order and such ordering principles as distance, space, location; and the meso, emanating from behaviour, specifically in terms of growing up and learning home range and the whereness of people and things. Seeing whereness 'in relation' leads to a consideration of geography and intersubjectivity, i.e. self in relation to others, movement, rest (nodes) and spaces (neighbourhood, community), with the latter leading to geography and culture, namely the self in relation to world-view and societal order. The economic, political and ideological shapes our geographical thinking, e.g. North–South, regional framework of government, centre–periphery, the connotations of here and there.

2   Next, geographical thinking is seen as shaping geographical (and other) behaviour. This can be illustrated by author's own behaviour and that of others (the latter being the context of research). It can also range from the everyday and commonplace to fantasy (including the stereotype).

3   Thinking geographically can be related to the isolation of research tasks and theorizing: we focus on problems because they are there existentially and locationally. But geographical focus is one of the 'natural' ways of looking at the world. We can theorise on the basis of geographical experience.

4   Relevance of thinking geographically in social theory, understanding and explanation.

I recognized that I had set, myself at least, a difficult task and wondered what I could say that would be more than an uncomfortable amalgam of what had already been said by, *inter alia*, James and Martin (1981) on historic concepts of space, Abler, Adams and Gould (1972) on spatial organization, Sack (1980) on concepts of space in social thought and human territoriality, Tuan (1974, 1977) on the relationships between space, person and culture, and some of the contributors to Gregory and Urry (1985) on the definition of the spatial. And what would it have to do with doing research? I was rescued by the essays of the contributors. These made me think again about the purpose of this chapter and the nature of research. I decided, therefore, to try and expose how we may think geographically and in many significant respects the only subject-matter I have is myself.

I have already expressed a great deal what I think about places and what they mean to me (Eyles, 1985). Further exposure may push me into what a kind but critical reviewer called the stop-it-or-you'll-go-blind category (Powell, 1985). But a brief excursion is felt to be necessary because rather different issues need confronting (thinking geographically need not be the same as thinking about places) and because I certainly lacked what Peter Gould graphically terms 'a calling to geography'. An important reason for this state of affairs may be seen in my socialization. I regard the period of late-teens and early twenties (including the time spent at university) as being the most important formative years for the development of my career as an academic. For me this period occurred during the mid- and late-1960s. During that time, with the fervour reserved for the new (or the rediscovered), it was believed that the patterns of inequality and exploitation increasingly observed by social science and human geography were caused by the ever-widening and homogenizing influences of capitalist economic and military power, and that the eradication of these patterns required the internationalization of protest and rebellion. There was little thought of place or space differentiation; rather it was seen as necessary to expose the economic (and political) processes causing domination and exploitation, and to develop theory that would reveal both these processes and the means of their eradication. We turned to marxism of a crude and mechanistic kind, which regarded space as an irrelevance in the social totality and which still has persuasive representatives in the discipline (e.g. Hurst, 1985).

My academic socialization during this formative period was dominated by the quantitative revolution arriving in Britain through the publication of Peter Haggett's (1965) book on locational analysis and its introduction in the Masters course at the London School of Economics. Despite the advances in data analysis and technical development brought by quantitative methods – and they have far better 'apologists' than I (see Billinge, Gregory and Martin, 1984) – they, as is now commonly known, tend to turn all that they are used to study into objects or 'data'. This reification of people and places again drove the significance of the spatial from me. A place was any place. It did not seem to matter if the locale of the study was Iowa, Brazil or East Anglia; technique was (nearly) all. Thus the importance of the geographical perspective was lost and much of my early work may be said to reflect that loss. And, to jump forward several years, it is only with interest in the theoretical debates of human geography and the social sciences, and with grappling with the implications of these debates for empirical investigations, that the significance of the geographical and the spatial has re-emerged.

On talking to and reading what others had written, I became increasingly aware that I was not alone in this respect. While, to generalize, it may be said that the significance of the spatial emerged with detailed, often process-oriented empirical investigations, particularly eloquent and convincing arguments may be found in Johnston (1986) and Massey (1984a, b, 1985). While Sayer (1985) is correct to point to the ways in which we can misconceive the relationships between the social and the spatial, Massey (1985, p. 12) summarizes the issues well: 'my summary critique of the critique of the 1970s would be, then, that "geography" was underestimated; it was underestimated as distance, and it was underestimated in terms of local variation and uniqueness. Space *is* a social construct – yes. But social relations are also constructed over space, and that makes a difference.' This does not imply that the spatial itself has determinate effects. The social and the spatial are not separate: neither are people and nature (see Williams, 1981; Sayer, 1979). 'Geography in both its senses of distance/nearness/betweenness and of the physical variation of the earth's surface (the two being closely related) is not a constraint on a pre-existing non-geographical social and economic world. It is constitutive of that world' (Massey, 1984a, p. 53). The spatial is not only the arena for the production and reproduction of social and economic relations, it also conditions their nature.

The significance of the spatial and its relations with the social are also explored by Massey and Allen and their contributors (1984). In her introduction, Massey (1984b) points to the relationships between society and social processes on the one hand, and the fact and form of the spatial organization of both on the other; between the social and the natural; between different elements, i.e. economy, social and political structure and so on. This last concern has begun to demonstrate the salience of space (and time) for the development of social theory (see, for example, Urry, 1981; Giddens, 1984). In that introduction, Massey also hints at another way in which 'geography matters' (and in which we may think geographically), when she argues that 'it is not just that the spatial is socially constructed; the social is spatially constructed too' (Massey, 1984b, p. 6). In this comment we may see a geography of everyday life, a view which owes much to humanistic geography. While the extreme view of this perspective would have it that everyone is a geographer, an argument which for me extends the term 'geographer' to become virtually meaningless, humanistic geography does allow for the sympathetic treatment of the experiential bases of social actions in space and space perceptions. There is then a taken-for-granted geographical world that is constitutive of our thoughts and actions (see Eyles, 1988) and which is manifested in the structure of language (Gould, 1985) and in the fact that all physical objects have spatial referents (Lee, 1976). To think geographically must enable us to bracket out the assumptions that give this world its taken-for-granted status in our own lives and in that of those we research to explore further the significance of the spatial. We must then, in Pickles' (1988) terms, problematize that which we take for granted. In this way we may become more conscious of the geographical.

Why, though, should we become more conscious of the geographical? To answer this question requires that we expose the reasons for research in human geography. If human geography is a social science its aim is to investigate social reality. While the constitutive relationship between the social and the spatial makes theoretical development difficult (see Massey, 1985; Urry, 1985), human geography must examine, in a theory-informed empirical way, concrete reality in particular localities. It must therefore examine the particular but, further, this examination must be geared towards scientific exploration, understanding and explanation. Our overall aim, as the contributors to this collection demonstrate, is generalization, representative or statistical (in the case of quantitative, often positivistic, endeavour), theoretical (as with interpretive research based on selected cases) or practical (as with policy-oriented work). I recognize that this emphasis on generalization may appear to be too simplistic, and note the discussions of Sayer (1984) on generalizations, determinations and synthesis. The term is used to try and highlight another difficulty that seems to have resurfaced in the re-emergence of the significance of the geographical, namely whether human geography is art or science. I concur with Morrill's (1984, p. 70) forceful argument 'that a retreat to a concept of geography as the contemplation of the uniqueness of places will be . . . disastrous'. If, therefore, the re-emergence does mean the idiographic and descriptive come to dominate, and these terms are not used in a pejorative way – there are some powerful arguments for geography as art (Hart, 1982; Meinig, 1983; Smith, 1988) – then the significance of human geography becomes downgraded for other disciplines, theoretical development and the wider audience of other social scientists and policy-makers. Thinking geographically (and the ways in which we so think) shapes our academic endeavour which impacts on our 'audience'. If reducing the importance of 'generalization' means we can no longer distinguish, for example, what is intended to be a building site from a palace of culture (because each and every case of construction is described for itself and in its own terms) then we shall move from irrelevance to impotence. As Morrill (1984, pp. 70–1) asks, is there 'really any alternative to science except that we must do it better'? And doing it better means employing a variety of scientific methods from social research, and also implies that we consider the implications and outcomes of thinking geographically.

So what does thinking geographically imply? It must at the very least mean that we become conscious of the spatial and the geographical and their significance and implications. This appears trite. But as Jenkins (1981) points out in his analysis of thinking and doing, the ways in which we think, and how these are related to how we act (in everyday life or in research), are rather complicated. His review of some of the philosophical and anthropological literature shows how different ways of thinking ('models') are interrelated, particularly operational ways (how we practically act) and representational ones (how we think things are). While his detailed argument need not detain us, he is at pains to clarify the meaning of ways of thinking or models. He suggests that a model 'is something which represents or stands for the perceived *structure* of something else *in order that particular operations of a projective or imaginative nature may be performed on it or with it*' (Jenkins, 1981, p. 95, emphasis in original). A model is therefore representative of, or homologous with, the structure of something, and is used to enable the performance of particular types of operations or actions. While models are not therefore unique to science, it must be pointed out that such a model is used in the research process to clarify (make conscious) the phenomena under investigation (the 'structure') and the investigative procedure itself (imaginative operations).

The importance of these operations may be itself clarified if we see them as ways of transforming knowledge from one type to another. Just as Jenkins's argument has been specifically related to the research process, so too maybe that of Thrift (1985) on types of knowledge. But in this usage we accept that human beings (including researchers) 'conventionally conjoin what may seem to be quite different types of knowledge' (Thrift, 1985, p. 372). There is though, first, unconscious knowledge, based on forgotten practices (see also Bourdieu, 1977); and secondly, practical knowledge, defined as informal (but not unstructured), learnt from interaction and the experience of observation and social action in particular contexts. Practical knowledge is unarticulated (part then of the taken-for-granted world and the world of continuous and repetitive conduct) and local with great importance attaching to analogy and metaphor. Thirdly, there is empirical knowledge which is cumulative, systematized and coordinated. It is the rationalization of knowledge, removed from the experiences and events it describes. Empirical knowledge is therefore often homogenized and objectified. Thrift continues by pointing to three main subtypes of empirical knowledge, namely that based on its application (e.g. cookery, gardening), on its codification (e.g. engineering, town planning) and its generation by the restricted model of the natural sciences. While Thrift (1985, p. 377) sees this knowledge – 'normal science' – as coming 'from practices whose conduct is resolutely oriented to the practical', we should add that this science often divorces itself from the practical by reifying that which emanates from this realm. The researcher must always be aware of the transformations that s/he is performing on knowledge, so that the practical, as well as the empirical, remains articulated. In this way the integrity of the phenomena under investigation – their contexts and relationships – is preserved. Thus the natural scientific way of thinking may be a powerful mode of investigation for certain purposes; it remains only *one* possibility. It is therefore not just a matter of thinking, and thinking geographically, but of how we so think. How we think affects what we think and to conceive of research just in natural scientific terms limits our possibilities. Thus, the strength of Antony Flew's (1975) book 'thinking about thinking' is diminished by his taking what I would regard as a narrow, scientistic and rationalistic approach to validity, truth and logic. If our arguments must posit sequential events (if . . . then) or deny the possibility of internal contradictions (either A or not A) then we hide our faces from the search for synthetic and internally formed explanation. We may note in passing that synthesis – knowledge about knowledge, gleaned from natural philosophy – is Thrift's (1985) fourth type. Further such explanation may even be found in the structural–functionalist school and their recognition that an activity may have both manifest and latent functions can be functional or dysfunctional. Thus the Hopi rain-dance functions manifestly to create rain but latently to enhance group solidarity by bringing the people together for collective ceremonial, while nepotism in dynastic China was functional for the maintenance of family relationships but possible dysfunctional for the efficient operation of the economy.

How may we conclude? Thinking geographically means becoming conscious of the significance of the spatial as practical (and unconscious) knowledge becomes articulated (and transformed) into empirical (and synthetic) knowledge. We need, therefore, not just to be aware of the rather mechanical and/or routine tasks of the research process – asking questions, searching out documents, analysing data and so on – but also of the nature and purpose of the research itself. Of course, many of the contributors are right when they say that intellectual curiosity sets us off, but after that we must be aware of our research aims, its and our own containing contexts (theoretical, personal, societal and practical) and where it stands in relation to the endeavours of others. We must therefore be resolute of purpose (it helps with the routine), but be flexible too, open to influence and willing to change. We must constantly and conscientiously think about what we are doing and how it is being done, part of these tasks being to think geographically. At times such thinking will apparently increase the tedium factor (and it may be that joy in research is found only when a revealing insight comes or when the project is finished, though that may be linked to loss as well). But the act of self-assessment (along with the critical appraisal of one's peers) is a necessary part of the research process. It leads, as Gould (1985, part VII) points out, not back to where we start from but to new beginnings, enriching our endeavour. And if part of this process is the interrogation and articulation of the geographical, then our calling or commitment may be further strengthened.

References

Abler, R. J. S., Adams, J. S. and Gould, P. R. (1972) *Spatial Organisation*. Prentice-Hall, Englewood Cliffs.
Billinge, M., Gregory, D. and Martin, R. (eds) (1984) *Recollections of a Revolution*. Macmillan, London.
Bourdieu, P. (1977) *Outline of a Theory of Practice*. Cambridge University Press, Cambridge.
Eyles, J. (1985) *Senses of Place*. Silverbrook Press, Warrington.
Eyles, J. (1988) The geography of everyday life. In D. Gregory and R. Walford (eds), *New Horizons in Human Geography*. Macmillan, London.
Flew, A. (1975) *Thinking about Thinking*. Fontana, London.
Giddens, A. (1984) *The Constitution of Society*. Polity Press, Cambridge.
Gould, P. R. (1985) *The Geographer at Work*. Routledge & Kegan Paul, London.
Gregory, D. and Urry, J. (eds) (1985) *Social Relations and Spatial Structures*. Macmillan, London.
Haggett, P. (1965) *Locational Analysis in Human Geography*. Arnold, London.
Hart, J. F. (1982) The highest form of the geographer's art, *Annals of the Association of American Geographers*, 72, 1–29.
Hurst, M. E. (1985) Geography has neither existence nor future. In R. J. Johnston (ed.), *The Future of Geography*. Methuen, London, pp. 59–91.
James, P. and Martin, G. (1981) *All Possible Worlds*. Wiley, New York.
Jenkins, R. (1981) Thinking and doing: towards a model of cognitive practice. In L. Holy and M. Stuchlik (eds), *The Structure of Folk Models*. Academic Press, London, pp. 93–121.
Johnston, R. J. (1986) Places matter, *Irish Geography*, 18, 58–63.
Lee, T. (1976) Cities in the mind. In D. T. Herbert and R. J. Johnston (eds), *Social Areas in Cities*. Wiley, Chichester, vol. 2, pp. 159–87.
Massey, D. (1984a) *Spatial Divisions of Labour*. Macmillan, London.
Massey, D. (1984b) Introduction: geography matters. In Massey and Allen (1984), pp. 1–11.
Massey, D. (1985) New directions in space. In Gregory and Urry (1985), pp. 9–19

Massey, D. and Allen, J. (eds) (1984) *Geography Matters!* Cambridge University Press, Cambridge.

Meinig, D. (1983) Geography as an art, *Transactions of the Institute of British Geographers*, 8, 314–28.

Morrill, R. (1984) Recollecions of the 'quantitative revolutions' early years. In Billinge, et al. (1984).

Pickles, J. (1988) From fact-world to life-world: the phenomenological method and social sciences research. In J. Eyles and D. M. Smith (eds), *Qualitative Methods in Human Geography*. Polity Press, Cambridge.

Powell, J. (1985) Review of 'Senses of place', *Australian Geographical Studies*, 23, 381–2.

Sack, R. (1980) *Conceptions of Space in Social Thought*. Macmillan, London.

Sayer, A. (1979) Epistemology and conceptions of people and nature in geography, *Geoforum*, 10, 19–43.

Sayer, A. (1984) *Method in Social Science*. Hutchinson, London.

Sayer, A. (1985) The difference that space makes. In Gregory and Urry (1985), pp. 49–66.

Smith, S. (1988) Constructing local knowledge. In J. Eyles and D. M. Smith (eds), *Qualitative Methods in Human Geography*. Polity Press, Cambridge.

Thrift, N. (1985) Flies and germs: a geography of knowledge. In Gregory and Urry (1985), pp. 366–403.

Tuan, Y. -F. (1974) *Topophilia*. Prentice-Hall, Englewood Cliffs.

Tuan, Y. -F. (1977) *Space and Place*. Arnold, London.

Urry, J. (1981) *Anatomy of Capitalist Societies*. Macmillan, London.

Urry, J. (1985) Social relations, space and time. In Gregory and Urry (1985), pp. 20–48.

Williams, R. (1981) Problems of materialism, *New Left Review*, 109, 3–17.

Index